Essentials

of **Psychological Assessment** Series

ORDER FORM

Please send this order form with your payment (credit card or check) to:
Wiley, Attn: Customer Care, 10475 Crosspoint Blvd., Indianapolis, IN 46256

QUANTITY	TITLE	ISBN	PRICE
_____	_____	_____	_____
_____	_____	_____	_____
_____	_____	_____	_____
_____	_____	_____	_____
_____	_____	_____	_____

Shipping Charges:	Surface	2-Day	1-Day
First item	$5.00	$10.50	$17.50
Each additional item	$3.00	$3.00	$4.00

For orders greater than 15 items,
please contact Customer Care at 1-877-762-2974.

ORDER AMOUNT _____

SHIPPING CHARGES _____

SALES TAX _____

TOTAL ENCLOSED _____

NAME_____

AFFILIATION_____

ADDRESS_____

CITY/STATE/ZIP _____

TELEPHONE _____

EMAIL_____

❑ Please add me to your e-mailing list

PAYMENT METHOD:

❑ Check/Money Order ❑ Visa ❑ Mastercard ❑ AmEx

Card Number _____ Exp. Date _____

Cardholder Name (Please print) _____

Signature _____

Make checks payable to **John Wiley & Sons.** Credit card orders invalid if not signed.
All orders subject to credit approval. • Prices subject to change.

To order by phone, call toll free 1-877-762-2974
To order online: www.wiley.com/essentials

WILEY

Essentials of Working Memory Assessment and Intervention

Essentials of Psychological Assessment Series

Series Editors, Alan S. Kaufman and Nadeen L. Kaufman

Essentials

of Working Memory Assessment and Intervention

Milton J. Dehn

Published by John Wiley & Sons, Inc., Hoboken, New Jersey.
Published simultaneously in Canada.

This publication is designed to provide accurate and authoritative information in regard to the subject matter covered. It is sold with the understanding that the publisher is not engaged in rendering professional services. If legal, accounting, medical, psychological or any other expert assistance is required, the services of a competent professional person should be sought.

Designations used by companies to distinguish their products are often claimed as trademarks. In all instances where John Wiley & Sons, Inc. is aware of a claim, the product names appear in initial capital or all capital letters. Readers, however, should contact the appropriate companies for more complete information regarding trademarks and registration.

For general information on our other products and services please contact our Customer Care Department within the United States at (800) 762-2974, outside the United States at (317) 572-3993 or fax (317) 572-4002.

Wiley publishes in a variety of print and electronic formats and by print-on-demand. Some material included with standard print versions of this book may not be included in e-books or in print-on-demand. If this book refers to media such as a CD or DVD that is not included in the version you purchased, you may download this material at http://booksupport.wiley.com. For more information about Wiley products, visit www.wiley.com.

Library of Congress Cataloging-in-Publication Data:

Dehn, Milton J.
    Essentials of working memory assessment and intervention / Milton J. Dehn.
        pages cm
    Includes bibliographical references and index.
    ISBN 978-1-118-63813-2 (pbk.) – ISBN 978-1-118-70557-5 (epdf) –
        ISBN 978-1-118-87673-2 (epub)
    1. Short-term memory. 2. Memory. I. Title.
    BF378.S54D437 2015
    153.1'3—dc23
                                                2015013591

Cover image: © Greg Kuchik/Getty Images
Cover design: Wiley

This book is printed on acid-free paper. ∞

Printed in the United States of America

10 9 8 7 6 5 4 3 2 1

For Paula, my soulmate.

CONTENTS

SERIES PREFACE

I n the *Essentials of Psychological Assessment* series, we have attempted to provide the reader with books that will deliver key practical information in the most efficient and accessible style. Many books in the series feature specific instruments in a variety of domains, such as cognition, personality, education, and neuropsychology. Other books focus on crucial topics for professionals who are involved in any way with assessment—topics such as specific reading disabilities, evidence-based interventions, or ADHD assessment. For the experienced professional, books in the series offer a concise yet thorough review of a test instrument or a specific area of expertise, including numerous tips for best practices. Students can turn to series books for a clear and concise overview of the important assessment tools and key topics, in which they must become proficient to practice skillfully, efficiently, and ethically in their chosen fields.

Wherever feasible, visual cues highlighting key points are utilized alongside systematic, step-by-step guidelines. Chapters are focused and succinct. Topics are organized for an easy understanding of the essential material related to a particular test or topic. Theory and research are continually woven into the fabric of each book, but always to enhance the practical application of the material, rather than to sidetrack or overwhelm readers. With this series, we aim to challenge and assist readers interested in psychological assessment to aspire to the highest level of competency by arming them with the tools they need for knowledgeable, informed practice. We have long been advocates of "intelligent" testing—the notion that numbers are meaningless unless they are brought to life by the clinical acumen and expertise of examiners. Assessment must be used to make a difference in the child's or adult's life, or why bother to test? All books in the series—whether devoted to specific tests or general topics—are consistent with this credo. We want this series to help our readers, novice and veteran alike, to benefit from the intelligent assessment approaches of the authors of each book.

This volume provides practitioners with a framework for planning, conducting, and interpreting an assessment of working memory, as well as a review of evidence-based interventions for working memory. The selective, multi-battery assessment approach elucidates a challenging type of evaluation that requires the compilation of an assessment battery from different tests. Dr. Dehn, an expert in the areas of processing and memory assessment, sets the stage by proposing an integrated model of working memory for assessment and intervention purposes. Next, the relations between working memory and specific types of academic learning are reviewed. Through step-by-step guidelines and worksheets, Dehn walks the reader through planning an assessment and interpreting test results, including how to determine intra-individual strengths and weaknesses among working memory components. He then offers detailed information on subtests from cognitive and memory scales that can be used to measure working memory. Finally, Dehn provides details on working memory exercises, strategies, and accommodations that can be used during intervention. Additional assessment and intervention resources—such as checklists, forms, and detailed directions—are available in the online resources that accompany this book. It is our hope that the knowledge, insights, and practices gained from this volume will lead to more accurate diagnoses and more effective treatment for individuals who struggle with learning and memory.

Alan S. Kaufman, PhD, and Nadeen L. Kaufman, EdD, Series Editors
Yale Child Study Center, Yale University School of Medicine

ACKNOWLEDGMENTS

I wish to express my gratitude to three individuals who reviewed the manuscript and provided very helpful feedback from a practitioner's viewpoint. They are:

Kim Charnofsky, MS, who works as a school psychologist and mental health facilitator in California.

Janice Barron, EdD, who works as an educational diagnostician and speech therapist in Texas.

Silvia De La Riva, EdD, who works as a bilingual school psychologist in California.

Essentials of Working Memory Assessment and Intervention

One

WORKING MEMORY MODELS

In their attempts to better understand the workings of the mind, psychologists develop explanatory models known as *constructs*. A hypothetical construct is inferred from data because it is not directly observable. For example, *intelligence* is a well-known and long-debated construct that cannot be directly observed or measured. This book is about *working memory* (WM), one of the most influential psychological constructs of the past 40 years. The behaviors associated with WM are measurable and real. However, the underlying construct associated with these behaviors remains hypothetical. Its exact nature, functioning, neurological structure, and even its name are still open to debate and refinement.

WM is the cognitive ability to briefly hold, maintain, or store information while processing the same or other information. Simply put, brief storage plus simultaneous cognitive processing equals WM. The brief storage aspect is commonly referred to as *short-term memory* (STM). Thus, the construct of WM includes STM, with WM having a supervisory role over the STM component (Baddeley, 1986). The supervisory role is just one of WM's executive functions. WM is complex; it has both cognitive and metacognitive dimensions (Dehn, 2014a).

What makes WM so interesting and so influential is that it is very limited in humans, and these limitations have significant consequences for all sorts of human endeavors. Without keeping information refreshed

> **DON'T FORGET**
> ....
> Working memory occurs whenever there is concurrent temporary storage and processing of information. Short-term memory provides the storage function. Thus, short-term memory is embedded within working memory. In this book, the term "working memory" includes short-term memory.

in WM, it will be retained only for a few seconds. In the typical adult, only four to seven pieces of information can be maintained in WM during cognitive processing (Cowan, 2001).

Psychologists were measuring WM long before the construct was even proposed. The *digit span* test goes back more than 100 years. This test includes *digits backward*, which requires the examinee to reverse the sequence of orally presented digits. Digits backward is now recognized as a robust measure of WM. Prior to the 1990s, the widely used *Wechsler Intelligence Scale for Children* incorporated the digit span subtest into a composite score it called *Freedom From Distractibility*, a label that describes one of WM's key functions but gave psychologists little understanding of what they were actually measuring.

CAUTION

Despite working memory's wide-ranging influence, the definition of working memory should remain narrow. For example, reasoning and working memory are not the same thing, even though reasoning heavily depends on working memory capacity.

When defining WM and discussing the roles that it plays in cognitive functioning, it is important to consider how WM is typically measured. The usual task requires the maintenance of oral or visual stimuli while processing those stimuli in some manner. What is actually measured is not the processing but the number of sequential items (a span) that is retained. All of the empirical data on how WM is related with cognitive abilities, academic learning, and daily functioning is based on such traditional span measures of WM. Consequently, the definition and application of the WM construct should not go beyond how it is measured. For example, WM should not be equated with intelligence, general executive functioning, or all conscious mental activity. When the definition goes beyond the measurement of the construct, then WM becomes too inclusive and less meaningful. Also, very broad applications of the construct create false impressions that WM training should lead to improved functioning in psychological processes that may not really be WM.

WORKING MEMORY'S INFLUENCE

Nearly all cognitive and metacognitive functions are closely interrelated with WM. For example, language expression, processing speed, reasoning, phonological processing, attentional control, and executive functions have high correlations with WM (see Chapter 2). Furthermore, nearly all aspects of learning, especially academic learning, depend on adequate levels of WM (see Chapter 4).

Finally, performance and application of skills, as well as cognitively challenging daily activities, depend on WM. A short list of activities that are influenced by WM capacity includes:

- Keeping up with the flow of a conversation and remembering what one was going to say.
- Noticing errors that are contained in a written sentence one just produced.
- Keeping track of one's place while counting.
- Being able to take detailed notes while listening at the same time.
- Remembering multistep directions that were just presented or read.
- Completing a task in a time-efficient manner.
- Coping with distractions while thinking.
- Comprehending what is being said or read.
- Remembering what one was going to do next.
- Keeping track of subproducts while doing mental arithmetic.
- Being able to switch between mental tasks.
- Being able to reason, such as comparing and contrasting two concepts.
- Integrating visual and auditory information.
- Efficiently memorizing information.
- Consciously retrieving a name or word that does not come immediately.

Obviously, a normal WM ability is essential for all kinds of cognitive, learning, and daily activities (Engle, 2002). Consequently, unusual shortcomings or deficits in WM can lead to all kinds of problems. Such problems include forgetfulness, inattentiveness, difficulty following directions, difficulty completing tasks, difficulty communicating, and various types of learning disorders.

BADDELEY'S WORKING MEMORY MODEL

The predominant model of WM was originally proposed by Baddeley and Hitch in 1974 and later expanded by Baddeley (1986, 2000). The Baddeley model of WM is the theoretical basis of the majority of research on WM. This multicomponent model has been validated through neuropsychological research and has been operationalized in measurement instruments. Baddeley defines *working memory* as "a system for the temporary holding and manipulation of information during the performance of a range of cognitive tasks such as comprehension, learning, and reasoning" (1986, p. 34). The original multifaceted model was made up of three components: a phonological loop, a visuospatial sketchpad, and a central executive. In 2000, Baddeley added another component—the episodic buffer (see Rapid Reference 1.1). Baddeley's model is hierarchical, with the central executive as the top-level, domain-free facet that controls all of the subcomponents.

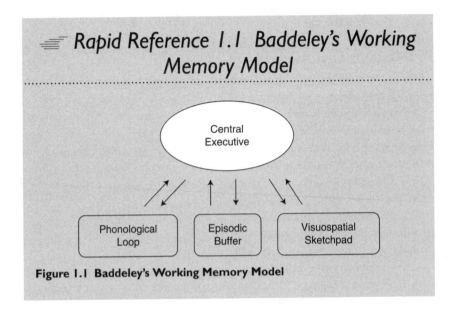

≡ Rapid Reference 1.1 Baddeley's Working Memory Model

Figure 1.1 Baddeley's Working Memory Model

The Phonological Loop

What Baddeley refers to as the *phonological loop* is also known as auditory, phono-logical, or verbal short-term memory. (In this text, this aspect of WM will be called *phonological short-term memory.*) The phonological loop is a limited capacity component that briefly stores verbal information in phonological form. Baddeley (1986, 2003a) divides the phonological loop into passive storage and subvocal, articulatory rehearsal. The number of unconnected verbal items (such as words from a list) that can be retained in the phonological loop depends on the time it takes to articulate them (Baddeley, 2003a). Individuals can recall only a sequen-tial span that they can articulate (aloud or subvocally) within 2 seconds (Ellis & Hennelley, 1980; Hulme & Mackenzie, 1992). For instance, if an individual's speech rate is two monosyllable words per second, his memory span will be about four monosyllable words. Thus, auditory STM span varies according to the length of the words and the individual's speech rate. Individuals with faster articulation rates can maintain more items than individuals who are slow articulators (Hulme & Mackenzie, 1992). Also, more monosyllable words can be retained than multi-syllable words. For adults, normal phonological loop span is approximately seven monosyllable units.

Despite the strong evidence that word length and articulatory rehearsal speed determine auditory STM span, other influences also affect memory span. One influence is prior knowledge. Meaningful phonological information may activate relevant long-term memory (LTM) representations, which may then facilitate immediate recall from short-term storage. For instance, the average adult has a longer span for meaningful words than for pseudo-words. The degree of chunking or grouping of items into larger units also affects span. For example, the separate digits "five" and "eight" can be chunked as "fifty-eight." Also, individuals can remember sentences that take several seconds to articulate because the sentences can be chunked into meaningful phrases or ideas.

Subvocal rehearsal seems to largely determine verbal span because whenever individuals are prevented from rehearsing, performance is markedly impaired. The typical interference task prevents rehearsal by requiring the participant to engage in an unrelated attention-demanding task, such as counting. The impact of disrupting phonological short-term rehearsal provides evidence of the importance of rehearsal to the short-term retention of information. Without rehearsal, less information will be retained, and the retention interval will last only a few seconds (Henry, 2001).

The Visuospatial Sketchpad

What Baddeley refers to as the *visuospatial sketchpad* is also known as *visual-spatial short-term memory* (the label that will be used in this text). The visuospatial sketch-pad is responsible for the immediate storage of visual and spatial information, such as the color of objects and their location. Like the phonological component, it consists of passive temporary storage and mostly automated rehearsal. Decay in the visuospatial sketchpad seems to be as rapid as phonological decay, taking place within a matter of seconds. Rehearsal of the information involves eye movement, manipulation of the image, or some type of visual mnemonic (Baddeley, 1986).

Neurologically, visual-spatial short-term storage has two dimensions: visual and spatial (Pickering, Gathercole, Hall, & Lloyd, 2001). The visual aspect is responsible for the storage of static visual information (e.g., shape, color, and size). The spatial dimension is responsible for the storage of dynamic information (e.g., location, motion, and direction). Visual-spatial short-term storage capacity is typically three to seven items for a matter of seconds.

Complex or abstract stimuli are more difficult to retain than simple or common stimuli that can be named. For example, blocks displayed in a matrix are easier to recall than a random display, and abstract figures are more difficult to recall than drawings of common objects. These findings indicate that structured visual-spatial information consumes less short-term storage capacity than unstructured. The fact that visual-spatial span is better for familiar material suggests that long-term memory representations are facilitating short-term visual-spatial memory, much like recognizable words extend phonological memory span.

Better recall for familiar images may also be accomplished by the recoding of visual-spatial information into verbal information, which is more likely to occur when images are recognizable and can be named. Once recoded, verbal rehearsal maintains the information that originally was visual-spatial (Richardson, 1996). By 10 years of age, most children verbally recode visual-spatial stimuli.

In Baddeley's model, the generation, manipulation, and maintenance of visual images also appear to involve the visuospatial sketchpad (De Beni, Pazzaglia, Meneghetti, & Mondoloni, 2007). Maintenance and manipulation of visual images are highly demanding, requiring more than the visuospatial sketchpad itself. Thus, WM's central executive must become involved whenever internally generated visual images are being consciously manipulated.

The Episodic Buffer

Baddeley's (2000) *episodic buffer* refers to the interaction between WM and LTM. This interaction takes new information currently being held and processed in WM and incorporates it with already existing LTM representations. For example, the episodic component combines visual and verbal codes and links them to multidimensional representations in LTM. The episodic buffer is involved in learning because this is where encoding into LTM takes place (Pickering & Gathercole, 2004). It is also involved in conscious efforts to retrieve desired information from LTM storage.

The episodic buffer can account for temporary storage of large amounts of information that exceed the capacities of the phonological and visuospatial storage systems (Baddeley, 2003a). This perspective is best explained by Cowan's (2005) *embedded process model*. Cowan proposes that there is a pool of recently activated LTM items. WM interacts with these activated pieces of information, quickly switching the focus of attention from one to another as the processing task demands change. Thus, the episodic buffer accounts for how individuals can handle more information than would be indicated by measures of WM span. Unfortunately, a standardized method of measuring the capacity of the episodic buffer has not yet been devised. Consequently, further discussion of the episodic buffer in this book will be limited.

The Central Executive

In Baddeley's model, the *central executive* is responsible for managing the three subcomponents, and it also regulates and coordinates all of the cognitive subprocesses involved in WM performance. The central executive is involved whenever an individual must simultaneously store and process information (Tronsky, 2005). For example, the central executive is responsible for managing dual-task situations, which typically involve processing information while trying to retain the same or different information. As described by Baddeley (1996b), the central executive is multimodal and does not have its own temporary storage, relying on the phonological loop and visual-spatial sketchpad for storage. In addition, it has limited capacity for the processes it conducts. Overall, the primary role of the central executive is to coordinate information from a number of different sources and manage performance on separate, simultaneous tasks (Baddeley, 1996b). For example, the central executive will be involved whenever visual and verbal information needs to be integrated.

Over the years, Baddeley (1986, 1996b, 2003b, 2006) has described several core central executive functions, including (a) focusing attention on relevant information while inhibiting the irrelevant information; (b) switching between concurrent cognitive activities; (c) applying strategies, such as conscious rehearsal; (d) allocating limited resources to other parts of the WM system; and (e) retrieving, holding, and manipulating temporarily activated information from LTM.

OTHER MODELS OF WORKING MEMORY

Although Baddeley's model is the most popular and has the most empirical and neurological support, there are other conceptualizations of how WM functions. Most of these have some empirical support as well. They also account for WM performance in ways that further enhance our understanding of WM. The other models mainly differ from Baddeley's in that they emphasize processing instead of storage, the control of attention, and the interactions between WM and LTM.

Daneman and Carpenter's Processing Efficiency Model

Daneman and Carpenter (1980) emphasize the processing dimension of WM, arguing that what appears to be smaller storage capacity may actually be the result of inefficient processing. They contend that complex mental operations utilize WM resources and the more efficient the mental processing, the more resources are available for short-term storage. Because processing efficiency varies by task, WM performance varies, depending on the task at the moment. For example, an expert in chess has better WM-related performance during a chess match than a novice does. However, the chess expert will not excel when a nonchess task is used to assess WM. Daneman and Carpenter believe that individuals do not vary as much in available storage capacity as they do in processing efficiency. They also believe that storage and processing capacity remain relatively constant during development. Age-related improvements in span result mainly from increased operational efficiency. Although this model views WM as including both storage and processing functions, the model reduces the need for modality-specific storage buffers (Just & Carpenter, 1992). For Daneman and Carpenter, WM essentially corresponds to the central executive in Baddeley's theory. From their perspective, performance on complex span tasks is due primarily to central executive processing efficiency, not storage capacity.

Kane and Engle's Executive Attention Model

Kane and Engle (Engle 1996, 2002; Kane, Conway, Bleckley, & Engle, 2001) portray WM as an executive attention function that is distinguishable from STM. Kane and Engle make the case that WM capacity is not about short-term span but rather about the ability to control attention in order to maintain information in an active, quickly retrievable state. They define *executive attention* as "an executive control capability; that is, an ability to effectively maintain stimulus, goal, or context information in an active, easily accessible state in the face of interference, to effectively inhibit goal-irrelevant stimuli or responses, or both" (Kane et al., 2001, p. 180). Executive attention not only allows switching between competing tasks but also maintains desired information by suppressing and inhibiting unwanted, irrelevant information. Therefore, the capacity of WM is a function of how well executive processes can focus attention on the relevant content and goals, not on the length of the retention interval or how much short-term storage is available.

Evidence for their model comes from studies in which high-memory-span participants demonstrate better attentional control than low-span subjects. High-span individuals are more adept at resisting interference than low-span subjects (Kane et al., 2001). Their ability to inhibit interference allows them to retain and process more information. Most of the interference is internally generated, often caused by associating current information with earlier information that is no longer relevant. Thus, individuals with a high WM span may not necessarily have a greater short-term storage capacity than those with a low span. Rather, WM span is constrained by the executive capacity to control attention and resist interference (Hester & Garavan, 2005).

Kane and Engle (2000) also emphasize the role of WM in retrieving and actively maintaining information from LTM. They believe WM is responsible for cue-dependent, focused searching that has a high probability of leading to correct recall. Furthermore, this cue-dependent process applies to retrieval of information just recently lost from short-term storage because of the removal of attention, extended time intervals, or distractions. Such information has often transferred to the pool of recently activated LTM items.

According to Kane and Engle (2000), low-WM-capacity individuals have more difficulty selecting and using correct cues to guide the LTM search process, resulting in too many irrelevant representations being retrieved and ultimately in failure to retrieve the sought-after information. Thus, individual differences in WM capacity are also related to individual differences in the ability to engage in a controlled, strategic search of LTM (Unsworth & Engle, 2007).

Kane and Engle emphasize a strong connection between WM and LTM. They view WM as a subset of recently activated LTM units (Unsworth & Engle, 2007). By continually focusing attention, WM maintains a few representations (typically about four) for ongoing processing. As attentional resources increase with age, more LTM structures can be activated concurrently.

Kane and Engle (2000) have also investigated the relationships WM has with higher-level cognitive functions. According to their theory, controlled attention is what binds all of the cognitive processes and functions, such as fluid reasoning, together. In contrast, the STM components are not significantly related to higher-level cognition.

In summary, Kane and colleagues are proposing that WM consists of domain-general controlled attention, which is mainly applied to retrieving and maintaining activation of LTM representations. Individual differences in WM reflect the degree to which distracters can be inhibited and relevant information can be actively maintained as the focus of attention (Kane et al., 2001). The theory makes inhibitory control the primary determinant of working memory capacity.

> **DON'T FORGET**
> ....
> Most models of working memory emphasize the close interaction between working memory and long-term memory. Working memory is constantly utilizing items from a recently activated pool of long-term memory representations. This activated pool can contain more than 20 items at a time (Anderson, 1983), thereby expanding the amount of information that working memory can handle.

Cowan's Embedded-Process Model

Cowan (2005) is an American psychologist who has greatly expanded the construct of WM, altered the view of WM capacity, and closely linked WM with LTM. His model emphasizes focus of attention, levels of activation, and expertise as essential properties of WM. Cowan's theory embeds WM within LTM while still recognizing WM and STM as separable from LTM. Essentially, Cowan believes that WM refers to information in LTM that is activated above some threshold.

Cowan's model mainly distinguishes between the activated part of LTM and the focus of attention (see Rapid Reference 1.2). Only the focus of attention has limited capacity, typically a few highly activated elements at a time. The larger pool of activated LTM items is not capacity-limited, but items can be lost through decay or interference (Oberauer, 2002). Items in the activated pool quickly move in and out of the focus of attention, depending on what is needed at the moment.

The focus of attention replaces the multiple separate storage buffers and the central executive of Baddeley's model. Cowan posits that a limited focus of attention restricts WM retention and processing, not storage capacity. In adults with normal WM capacity, the focus of attention can handle about four chunks of activated information at a time. Studies of retrieval speed (McElree, 1998) provide support for Cowan's model by finding that items expected to be in the focus of attention are retrieved more quickly than recently activated items that are no longer the focus of attention.

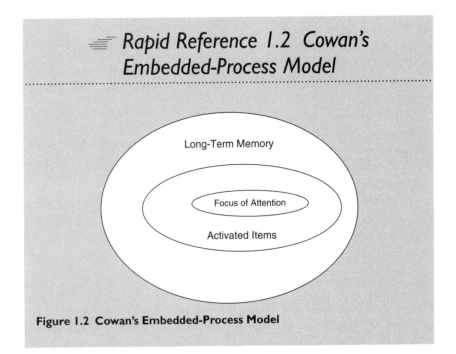

Rapid Reference 1.2 Cowan's Embedded-Process Model

Figure 1.2 Cowan's Embedded-Process Model

Ericsson and Kintsch's Long-Term Working Memory Model

Given the close connection between WM and LTM, it is not surprising that there are advocates (Ericsson & Kintsch, 1995) for a *long-term working memory*. According to this view, WM is not structurally distinct from LTM. Essentially, WM is the skillful utilization of information stored in LTM. Although WM may not be separable from LTM in this model, it still performs the same functions, such as processing select sensory input and encoding new information into long-term storage.

The notion of long-term WM changes the perspective on storage capacity. Instead of how many chunks can be held in short-term storage, capacity entails how many long-term representations can be in a highly active state at any one time (Richardson, 1996). As suggested by Cowan (2005), the typical individual can hold and manipulate about four pieces of information concurrently. Similar to decay in STM models, activated portions of LTM must quickly return to an inactive state so that there is room for other long-term representations as they become activated. This perspective opens the door to the possibility that much of what is immediately retrieved is actually being retrieved from long-term, not short-term, storage. This leads to several educational implications, among them the benefits of long-term mnemonics on WM functioning.

Ericsson and Kintsch suggest that the skillful use of information held in LTM depends on expertise and the use of mnemonics, both of which enable individuals to use LTM as an efficient extension of WM. Extended WM seems to depend mainly on grouping items into chunks and then associating the chunks with familiar patterns, such as schemas, already stored in LTM. The process of reading comprehension is consistent with Ericsson and Kintsch's model. Comprehension over extended parts of text would not be possible without LTM involvement. As the reader progresses through text, a representation is constructed in LTM. This representation is continually expanded to integrate new information from the text, with relevant parts remaining accessible during reading. Ericsson and Kintsch view the accessible portions of this structure as an extended WM. Their argument seems plausible, given that text comprehension increases dramatically from childhood to adulthood without concomitant increases in short-term and WM capacity.

The Relationship Between Working Memory and Long-Term Memory

Most of the long-term WM theorists agree that WM is a separate cognitive process, even if it might be embedded within LTM. In contrast, advocates for a separate WM view LTM and WM as structurally separate memory systems, each with its own storage area. This viewpoint is consistent with neuroscience evidence. For example, when individuals work at WM tasks, it is the dorsolateral prefrontal cortex and related STM storage areas that are the most active, rather than the hippocampus, which is an LTM structure (see Chapter 3 for neuroanatomy details). Also, amnesic cases illustrate (Corkin, 1984) that STM and WM can function adequately while LTM is impaired. However, there is no doubt that WM and LTM are highly interrelated. Thus, models of WM that focus only on the WM-STM connection may be missing valuable insights into the functioning and dysfunctioning of human memory systems.

THE CONTROVERSY REGARDING WORKING MEMORY CAPACITY

Most models represent WM as a unitary system where processing and storage compete for a limited, common pool of resources. This shared-resources position is known as the *general capacity hypothesis* (Engle, Cantor, & Carullo, 1992). On a moment-to-moment, flexible basis, resources are shared between the STM and LTM storage components and the executive component. Unless the individual consciously prioritizes storage, processing demands receive priority. When the processing demands of the task are high, such as trying to solve a complex mental arithmetic problem, WM capacity cannot meet demand. The result is information loss, an inability to complete the task, or, at the very least, slower processing (Engle et al., 1992). In typical cognitive activities, the difficulty of the processing task is inversely related to memory span.

Humans are capable of simultaneously storing and processing information. In order to do so, they must continually and rapidly switch back and forth between storage and processing (Barrouillet, Gavens, Vergauwe, Gaillard, & Camos, 2009). During the storage phase they are rehearsing the material to prevent decay, and during the processing phase at least some of the items in storage are neglected. Accordingly, span reduction results from limited, disrupted, infrequent, or too-late rehearsal opportunities. Thus, the amount of information an individual can simultaneously maintain and process partly depends on the efficiency of switching. However, attention-demanding processes reduce the proportion of time that can be allocated to rehearsal (Barrouillet, Bernardin, Portrat, Vergauwe, & Camos, 2007). On the other hand, efficient processing releases additional resources for maintaining storage, thereby increasing memory span. Therefore, improvements in WM performance may be due to increased processing efficiency, rather than increases in storage capacity per se.

Conscious and systematic switching is challenging. Switching is also a process that draws from overall WM capacity. Thus, more efficient and automated switching detracts less from storage and the task at hand. Most children are unable to switch back and forth prior to the age of 7 (Barrouillet et al., 2009). At early ages, children focus only on the processing task, at the expense of maintaining information in STM. Switching efficiency apparently develops gradually. The rate of switching so that rehearsal can occur is twice as high for 14-year-old children as it is for 8-year-old children (Barrouillet et al., 2009). When children are developmentally ready, they can be taught how to switch. WM exercises that incorporate switching training are discussed in Chapter 7. In contrast to the position that WM has limited resources that are shared between storage and processing, some cognitive psychologists (Halford, Wilson, & Phillips, 2001) postulate that there are separate capacity limits for storage (STM components) and processing (executive WM). This claim, known as the *separate resources hypothesis*, is in accord with the beliefs that storage and processing demands are quite different. From this viewpoint, the capacity of the central executive determines the rate and extent of information processing, whereas STM span reflects the storage capacity of the phonological loop or visuospatial sketchpad (Baddeley, 1990). Short-term storage components each have their own capacity limitations, which are distinct from executive WM capacity.

There is empirical evidence supporting the separate resources hypothesis. As expressed by Towse, Hitch, and Hutton (1998), "Storage is independent of concurrent processing load, and processing performance is independent of concurrent storage load. The relationship between processing and storage arises because the time spent in processing affects the amount of forgetting that accrues" (p. 219). Also, there are numerous examples (reviewed by Oberauer, 2002) of short-term retention being unimpaired by concurrent secondary processing tasks. Moreover, the amount of information retained in storage seems unaffected by the degree of processing. Even in demanding dual-task experimental designs, participants typically perform well on both storage and processing (Seigneuric, Ehrlich, Oakhill, & Yuill, 2000). In instances where there is a decrement in storage (Duff & Logie, 2001), it is not the substantial drop predicted by the common resource model. Overall, contemporary research has pretty well established that executive WM and STM capacities are not necessarily limited to a common pool of general resources.

Nonetheless, there appear to be some shared general resources. Neuropsychological evidence supports this conclusion: STM storage and executive WM operate from separate structures in the brain, but are directly connected and highly interactive when information in STM storage is being processed (see Chapter 3). Storage seems to suffer most when it is neglected because the individual does not intermittently rehearse the material being held there.

Furthermore, other cognitive factors clearly impact capacity (see Chapter 2). For example, the ability to control attention and inhibit interference and the extent of long-term memory activation all play a role. Processing speed is especially important because slow processing extends the processing interval during which no attention is paid to the items in storage. Processing efficiency and the application of strategies impact retention and performance.

This understanding of WM limitations and capacity has assessment implications. First, span should be measured under minimal or no processing demands and also when there are high processing demands. The first condition is referred to as *simple span* and is measured by such tasks as *digits forward*. Performance on simple span tasks represents STM storage. The latter condition is known as *complex span* and is measured by such tasks as digits backward. Performance on complex spans represents overall WM capacity (Gibson et al., 2012). Another way of framing this is that the STM components should be assessed separately from the WM components. Second, the examinee should be observed and queried in regards to switching and other strategies. Finally, related cognitive processing components, such as processing speed, should be considered.

> **CAUTION**
> ....
> Although the average adult can retain a verbal sequential span of seven chunks in short-term storage, the maximum number of information chunks that can be simultaneously processed by working memory is typically four.

Regarding overall WM capacity, Cowan (2001) presents extensive convergent evidence that normal adult WM capacity is four chunks. This is distinct from normal adult STM span, which is typically seven words. Cowan views this WM capacity limit as nearly universal, applying across individuals, across modalities, and across levels of expertise. In his view, what varies is the size of the chunks, not the number of chunks. The rule of four chunks applies to normal situations in which individuals are passively attending to information and in which most of the WM processing is automatic. When individuals use a rehearsal strategy to supplement the limited storage function, capacity can be extended to six or seven chunks. Despite Cowan's convincing evidence, some recent studies (reviewed by Verhaeghen, Cerella, & Basak, 2004) have indicated that the typical focus of attention is actually only one item, not four. For example, Oberauer (2002) contends that, at any one time, the focus of attention holds only the single item that is the object of the current or next cognitive operation.

RETENTION INTERVALS

In addition to limits on the amount of information that can be retained and processed, STM and WM are constrained by elapsed time. It has been frequently suggested that the typical retention interval for unrehearsed information is about seven seconds. However, verbal memory traces may fade or decay in as little as two seconds (Baddeley, 1986). It is impossible to specify a normal retention interval in seconds because of confounds that are introduced by rehearsal strategies, long-term retrieval, and processing load. Nonetheless, it is safe to assume that most information that enters STM and is processed in WM is highly degraded within 7 to 15 seconds and completely erased from the short-term store within 20 to 30 seconds (Cowan, 2005; Richardson, 1996). The only exception is when the stored information is being continually processed or rehearsed, in which case the retention interval can be extended indefinitely.

What appears to be a span limitation may actually be a temporal limit. As discussed earlier, individuals can recall about as much as they can articulate, or repeat, in about two seconds (Baddeley, 1986). This finding explains why individuals can recall more short words than long words. The finding also implies that phonological STM holds information for only two seconds unless it is maintained through covert or overt articulatory rehearsal.

While subvocal rehearsal extends the retention interval, it does not necessarily extend the number of items that can be recalled. This has led some researchers (Nairne, 2002) to conclude that span capacity rather than elapsed time is the main factor in forgetting. Nonetheless, there is clearly an inverse relationship between length of interval and length of span. Longer intervals without rehearsal undoubtedly constrict the span (Bayliss, Jarrold, Baddeley, & Gunn, 2003). It appears that extending the duration of the retention interval probably accounts for most of the reduced span performance in complex WM tasks (Conlin, Gathercole, & Adams, 2005).

Distinguishing between STM capacity and WM capacity may clarify some of the discrepancies found across studies. Without rehearsal, passive retention in phonological STM may be as little as two seconds. With rehearsal, this interval can be extended, and, with chunking, the number of items can be increased. That is why it is important to assess different types of WM capacity and to use measures that prevent rehearsal strategies or take strategies into account.

COGNITIVE LOAD THEORY

Cognitive load theory (Van Merrienboer, Kirschner, & Kester, 2003) emphasizes the limited cognitive capacity of WM and how easily WM can become overloaded during academic learning (T. de Jong, 2010). *Cognitive load* is the processing dimension of WM. Specifically, cognitive load is the proportion of time during which a given processing task occupies WM's focus of attention (Barrouillet, Portrat, & Camos, 2011). Cognitive load does not include the storage dimension of WM but has a direct influence on how much is maintained in storage. As cognitive load increases, there is a corresponding decrease in how much information is retained (Barrouillet et al., 2009). The more that a processing task demands attention, the fewer WM resources are available for rehearsing the information in STM storage components. The processing-storage relationship is bidirectional. Focusing too much on maintaining information through rehearsal can impede processing, slowing it down or causing processing errors.

DON'T FORGET

As cognitive load increases, the amount of information retained in short-term storage decreases.

Cognitive load theory is similar to the general capacity hypothesis discussed earlier. When attention is required for processing, it is not available for the maintenance of memory items and consequently the items fade away. Effective time sharing of attention involves rapid, back-and-forth switching of attention from processing to maintenance (rehearsal). The crucial variable is the amount of time that is occupied by the processing task (Liefooghe, Barrouillet, Vandierendonck, & Camos, 2008). Memory items are lost when the processing demands are such that the switching cannot occur at all or cannot occur in time to prevent loss of information. Switching in and of itself also adds to cognitive load.

Cognitive load theorists attempt to address cognitive overload in the classroom by identifying causes of high load and by promoting instructional design that minimizes load (T. de Jong, 2010). During instruction and learning, part of the cognitive load is inherent to the content and material to be learned, part is caused by the instructional behaviors of the teacher, and part is created by the learner's internal processing of the information (Kirschner, 2002). The concern is that learning is reduced when too much cognitive load causes loss of information before it can be encoded into LTM. See Chapter 4 for details on what causes high cognitive load in a learning environment.

THE INTEGRATED MODEL OF WORKING MEMORY

The purpose of psychological theories, models, and research is to further understand the functioning of the human brain, in this case WM. For this scientific information to be useful for real-world assessment and intervention purposes it needs to be operationalized so that WM ability can be effectively and validly measured. The *integrated model* proposed in this text draws from several WM models to frame and organize WM components and functions in a manner that facilitates assessment and intervention. The integrated model, first introduced in Dehn (2008), does not propose any new constructs or structures, but rather integrates models and research so that a whole and comprehensive portrayal of WM is created. Recent research from neuropsychology and neuroscience is considered so that the integrated model is true to what is known about WM neurological structures and functions. The model also incorporates related cognitive functions that need consideration during an assessment of WM (see Chapter 2). Finally, the integrated model is designed to enhance identification of WM weaknesses, deficits, and impairments. The assessment and intervention chapters in this text will reflect the structure of the integrated model.

Short-Term Memory

All of the contemporary models divide WM into processing and storage dimensions. The brief storage components have traditionally been referred to as *short-term memory*. Before the construct of WM was introduced by Baddeley and Hitch (1974), human memory was divided into STM and LTM. Baddeley's model and most other models embed STM within WM, and define it as the storage aspect of WM. This incorporation of STM clouds the independent aspects of STM. The models seldom acknowledge STM as a separate neurological function with its own processing and storage areas. However, to omit STM from separate consideration and assessment is a mistake because it does function automatically at a subconscious level, without necessarily requiring supervision or involvement from WM. It is only when WM is utilizing specific information held in STM that the two systems work in an integrated fashion.

In the integrated model, WM is considered one of many executive functions. As humans speak, the executive function of self-monitoring detects speech and language errors, leading to immediate self-corrections. Yet, language is not considered a subsystem of self-monitoring. Similarly, STM should not be considered only a subsystem of WM. Support for this argument can be found in research that has found weak correlations between short-term auditory memory span and the capacity of the WM central executive (Pennington, Bennetto, McAleer, & Roberts, 1996; Swanson, 1994). Furthermore, factor analysis of memory performance has revealed that STM and WM operate fairly independently of one another (Engle, Tuholski, Laughlin, & Conway, 1999; Swanson & Howell, 2001). Factor analysis of memory scales has also supported the distinction between STM and WM (Passolunghi & Siegel, 2004).

In the integrated model of WM, STM consists of instantaneous and automated subconscious processes. After perceptual processes have interpreted sensory input, information briefly passes through STM on its way to automatically activating relevant information stored in LTM, such as the meaning of a word that has just been heard. STM also temporarily holds information while it is encoded into LTM. Neither of these automated processes requires conscious participation from WM. Therefore, much of the information handled by STM bypasses WM. Nonetheless, there is nearly constant interaction between executive WM processes and STM storage components. When this type of interaction occurs, it is labeled *verbal WM* or *visual-spatial WM* to distinguish it from the automated, more independent functioning of STM (see Rapid Reference 1.3). In the integrated model, the two STM components are called *phonological STM* and *visual-spatial STM*.

Phonological Short-Term Memory. Phonological STM briefly stores speech-based information in phonological form. Phonological STM continually receives information from auditory sensory stores and automatically activates related items held in long-term storage, such as phonologically similar items. In essence, phonological STM is identical to Baddeley's phonological loop except that subvocal rehearsal is not always a function of phonological STM. Conscious, directed rehearsal efforts are active processes that fall under the purview of executive WM. However, processing occurring below the level of awareness, such as automated rehearsal, is part of phonological STM.

Visual-Spatial Short-Term Memory. This is another STM subcomponent that briefly stores visual (object and color) and spatial (location and direction) information. This subcomponent is the same as Baddeley's visuospatial sketchpad, except that the generation and manipulation of mental images are assigned to WM level. Visual-spatial information is refreshed automatically and continually as objects in the environment change and as the focus of attention changes.

Verbal Working Memory

Verbal WM occurs whenever WM processes utilize verbal information that was just retrieved from LTM or was just perceived and is being temporarily held in phonological STM (see Rapid Reference 1.3). The integrated model does not view recently activated information from LTM as being stored in STM, but rather as

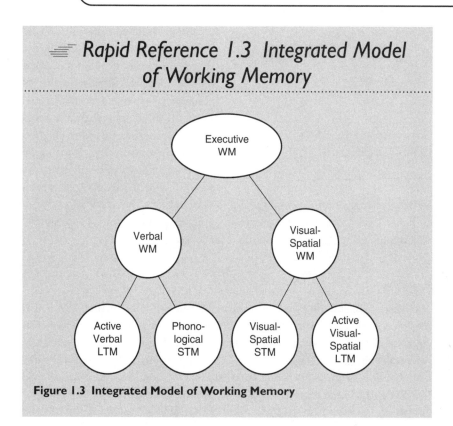

≋ Rapid Reference 1.3 Integrated Model of Working Memory

Figure 1.3 Integrated Model of Working Memory

being held in an active region of LTM. This allows WM to quickly go from one recently activated piece of information to another as the focus of attention shifts. This effectively increases WM capacity so that it can process more information concurrently than could be held in very limited STM. For example, Anderson (1983) found that the recently activated LTM region may hold more than 20 LTM units at a time.

Interaction only between WM and STM will not last long, unless the individual has no relevant LTM representations from which to draw, such as someone who has no prior knowledge of a topic. Thus, WM is usually working with both STM and activated LTM units at the same time. An example of this complex interaction would be the processes that occur during reading comprehension. The reader is briefly holding recently decoded words and phrases while at the same time utilizing prior knowledge that has just been activated.

DON'T FORGET

The verbal and visual-spatial processing components of working memory draw information from both short-term storage and recently activated long-term memory representations.

Verbal WM consists of complex WM operations in which analysis, manipulation, and transformation of phonological, auditory, or verbal material take place. One of the primary functions of verbal WM is to extract a meaningful representation that corresponds to the phonological information taken in by phonological STM (Crain, Shankweiler, Macaruso, & Bar-Shalom, 1990). In contrast to phonological STM, verbal WM is viewed as higher-level, meaning-based processing, whereas phonological STM is simple, passive processing that is more phonologically based.

Visual-Spatial Working Memory

The main distinction between visual-spatial STM and visual-spatial WM is that the STM component involves only passive retention of information, whereas visual-spatial WM adds a processing component, such as reversing the sequence of objects held in STM storage or manipulating an image that was recently activated in LTM. Similar to verbal WM, visual-spatial WM combines information held in STM and LTM. Visual-spatial WM is also involved in creating and manipulating visual images. Until recently, visual-spatial WM was seldom acknowledged as a separate WM component. For a review of empirical support for visual-spatial WM, see Alloway, Gathercole, and Pickering (2006).

Executive Working Memory

According to Baddeley (2003b), there is no verbal or visual-spatial division of WM, except at the STM level. Rather, he views his central executive as modality-free. The functions Baddeley attributes to the central executive are the same as those conducted by verbal and visual-spatial WM in the integrated model. However, the integrated model not only divides WM into verbal and visual-spatial but also retains the concept of a higher-level executive WM that specializes in executive functions not necessarily carried out during specific verbal and visual-spatial processing (see Rapid Reference 1.3).

In the integrated model, executive WM regulates and coordinates all of the cognitive processes that interact with information from either STM or WM. One observable indication that higher-level executive WM is in play is when the task involves integration of verbal and visual-spatial information. Thus, executive WM is not modality-free but multimodal. Multitasking regardless of the modalities involved would also require executive WM. The unique features of executive WM relative to the modality-specific WM components include the application of strategies that extend the capacity and duration of both the STM and WM subcomponents.

Executive WM operations are both conscious and unconscious. WM theories and research have focused mainly on reportable, conscious functioning. However, a myriad of unconscious specialized operations, such as inhibition, carry out detailed WM functions (Baars & Franklin, 2003). These functions are able to operate subconsciously because they have become automated. Unconscious, automated processing is crucial to successful WM performance because it is believed that automated processing does not draw on the measurable capacity of WM. Nonetheless, automated processes operating below the level of awareness tend to be readily accessible, being called into consciousness whenever effortful processing is required. Operations that were once conscious but became unconscious as their function became automated are the most accessible (Baars & Franklin, 2003).

The other primary executive functions are inhibition, switching, and updating. *Inhibition* is the ability to attend to one stimulus while screening out and suppressing the disruptive effects of automatically generated or retrieved information that is not pertinent to the task at hand. Inhibition also discards previously activated but no longer relevant information and suppresses incorrect responses. In effect, inhibition controls and reduces interference. *Switching*, or shifting, refers to the ability to alternate between different tasks, sets, and operations, such as switching retrieval plans or switching between processing and rehearsing. *Updating* is the ability to keep up with the ongoing flow of information. Updating is a constant process of revision whereby newer, more relevant information replaces old, no longer relevant information (Swanson, Howard, & Saez, 2006).

Interaction With Long-Term Memory

LTM is a vast storehouse of information, much of which is encoded, consolidated, and retrieved through subconscious automated processes. For the most part, LTM can operate independently of WM. For example, when decoding text, a fluent reader automatically retrieves known words and comprehends them without the involvement of WM.

Perhaps the closest interaction between WM and LTM occurs during learning and encoding of information into LTM. For example, when a student listening to a presentation hears new information about a familiar subject, relevant information in LTM is activated. WM then holds and processes the information, making associations between the new information and activated prior knowledge. The new associations then become encoded into LTM. Another interactive function of WM is to support conscious, effortful retrieval from LTM when the desired information is not automatically and immediately retrieved (Rosen & Engle, 1997). Effortful retrieval from LTM also occurs whenever specific information is demanded of the individual.

The relationship is reciprocal; LTM supports WM as much as WM supports LTM. This is because WM capacity and functioning are affected by the knowledge and skill base in LTM. As knowledge and skills become consolidated and automated in LTM, less processing is required by WM. Moreover, LTM representations may directly enhance short-term and WM spans. When information enters STM, relevant items are immediately activated in LTM. When the information is lost from STM, LTM immediately, automatically, and subconsciously sends cues to WM so that the decayed information can be reconstructed (Nairne, 2002). This interaction explains why individuals are able to remember some newly presented information for longer than a few seconds.

Capacity of Working Memory Operations

In the integrated model of WM, functional capacity, while still limited, may be greater than indicated by span measures. Humans often accomplish WM feats that go beyond predictions based on typical memory spans of only a few items. Incorporating an activated pool of LTM items greatly expands the amount of information available to WM. However, the WM processing dimension still has very limited capacity. Consistent with Cowan's embedded process model, the integrated model proposes that simultaneous processing in WM is limited to approximately four units of information in a typical adult and perhaps only one or two units in a young child. However, the size of the units or chunks may vary, depending on the content and the individual's level of expertise.

The integrated model also proposes that WM performance is determined by how effectively the individual utilizes his innate capacity. For example, the development of automaticity or expertise in a particular skill or content area will enhance WM performance by increasing the size of the information chunks that are manipulated. Applying effective memory strategies from simple rehearsal to more elaborate strategies will also enhance WM performance.

Finally, the integrated model recognizes the influence of cognitive load on WM processing and short-term retention. As cognitive load increases, the amount of information that can be concurrently retained diminishes. Only frequent switching between processing and maintaining items in storage can ameliorate this effect.

SUMMARY

In the integrated model of WM proposed herein, STM, WM, and LTM are all distinct but interrelated memory systems. WM is the interface between STM and LTM, working both with units temporarily retained in STM and with recently activated units from LTM (Rose & Craik, 2012; Unsworth & Engle, 2007). At any point in time, the focus of WM might be material from short-term storage, elements from long-term storage, or a combination of the two.

Without assistance or management from WM, STM and LTM can both function independently. STM can retain information without involvement from WM, although the retention interval is quite short. STM also automatically and independently activates relevant information in LTM. For its part, LTM can automatically and independently encode information briefly held in STM, and it can also function independently in activating and retrieving information.

However, whenever temporarily held or recently activated information requires effortful, conscious processing, WM clearly comes into play. When the interaction is primarily verbal, it is considered verbal WM; when the interaction is primarily visual-spatial, it is considered visual-spatial WM; and when higher-level multi-modal executive functions come into play, it is considered executive WM.

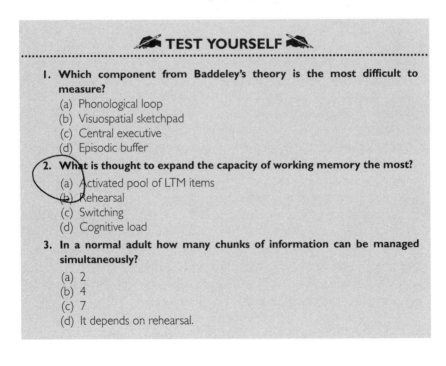

🔨 TEST YOURSELF 🐟

1. **Which component from Baddeley's theory is the most difficult to measure?**
   (a) Phonological loop
   (b) Visuospatial sketchpad
   (c) Central executive
   (d) Episodic buffer

2. **What is thought to expand the capacity of working memory the most?**
   (a) Activated pool of LTM items
   (b) Rehearsal
   (c) Switching
   (d) Cognitive load

3. **In a normal adult how many chunks of information can be managed simultaneously?**
   (a) 2
   (b) 4
   (c) 7
   (d) It depends on rehearsal.

4. **Consistent with the integrated model, verbal working memory should be measured separately from phonological short-term memory.**
   (a) True
   (b) False

5. **Which is not a key function of executive working memory?**
   (a) Updating
   (b) Shifting
   (c) Monitoring
   (d) Inhibition

6. **Regardless of age, the length of an individual's phonological STM span is limited to how many monosyllable words the individual can articulate within ___ seconds.**
   (a) 2
   (b) 5
   (c) 7
   (d) 15

Answers: 1. d; 2. a; 3. b; 4. True; 5. c; 6. a

Two

COGNITIVE PROCESSES HIGHLY RELATED WITH WORKING MEMORY

W M is closely interrelated with several cognitive processes, as well as metacognitive executive processes (McNamara & Scott, 2001). Many of these relations are moderate to high, with some correlations as high as .9. In Rapid Reference 2.1 correlations from the Woodcock-Johnson IV (WJ IV; McGrew, LaForte, & Schrank, 2014) are used to illustrate the strong correlations between WM and other cognitive processes. These strong relations indicate that WM is a core cognitive process. Thus, much of successful cognitive activity depends on the interplay between WM and cognitive processes. Some of these relationships are hierarchical, some are reciprocal, and some are between parallel processes. Sometimes there is such close interaction that it is difficult to distinguish between WM and a related process. For example, the control of attention is a process that is difficult to untangle from executive WM processes.

Because many of the relationships are reciprocal, deficient cognitive processes can reduce WM's efficiency and performance, whereas strong cognitive processes can enhance WM. For example, exceptionally fast processing speed may compensate somewhat for a subaverage WM. For its part, WM capacity constrains related cognitive processes, such as fluid reasoning (Conners, Rosenquist, & Taylor, 2001). An impaired WM system may place serious limitations upon other cognitive functions that in themselves do not involve the retention of information. At times, even a WM with normal capacity and efficient functioning can have deleterious effects on other processing. For example, when an individual is trying to maintain information in short-term storage, a computational task may take longer to complete, with increased risk of errors.

The effect that WM load has on another process reflects the level of dependence the related process has on WM. The effect also could indicate that WM and other cognitive functions draw from the same pool of processing resources.

Rapid Reference 2.1 Correlations Between the WJ IV Working Memory Cluster and Related Cognitive Clusters, Ages 6 Through 8

General Intellectual Ability	.72
Fluid Reasoning	.54
Processing Speed	.42
Auditory Processing	.56
Long-Term Retrieval	.40
Visual-Spatial Processing	.37

Also, the interdependency of WM and associated processes means that growth and development in other cognitive processes will contribute to the expansion of WM capacity. For example, WM capacity expands along with a child's growing attention span.

From an assessment perspective, knowing which cognitive abilities are closely connected with WM is important. When WM is deficient, related cognitive processes should also be assessed. Similarly, when a closely related cognitive process is deficient, WM should be tested in a comprehensive manner. When analyzing assessment results, the examiner should hypothesize as to how the cognitive processes involved are influencing each other (see Chapter 5).

GENERAL INTELLIGENCE

There is strong evidence from several studies that WM, more than any other cognitive factor except fluid reasoning, may account for individual differences in general intelligence (Ackerman, Beier, & Boyle, 2002b; Cowan, 2005; Kyllonen, 1996). The correlations between WM capacity and general intelligence, also known as "g" and "IQ," have generally been around .6 (for a review see A. Conway, Kane, & Engle, 2003), with WM accounting for a third to half of the variance in g. Kyllonen and Christal (1990) were the first to assert that "WM is *the* general factor in cognition" (1990, p. 401). Subsequent studies have replicated their original findings. For example, Sub, Oberauer, Wittmann, Wilhelm, and Schulze (2002) found general WM capacity to be highly related with general intelligence. A recent study reported that WM predicted 66% of the variance in g (Giofre, Mammarella, & Cornoldi, 2013).

Other factor analytic studies have found WM to have the highest correlation (.93) with g, supplanting fluid reasoning as the primary, first-order factor (Colom, Rebollo, Palacios, Juan-Espinosa, & Kyllonen, 2004). The relationship is so strong that g is almost perfectly predicted by WM capacity, making WM capacity the best predictor of g (intelligence). The relationship is bidirectional; g is also a good predictor of WM. Findings of such strong relations have led some to claim that WM and intelligence are unitary constructs. However, the current consensus seems to be that WM capacity and g are highly related factors but are not identical (A. Conway et al., 2003; Kyllonen & Christal, 1990). Also, WM and g may be highly correlated because measures of each construct share multiple cognitive processes, not because WM and g share one general factor (A. Conway, Macnamara, & de Abreu, 2013).

The strong relation most likely results from the necessity for WM involvement whenever complex cognitive activity occurs. That is, a considerable amount of information must be actively maintained in WM during most complex cognitive functioning. The WM components that most account for the relationship are the verbal and executive components (see Rapid Reference 2.2). For example, when complex processing is required, executive WM focuses attention, maintains activation of goal-relevant information, and inhibits interference. Actively maintaining a memory representation while inhibiting distracting interference may account for much of the variance WM and g have in common (Kane & Engle, 2002). In contrast, STM tasks that measure simple storage typically do not have significant relations with g.

Some advocates of the WM construct (Alloway & Alloway, 2010) have argued that WM is a better predictor of academic learning than is full-scale IQ. WM scores not only have strong relations with IQ scores but also are highly predictive of academic learning (see Chapter 4). In the recently released Woodcock-Johnson IV, the instrument's cognitive battery

> **DON'T FORGET**
>
> Working memory is now recognized as one of the best measures of intelligence, but there is more to intelligence than what is measured by a working memory test.

> **CAUTION**
>
> High correlations between two factors do not mean that the entities involved are one and the same. Also, correlations do not prove causality or which of two factors involved is more dependent on the other.

≡ Rapid Reference 2.2 Specific Working Memory Components Most Highly Related With Cognitive Processes*

Processes	Phonological STM	Visual-Spatial STM	Verbal WM	Visual-Spatial WM	Executive WM
Intelligence			X		X
Fluid Reasoning					X
Executive Functions					X
Attention				X	X
Oral Language	X		X		
Auditory Processing	X				
Phonological Processing	X		X		
Processing Speed	X	X	X	X	X
Visual-Spatial Processing		X		X	
Sequential Processing	X				
LTM Encoding	X	X	X	X	X
LTM Retrieval					X
Metamemory					X
Strategies					X

*This table can also be found in the online resources.

WM score was found to be one of the best predictors of its academic achievement battery scores (McGrew et al., 2014). Nonetheless, intelligence and cognitive abilities tests measure a broader range of functions and processes than WM tests measure. Consequently, overall cognitive ability should also be considered when there are academic learning concerns.

FLUID REASONING

Fluid reasoning is the ability to reason, form concepts, and solve problems, particularly when confronted with a novel task or unfamiliar situation. (A list of these cognitive processes with definitions that can be used in psychological reports can be found in the online resources.) Historically, fluid reasoning has been considered one of the primary intelligence factors, if not the essence of *g* (Carroll, 1993). Reading comprehension and mathematical reasoning are academic skills that draw heavily on fluid reasoning. Like executive processing, with which it is also intertwined, fluid reasoning is a cognitive process that does not reach full development until early adolescence.

Several studies have found extremely high correlations between fluid reasoning and WM capacity. In research reviewed by A. Conway et al. (2013), WM span tasks correlate between .72 and .85 with fluid reasoning. Kyllonen and Christal (1990) even found correlations as high as .90. The strong relationship between fluid reasoning and WM holds true over a broad range of different tasks (Sub et al., 2002). The close relation between WM and fluid reasoning is also supported by neuroimaging studies that found the same regions of the prefrontal cortex to be involved during both types of tasks (Kane & Engle, 2002). It is believed that WM provides the *mental workspace* that fluid reasoning needs in order to function, such as when items are being compared and contrasted.

The high correlations between the two variables may result from a third variable that they are both related to. What WM and fluid reasoning may have in common is some aspect of controlled attention (Engle, Tuholski, et al., 1999). Another explanation for the strong link between WM and fluid reasoning is offered by A. Conway, Cowan, Bunting, Therriault, and Minkoff (2002) who contend that performance in both domains depends on successful application of strategies, an aspect of executive functioning.

Some researchers (Kyllonen & Christal, 1990) suggest that individual differences in fluid reasoning are due to differences in WM capacity. For example, Kail (2007) reported longitudinal evidence demonstrating that an increase in WM capacity is one of the factors driving developmental growth in inductive reasoning. Despite this evidence, a reciprocal relationship is implicated, with differences in fluid reasoning at least partially explained by WM capacity and differences in WM partially reflecting one's ability to reason effectively (Shelton, Elliott, Matthews, Hill, & Gouvier, 2010).

The WM component that has the strongest relationship with fluid reasoning is executive WM. In contrast, phonological STM does not appear to have a strong connection with fluid reasoning (Engle et al., 1999). As with other processes, strong fluid reasoning abilities may help to compensate for an impaired WM; for example, fluid reasoning may produce a correct response when details have been partially forgotten. Although some investigators argue that fluid reasoning and WM are identical constructs (Buehner, Krumm, Ziegler, & Pluecken, 2006), the consensus is that WM and fluid reasoning are not identical factors, despite their extremely close relationship.

THE BIG THREE

When cognitive abilities, including WM, are factor-analyzed to determine underlying latent traits, the first factor that nearly always emerges is the general intelligence factor referred to as "*g*" (Carroll, 1993). A recent study by Dehn (2014a) found the second factor to be a combination of the WM, executive functions, and attention subscales in the teacher rating scale known as the *Children's Psychological Processes Scale* (CPPS; Dehn, 2012). This factor was named Self-Regulatory Processes because it seems to be primarily measuring the self-regulatory aspects, such as inhibition, that are involved in cognition.

> ## DON'T FORGET
> ....
> Working memory, attention, and executive functions can be considered *The Big Three* in working memory assessment.

The discovery of this factor on the CPPS is consistent with theories of WM, empirical evidence, and neuroanatomy. These three processes are closely related with each other in more than one way. First, WM is considered to be one of the executive functions (McCloskey & Perkins, 2013). Second, executive functions and control of attention are highly interrelated (Barkley, 1997b). Third, there is a strong relationship between attention and WM (see section later in this chapter). Moreover, what binds them together has a neurological basis: The source of their functioning seems to be located in the prefrontal cortex of the brain. Consequently, from a WM perspective, attention, executive functions, and WM should be considered *The Big Three*. These three hang together in a cluster that is second only to the general intelligence factor. Therefore, executive functions and attention should be included in every evaluation of WM.

EXECUTIVE FUNCTIONS

Executive functions include mental processes responsible for cuing, directing, and coordinating multiple aspects of perception, cognition, emotion, and behavior during purposeful, goal-directed, problem-solving behavior (McCloskey & Perkins, 2013). The different executive functions, which are analogous to a board of directors, monitor and manage cognitive functions. The complexity of executive functioning is illustrated by McCloskey and Perkins (2013), who identify 32 different self-regulation executive functions organized under the six executive clusters of attention, engagement, optimization, evaluation, efficiency, and memory. Nearly all experts in executive functions agree that WM is one of the executive functions. However, they are, for the most part, referring only to the executive component of WM. Such executive WM processes are called into action whenever automated STM and LTM processes are insufficient for the task at hand. Therefore, the relationships under consideration here are between executive WM and other executive processes.

It is important to distinguish between general executive functions and WM executive functions. General executive processes should not be viewed as the equivalent of WM (St. Clair-Thompson, 2011). Certainly, WM can vary independently of other executive functions (Bayliss, Jarrold, Baddeley, & Gunn, 2003). For example, WM may have little to do with such executive functions as initiating an activity or with the regulation of emotions. Nonetheless, WM may actually underlie and influence a wide range of executive processes. For example, planning, which is considered an executive process, requires the use of WM resources. Other aspects of executive functioning that play a role in WM performance are discussed under the Metamemory and Strategies sections at the end of this chapter.

ATTENTION

Attention is a complex, multifaceted psychological process that influences cognition, learning, behavior, and performance (Chun, Golomb, & Turk-Browne, 2011). There are several types of attention, including focused, sustained, and divided attention. Learning and the efficiency of cognitive operations, such as WM, require adequate attentional capacity and control. Individuals with higher levels of attentional control are better able to inhibit distractions, as well as receive, process, and encode information. Cognitive goals are best accomplished when the individual is able to focus attention on the relevant processing and information. There is an exceptionally strong relationship between WM and attention, making them difficult to distinguish by observation alone. For example, children with WM deficits are often mis-identified by their teachers as having attention problems (Cornish, Wilding, & Grant, 2006).

The control, focusing, maintenance, and dividing of attention are core functions of executive WM (Cornish et al., 2006; Soto, Heinke, Humphreys, & Blanco, 2005). Focused attention is necessary during almost every aspect of WM functioning (Engle, Kane, & Tuholski, 1999). WM is also responsible for resisting interference and for shifting attention from one task to another, without losing relevant information. Individuals who score high on tests of executive WM capacity are better at focusing attention and inhibiting distracting information than are low-span individuals (A. Conway, Cowan, & Bunting, 2001). Conversely, individuals with poor attentional control are likely to have concomitant difficulties in some aspects of WM.

What binds executive WM and attentional control together is that they are both executive functions (McCabe, Roediger, McDaniel, Balota, & Hambrick, 2010). All three are also linked neurologically because they share the same control structure in the prefrontal cortex (see Chapter 3). It has been proposed that the ability to inhibit interference may be the underlying trait that accounts for both attentional control and executive WM performance (Barkley, 1997a; Cornish et al., 2006; Schecklmann et al., 2014).

However, there are indications that inhibitory control levels do not underlie WM, but rather executive WM influences inhibition (Alderson, Rapport, Hudec, Sarver, & Kofler, 2010). Evidence for this is that higher cognitive load reduces inhibitory control and the focusing of attention. For example, inattentive behavior in the classroom may be due to cognitive overload. As cognitive load increases, the executive control of attention is reduced (Hester & Garavan, 2005), resulting in a diminished ability to exert inhibitory control over extraneous, irrelevant processing and information. Consequently, focus is lost, the mind wanders, and the task is abandoned (Gathercole & Alloway, 2008).

DON'T FORGET

Although control of attention is a function of executive working memory, attention and working memory should not be considered the same construct or neurological function because there is much more to both functions than the sub-processes they share.

With controlled attention and other aspects of attention frequently identified as core functions of executive WM, there is a tendency to consider attention and WM to be one and the same construct (Olivers, Meijer, & Theeuwes, 2006). However, WM and attention should not be considered one and the same, even though control of attention is part of WM (Buehner, Mangels, Krumm, & Ziegler, 2005). The main reason for maintaining the distinction between these two neurological systems is that there is much more to WM than attentional control, and there is much more to attention than focusing attention on the current cognitive task. For example, WM also has responsibility for retrieval of items from LTM and for maintaining information in STM. Attention includes such fundamental processes as arousal and controlling impulsivity.

ATTENTION-DEFICIT/HYPERACTIVITY DISORDER

Individuals with attention-deficit/hyperactivity disorder (ADHD) typically perform poorly on measures of WM (Klingberg, Forssberg, & Westerberg, 2002). Prevailing models of ADHD (Barkley, 1997a, 1997b) suggest that WM impairments are central to ADHD because WM deficits and ADHD both are associated with specific deficits in executive skills (Wu, Anderson, & Castiello, 2006). Barkley, a recognized expert in ADHD, has asserted that the core deficit of ADHD is the inability to use inhibitory processes when needed. Inhibition, an executive process, also performs a crucial function for WM by suppressing and deactivating information that is not relevant to the task at hand (Cowan, 2005). When inhibition fails, irrelevant information interferes with the retention and processing of information that should be the focus of attention, negatively impacting WM performance.

Numerous studies have found ADHD children and adolescents to have co-occurring deficits in WM. T. Brown, Reichel, and Quinlan (2009) reported that over 74% of the ADHD youth in their sample displayed a significant impairment in WM. In a meta-analysis of 26 studies on WM impairments found in children with ADHD, Martinussen, Hayden, Hogg-Johnson, and Tannock (2005) concluded that children with ADHD exhibit deficits in multiple components of WM. Martinussen et al. suggest that poor academic progress in children with ADHD may be the result of WM deficiencies rather than a direct consequence of inattention, a suggestion that has important implications for assessment and education.

The specific types of WM deficits seem to depend on the subtype of ADHD (Quinlan & Brown, 2003). Martinussen and Tannock (2006) found that children with the ADHD combined subtype perform worse than normal students on all STM and WM components, whereas the primarily inattentive subtypes are deficient only in visual-spatial and executive WM. They also found that the primarily hyperactive-impulsive subtypes may not display any significant WM deficits. When those who are primarily hyperactive-impulsive do have a WM impairment, it tends to be in the executive domain (Martinussen & Tannock, 2006). Thus, children with ADHD are not necessarily impaired in all aspects of WM. For example, they generally do not possess deficits in verbal WM or phonological STM unless they have ADHD combined subtype or have a comorbid learning disability.

For children with ADHD, the overall finding is that a deficit in executive WM is most likely to co-occur. Kasper, Alderson, and Hudec (2012) found that 81% of children with ADHD have deficits in executive WM. The second most likely WM deficit among ADHD children is in visual-spatial WM (Alderson et al., 2010; van Ewijk et al., 2014). Children with ADHD generally do not exhibit a deficit in phonological STM. Therefore, examiners should assess all WM components to avoid a misleading impression regarding an ADHD examinee's WM ability. LTM retrieval ability should also be assessed because it has been recently discovered that individuals with ADHD have difficulty retrieving relevant information from LTM (Gibson, Gondoli, Flies, Dobrzenski, & Unsworth, 2010).

The consensus among researchers is that WM is more strongly related to symptoms of inattention than to symptoms of hyperactivity-impulsivity. Some researchers have even asserted that verbal and executive WM deficits may be a common neuropsychological weakness in children who have both primarily inattentive ADHD and a learning disability. Perhaps the most important educational implication from this research is that a WM impairment may be the cognitive factor that actually underlies the academic learning problems experienced by children diagnosed with ADHD.

> # DON'T FORGET
> ....
> A high number (approximately 75% to 80%) of children with ADHD will also have impairment in working memory, especially executive working memory.

An overloaded WM may even have an impact on hyperactivity level. As cognitive load increases and inhibitory control declines, individuals with ADHD exhibit more hyperactivity (Hudec, Alderson, Kasper, & Patros, 2014; Rapport et al., 2009). Accordingly, Klingberg (2010) discovered that WM training reduced ADHD symptoms, including hyperactivity.

ORAL LANGUAGE

Oral language is a broad processing area that incorporates many basic psychological processes, from phonological encoding to word retrieval, as well as several specific linguistic processes, such as the processes involved in morphology and syntax. The acquisition of vocabulary occurs through language processes, but vocabulary level is not itself a process. Oral language divides into receptive and expressive language. Auditory processing and phonological processing can be considered subtypes of oral language.

Researchers in the field of linguistics generally concur that there is a strong relationship between language processes and WM (for a review, see Leonard et al., 2007). There is empirical evidence that linguistic processes are constrained by WM capacity (Moser, Fridriksson, & Healy, 2007). Some linguists believe that language processing has its own functionally separate WM, distinct from WM that serves other types of processing (Just & Carpenter, 1992). For instance, verbal WM is viewed as a language subsystem specifically designed for mediating language comprehension. Others contend that verbal WM and linguistic processing are so interrelated that they are not even distinct entities (MacDonald & Christiansen, 2002). However, most psychologists believe that

WM, even verbal WM, serves more general verbal processing, such as assisting with reading comprehension.

AUDITORY PROCESSING

Auditory processing is the ability to perceive, analyze, synthesize, and discriminate speech and other auditory stimuli. It is not the sensory aspect of audition, but rather what the brain does with sensory information received through the ear. Auditory processing subsumes such narrow abilities as phonetic coding, speech sound discrimination, resistance to auditory stimulus distortion, memory for sound patterns, maintaining and judging rhythm, musical discrimination and judgment, absolute pitch, and sound localization (J. Schneider & McGrew, 2012). Studies have reported moderate correlations between general auditory processing and WM (Hitch, Towse, & Hutton, 2001). Auditory processing is primarily receptive, whereas oral language and phonological processing are both receptive and expressive.

PHONOLOGICAL PROCESSING

Phonological processing is an aspect of oral language and auditory processing that involves manipulation of the phonemes that make up words (Gillon, 2004). Phonological processing involves recognizing, segmenting, and blending phonemes into whole words. Phonemes, the smallest units of speech, are combined to form syllables and words. The English language consists of about 44 phonemes. Phonemic awareness—the understanding that words (spoken and written) can be divided into discrete sounds—is an important dimension of phonological processing. The first indication that young children have developed phonemic awareness is that they are able to discriminate between speech sounds. Being able to rhyme and alliterate, or say words that start with the same sound, is another indication that phonemic awareness is developing.

Phonemic awareness is the single best predictor of early literacy development and reading performance (Kamhi & Pollock, 2005; National Reading Panel, 2000). Children who are better at detecting phonemes learn to decode words more easily by breaking down words into sound units. Most children who become proficient readers have strong phonemic awareness prior to formal reading instruction (see Chapter 4).

The WM component that is most closely related with phonological processing is phonological STM. Some verbal WM comes into play when phonemes are consciously blended to form words. Studies (reviewed by Wagner, 1996) have found measures of phonological awareness and phonological STM to be highly correlated with each other. The consensus among researchers is that the two processes have a reciprocal effect on each other (Cohen-Mimran & Sapir, 2007). Adequate phonological STM is necessary for proficient phonological processing; conversely, phonological processing ability affects STM span (Hulme & Mackenzie, 1992). To some extent, phonological processing and phonological STM seem inseparable; they are certainly strongly associated throughout development. It is possible that phonological processing is the underlying process that determines the capacity of phonological STM.

PROCESSING SPEED

Processing speed refers to how quickly the brain processes information and how efficiently simple cognitive tasks are executed over a sustained period of time. Broad processing speed can be divided into "simple" processing speed, which reflects the mental speed required to perform undemanding attentional tasks, and "complex" processing speed, which reflects the total time to complete more demanding tasks, such as a task that involves decision making. Simple processing speed is typically tested with tasks requiring the examinee to perform relatively easy, overlearned procedures that require little reasoning or higher-level complex processing.

Processing speed is highly interrelated with all aspects of WM and STM, and processing speed appears to have a strong influence on the growth of WM capacity. Ackerman, Beier, and Boyle (2002a) reported a correlation of .48 between WM tests and processing speed ability. Fry and Hale (1996) reported that 71% of the age-related changes in WM capacity are related to developmental changes in processing speed. Undoubtedly, the processing and storage capacity of WM is extremely dependent on the general speed of cognitive processing. Nonetheless, there is ample evidence for the functional separation of processing speed and WM (Leonard et al., 2007).

Processing speed heavily influences WM because memory processing and storage are time-related (Swanson et al., 2006). Faster processing speed allows more information to be processed in less time, thereby increasing the functional capacity of WM. Faster speed also reduces the interval over which information must be maintained, resulting in less short-term forgetting. Other ways faster processing speed enables WM processing and storage are: making it possible to shift more rapidly between competing tasks (Kail & Hall, 2001); increasing the speed at which information is encoded into an LTM representation; and increasing the speed at which long-term memories are activated and retrieved. Faster processing speed also allows more efficient access to representations maintained in STM or the activated LTM pool. In contrast, slow processing speed creates the possibility of loss of information from a normal WM before the cognitive or academic task can be completed (Compton, Fuchs, Fuchs, Lambert, & Hamlett, 2012). When WM is deficient, a relative strength in processing speed might help to compensate for the weakness (Compton et al., 2012). In general, individuals who process information more rapidly have more time to encode, rehearse, and process the to-be remembered material, resulting in improved short-term and long-term retention.

The influence of processing speed on phonological STM span has been explored in depth. As discussed in Chapter 1, increases in speech rate are highly related with the growth of STM span. Processing speed mediates articulation rate and rehearsal rate, which in turn determine the number of items that can be rehearsed before decay. Thus, faster processing speed extends STM span. In the case of curtailed phonological short-term capacity, processing speed can compensate somewhat by rapidly encoding information into long-term storage or rapidly moving information into WM for higher-level processing.

VISUAL-SPATIAL PROCESSING

Visual-spatial processing is the ability to perceive, analyze, synthesize, manipulate, and transform visual patterns and images, including those generated internally. The visual and spatial dimensions are easily differentiated. The visual aspect involves processing of stimulus characteristics, such as shape and color. The spatial dimension processes the location and movement of visual stimuli; for example, mental rotation of an image requires spatial processing.

Visual-spatial processing is closely related with the visual-spatial dimensions of WM and STM (Hitch et al., 2001). Visual-spatial STM is responsible for constantly refreshing the perceptual image of the visual field, even when the field is unchanging. Integration of visual-spatial processing and refreshing in STM seems necessary in order for individuals to remain oriented in space and be aware of the current location of moving objects. When individuals must consciously recall or manipulate objects or mental images, then visual-spatial WM becomes involved.

SEQUENTIAL PROCESSING

Sequential processing, also referred to as *successive processing*, is the maintenance of serial order and the sequential arrangement and encoding of information. Stimuli arranged sequentially form a chainlike progression in which each stimulus is related to the one it follows. Sequential processing is required in order to understand speech and decode written material. Most sequential processing is automatized and supported by phonological STM. However, there is more to phonological STM capacity than the ability to retain sequences. Demands to recall information sequentially will enlist WM resources, especially conscious rehearsal.

LONG-TERM MEMORY

As discussed in Chapter 1, WM interfaces with LTM as much as or more than it does with STM. The primary interaction occurs when WM utilizes recently retrieved information from LTM to accomplish a cognitive goal. Recently activated LTM items are temporarily held in a readily accessible pool without the need for rehearsal. WM switches back and forth between the items in this pool until the cognitive activity is completed. Also, WM supports LTM during conscious and effortful encoding and retrieval. For its part, LTM supports WM and STM by helping to reconstruct information that has been lost from short-term storage (J. Turner, Henry, & Smith, 2000). Yet, WM and LTM are separate memory systems with unique neurological structures. Thus, one system may be a relative strength or weakness compared with the other.

> ## DON'T FORGET
> ....
> Whenever an individual is referred for memory problems, both working memory and long-term memory should be assessed.

Any time an individual is referred for memory concerns, the evaluation should include both memory systems, even when the referring party believes it is only a WM or an LTM problem. This is because the referring party may be accurately reporting observations but attributing the problem to an incorrect memory system. Consequently, practitioners who assess WM also need to be versed in basic LTM processes and neurological structures. The main LTM processes are encoding, consolidation, and retrieval. The emphasis will be on encoding and retrieval because consolidation is primarily subconscious and is not impacted by WM functioning. (For details on assessment of LTM see Dehn, 2010.)

Encoding

Encoding refers to the process of transforming sensory and perceptual information into a representational code that can be stored in LTM. Encoding differs according to the type of sensory or processing system involved, as well as by the content. The form and extent of encoding are in part determined by the stimulus and in part determined by the individual's interpretation of the event or material. Consequently, any given experience or piece of information can be encoded in multiple formats and multiple brain locations (S. Brown & Craik, 2000). For example, verbal information may be encoded in terms of its phonological features, or it could be coded in terms of its semantic characteristics. Also, multiple modality encoding may occur, such as when information is encoded in both an auditory and visual mode. For example, when someone views an object and names it at the same time, both auditory and visual information is encoded.

Most encoding is relatively automatic and unconscious as information passes directly from perceptual structures, sensory memory, and STM into LTM stores. Automatic encoding operates at a constant level under a variety of circumstances. It occurs without intention and does not involve practice or repetition. The automatic processes encode certain attributes, such as spatial or temporal, of whatever event is occurring. Because it is automated, this type of encoding makes no demands on WM (Hasher & Zacks, 1979).

In contrast, conscious, effortful encoding is intentional and its efficiency increases with practice. Effortful encoding typically involves thoughtful processing or mnemonic strategies, and it consumes some WM, thereby limiting the ability to simultaneously engage in other cognitively demanding tasks, while also reducing the amount that can be retained in short-term storage. When WM experiences high cognitive load, new information is lost before it is encoded into LTM. Poor performance on learning and LTM encoding tasks, such as memorizing a word list, may be due to encoding limitations, WM deficiencies, or both. Used effectively, both WM and LTM strategies can enhance encoding so that information will be more memorable.

In addition to strategies, several other variables can influence the effectiveness of encoding. Foremost among them is attention. Focused attention is essential for successful encoding of memories. Encoding of explicit information often fails because insufficient attention is devoted to the stimulus at the time of encoding (Schacter, 1999). For example, divided attention during encoding substantially reduces later recall (Emilien, Durlach, Antoniadis, Van Der Linden, & Maloteaux, 2004). Another variable is preexisting knowledge already stored in LTM. Prior knowledge not only influences how an event or information is perceived but also provides memory structures and representations with which the incoming information can be integrated.

DON'T FORGET

Conscious, effortful long-term memory encoding and retrieval require working memory resources, but automated, subconscious encoding and retrieval do not.

Without encoding, there are no long-term memories. Moreover, effective encoding is a prerequisite for subsequent memory processing. How information is encoded partially determines how long it will remain in storage and how easily it can be retrieved. For example, a considerable amount of empirical evidence indicates that retrieval is more effective when encoding variables match retrieval variables. However, even with normal encoding there is no guarantee of long-term retention and retrieval.

Consolidation

Consolidation refers to an extended, multistage, subconscious process whereby a memory becomes more stable and resistant to interference and forgetting. It is a post-encoding process that involves maintenance, restructuring, and storage of new information (D. Siegel, 1999). During consolidation, new memories that are initially stored in and near the hippocampus are transferred to cortical areas for more permanent storage (see Chapter 3; McClelland, McNaughton, & O'Reilly, 1995). Consolidation is not yet entirely understood, but research in this area has established that information that is not encoded is rapidly forgotten, consolidation mainly occurs during sleep, and consolidation modifies memories. Although the brain's long-term storage capacity appears to be unlimited, its ability to consolidate new memories before they are forgotten or become irretrievable certainly is limited (Wixted, 2004).

Neuropsychological evidence for consolidation comes from cases of acquired retrograde amnesia that have been caused by head injuries or hippocampal atrophy. In such individuals, more recent memories are lost while more distant memories are spared. This phenomenon is attributed to incomplete consolidation. After encoding and initial learning, memories exist in a fragile state in the hippocampus. When the hippocampus is damaged, recent memories that are still undergoing the process of consolidation have not yet been transferred to cortical regions and therefore are permanently lost.

From an assessment perspective, consolidation failure is implicated when there is abnormally fast forgetting, or when free recall and recognition are equally deficient. In such instances, it is unlikely that the sought-after information remains in long-term storage. The reason it is not retained in storage is that it was not consolidated. If it had been consolidated, it would have been fairly impervious to forgetting. An example of poor consolidation is a student who appears to have learned something new but then has no recollection of it the next day.

Retrieval

Retrieval refers to the processes involved when one accesses information that is stored in LTM. Retrieval actually involves two types of processes: a spontaneous, automatic process that brings information into consciousness and a controlled, strategic process that guides a search for information. The automatic process is initiated by external cues. The controlled process may be activated by external or internal cues. According to Koriat (2000), the consciously controlled process might best be framed as goal-oriented problem solving that begins with a goal and proceeds strategically until the solution is found.

WM is important for a controlled search in LTM (Unsworth, Brewer, & Spillers, 2013). Effortful, conscious, strategic retrieval needs WM to control, monitor, coordinate, evaluate, and revise search processes while holding partially retrieved information in temporary storage and inhibiting irrelevant information. Thus, WM deficiencies can add to retrieval problems.

Of all the LTM problems, retrieval failures seem the most pervasive, probably because everyone experiences them frequently. When retrieval failure occurs, the individual usually "knows" the information is in storage, but can't access it at that moment. Retrieval failure can have many causes. First, successful retrieval is critically dependent on cues that are created or associated during encoding. Successful, effortful retrieval depends on how well the individual can regenerate the cues to which the memory is associated. Second, retrieval failure is often created by interference caused by prior retrieval of related but incorrect information. Third, successful retrieval is dependent on organized memory structures where related events and concepts are interlinked. Fourth, retrieval difficulties may be due to a deficient WM. Although the amount of storage capacity in LTM may be unlimited, the ability to retrieve any and all memories on demand is limited.

Another aspect of retrieval that can cause memory performance problems is retrieval speed or fluency. Retrieval speed is as important as accuracy in determining the overall efficiency of retrieval. Slow retrieval speed may have a neurological basis and may be just one aspect of slower cognitive processing speed. However, the speed and efficiency of retrieval also depend on the degree of interconnectivity among memory representations of related concepts and events (Klimesch, 1994).

Recall Versus Recognition

There are two main types of conscious retrieval: *recall* and *recognition*. Recall refers to retrieval without any deliberate or direct external prompts and cues, whereas recognition refers to selecting the response from a set of provided items. During a recognition task the individual examines the response options and either immediately recognizes one of the responses or feels that one of the responses is familiar. In a normally functioning memory, more correct information is retrieved through recognition than through recall because recognizing an item is easier than freely recalling it. Hence, recalling an item requires more readily available information in storage than recognizing an item (Haist, Shimamura, & Squire, 1992).

The distinction between recall and recognition is important because comparison of the two can provide insight into whether an LTM performance problem is primarily a storage or a retrieval problem. Most individuals can correctly recognize more information than they can accurately recall without cues. However, when recognition surpasses free recall by a highly unusual amount, it indicates that the information is in storage but the individual is having difficulty retrieving the information on demand. In such instances, storage problems can be ruled out while a retrieval impairment is implicated. When recognition of information is not substantially better than free recall of the same information, the implication is that the information was never consolidated, has been forgotten, and is now no longer stored in LTM.

METAMEMORY

Metamemory, a type of metacognition, refers to knowledge about and regulation of memory systems, processes, and functions (W. Schneider, 2010). One's knowledge and beliefs about human memory influence how one consciously attempts to influence memory performance. For example, knowing the differences between STM and LTM will lead one to realize that being able to immediately recall information does not mean it will be recalled as well a day later. An important aspect of metamemory is self-awareness of personal memory strengths and weaknesses—for instance, knowing that one has stronger visual-spatial than verbal memory. Metamemory also includes self-regulation of memory functions, such as making a conscious effort to rehearse or to retrieve information. The self-regulation aspect of metamemory is part of general executive functioning and executive WM in particular.

Poor metamemory development is associated with limited use of memory strategies because the individual does not understand why, how, and when to use strategies. For example, an adolescent with delayed metamemory development may believe that all memory strategies are ineffective, and, as a result, is unlikely to invest much effort in learning and using a strategy. As metamemory develops there is a corresponding increase in memory strategies and their application (J. Harris, 1996). For metamemory assessment recommendations, see Chapter 5.

> **DON'T FORGET**
> ....
> Poor development and use of WM strategies may be due to poorly developed metamemory. Minimal strategy use may also be due to a limited WM capacity that is unable to handle the additional cognitive load that occurs during learning a strategy.

STRATEGIES

WM performance is also related with the development and application of effective strategies. WM functioning improves with the application of strategies. For example, children who use rehearsal to maintain information in short-term storage are able to immediately retain and recall more information. Other strategies that enhance WM performance include chunking and visualizing verbal information. The application of strategies is a function of executive WM. Individuals with a weakness in executive WM are usually less strategic.

Students with learning disabilities and memory impairments also tend to be less strategic, even when they are aware of strategies. One reason these students employ strategies infrequently is that strategy learning and use add to cognitive load. As cognitive load increases, less information is retained in STM and WM (Barrouillet et al., 2011), causing frustration and abandonment of a potentially effective strategy.

> ## 🐾 TEST YOURSELF 🐾
> ....
>
> 1. **Which of the following is *not* one of the "Big Three" in WM assessment?**
>   (a) Attention
>   (b) Executive functions
>   (c) Fluid reasoning
>   (d) Working memory
> 2. **Control of attention is an executive WM function.**
>   (a) True
>   (b) False

3. **Which LTM process does *not* draw on WM?**
   (a) Encoding
   (b) Consolidation
   (c) Retrieval
   (d) Recognition

4. **Strong related processes cannot compensate for specific WM deficits.**
   (a) True
   (b) False

5. **Failure to correctly apply a memory strategy is most likely due to:**
   (a) Poor metamemory
   (b) Poor phonological STM
   (c) Poor LTM
   (d) Poor fluid reasoning

Answers: 1. c; 2. True; 3. b; 4. False; 5. a

Three

DEVELOPMENT, NEUROANATOMY, AND RISK FACTORS

DEVELOPMENT OF WORKING MEMORY

As discussed in the previous chapter, WM development does not occur in isolation. Advancement of several cognitive abilities depends on the development of WM, and WM, in turn, depends on the growth of other abilities, such as processing speed and phonological processing. Thus, a normal course of WM development from infancy to adolescence is important for overall cognitive development.

Simple STM spans increase two- to threefold between the ages of 4 and 16, with more gradual improvement after age 8 (Gathercole, 1999). At age 4, the typical child can recall an average of three digits in order. By 12 years of age, the span has doubled to about six digits, and by 16, digit span has plateaued at seven to eight digits (Hulme & Mackenzie, 1992). Complex WM spans, which are shorter than simple spans, are increasing in a similar fashion from early childhood to adulthood (see Rapid Reference 3.1).

Increases in complex WM spans are mostly the result of greater WM processing capacity. As WM processing abilities develop, children process information more quickly, handle more information at a time, deal with more complex information, have more automatized procedures, focus attention better, and inhibit interference better. Underlying the improved ability to handle greater cognitive load are improvements in operating efficiency and speed, as well as increased use of strategies (Gathercole & Baddeley, 1993). Deploying strategies changes how goals are accomplished and how tasks are approached and managed. As individuals develop, strategy use becomes more frequent, consistent, and sophisticated.

STM components appear to be present early in infancy, whereas executive WM does not clearly emerge until 4 to 6 years of age. The development of object permanence depends on visual-spatial STM. Infants display object permanence as early as 4 to 8 months of age. Later in infancy, children begin to imitate speech

≡ Rapid Reference 3.1   Span Length by Age

Age	Phonological STM	Verbal WM	Visual-Spatial STM	Visual-Spatial WM
4	3 items		2–3 items	
6		2 items		2 items
12	6 items	4 items	5–6 items	4 items
16	7–8 items			

sounds, a skill that requires phonological STM. WM components appear to be present in children as young as 4 years of age (Hitch, 1990). Gathercole, Pickering, Ambridge, and Wearing (2004) determined that Baddeley's tripartite WM structure is basically in place by age 6. From 6 onward, there is no evidence of any significant change in structure.

Although the WM functioning of children and adults is generally equivalent in terms of structure and processes, there are some notable differences. In early childhood, WM may consist of little more than STM processes. In general, young children seem to depend more heavily on phonological STM than do adults. In particular, the phonological features of words are more influential in children's processing, whereas adults rely more on semantic associations, as indicated by the finding that phonological similarity and nonwords are less disruptive to adult functioning (Conlin & Gathercole, 2006). Also, as development proceeds, children utilize verbal WM processes more than basic phonological STM alone.

As executive WM functions grow, there is a greater degree of interdependence between the functioning of the executive and short-term storage components. For example, in the Gathercole et al. (2004) study, the correlation between the executive WM and phonological STM increased from .73 at age 6 to .90 or greater for 10- to 15-year-olds. The growing interdependence is probably a function of more executive coordination, as well as increased strategy use. Moreover, growth in related processes and the acquisition of skills alter the nature of WM functioning. Also, the complexity of the task and the level of expertise affect how different WM functions are tapped.

Phonological STM

As discussed earlier, phonological STM begins during infancy and expands rapidly into middle childhood. Growth in span is the outcome of several factors:

faster processing speed, increased speech rate, greater efficiency of WM processes, attainment of expertise and automaticity, development of related cognitive processes, growth in knowledge and skills, and the conscious application of strategies after age 7. Faster processing speed and speech rate, along with more support from LTM, are probably the main determinants.

The traditional explanation for growth in phonological STM span is that age-related improvements in span depend primarily on increases in speech rate (Hulme & Mackenzie, 1992). Increases in articulation rates during childhood are thought to enhance the effectiveness of subvocal rehearsal processes and hence reduce the decay of memory items in the phonological store (Swanson & Howell, 2001). While the retention interval of phonological STM (as little as 2 seconds) is thought to remain constant during development and aging, the number of items retained increases as more words can be rehearsed in the same amount of time. Faster articulation during oral recall also reduces the total retention interval, meaning that more words can be recalled before they decay (Henry & Millar, 1993).

The development that has the most significant impact on span growth is the emergence of subvocal rehearsal around 4 years of age. Rudimentary subvocal rehearsal at this age is a precursor of the more deliberate and strategic rehearsal procedures that develop around 7 years of age (Gathercole & Pickering, 2000).

In childhood, phonological STM plays a greater role in cognitive functioning than it will later in life. Although phonological STM span is a significant predictor of general cognitive ability in childhood, it is not a reliable predictor in adolescence and adulthood when WM has the stronger relation (Hutton & Towse, 2001).

Verbal WM

The explanation for expanding verbal WM span is that WM operations become faster and more efficient, leaving more resources available for storage and reducing the time items are held in storage. Verbal WM span doubles in length from two items in 5- to 7-year-olds to four items in 11- to 12-year-olds, at which point it approximates adult levels (Cowan, 1999; Gathercole, 1999). The length of complex verbal span is only one indication of how much information can be managed by verbal WM because verbal WM also draws on recently activated information from LTM. Accumulating knowledge and faster retrieval speed enhance the contributions from LTM.

Visual-Spatial STM

Four-year-old children can typically remember a sequence of two to three pictures (Gathercole & Baddeley, 1993). Then the capacity of visual-spatial STM doubles between the ages of 5 and 11, when span reaches an adult level of approximately four items (Riggs, McTaggart, Simpson, & Freeman, 2006). Unlike phonological and verbal spans, much of the improvement seems to result from actual growth in capacity, rather than improved system efficiency or use of strategies.

Visual-Spatial WM

Throughout development, visual-spatial WM span is somewhat less than STM visual-spatial span because of the additional cognitive load involved. As individuals mature, visual-spatial WM becomes more closely associated with both verbal and executive WM. In adults, measures of verbal and visual-spatial WM share approximately 40% of their variance (Kane et al., 2004). The reason for this increasing common variance is the recoding of visual-spatial information into a verbal code. Visual-spatial to verbal recoding emerges between the ages of 6 and 8 years. Prior to recoding, children must remember nonverbal information in visual-spatial form. The recoding process capitalizes on the superior verbal storage and rehearsal processes that most individuals possess. When called on to recall recently perceived visual-spatial information, the stored verbal code is used to reconstruct the images or spatial orientation. The ability to use verbal WM to encode and retain visual-spatial information contributes to the expansion of visual-spatial WM capacity. Tasks that involve retention of complex visual-spatial information place heavy demands on the executive component (Gathercole & Baddeley, 1993). In the elderly population, age-related declines are more severe in visual-spatial WM than in verbal WM (Johnson, Logie, & Brockmole, 2010).

Executive WM

Neuropsychological studies have documented that growth in executive WM is related to prefrontal cortex maturation (Kane & Engle, 2002). Hence, full development of the executive component occurs later than that of the phonological, visual-spatial, and verbal components. Inhibition of irrelevant information, one of the primary functions of executive WM, has frequently been measured and provides a means of tracking executive development. Whereas 9-year-old children have considerable difficulty preventing unrelated information from entering WM, 14-year-olds have much better developed inhibitory mechanisms (Swanson & Howell, 2001). Thus, younger children may need more executive resources to inhibit or resist potential interference from irrelevant items, leaving fewer executive resources for other tasks. Efficient allocation of executive resources also depends on engagement of effective strategies.

Because the frontal lobes are slow to mature, executive WM develops until 16 to 17 years of age (Luciana, Conklin, Hooper, & Yarger, 2005). In old age, the decline of executive WM seems to precede that of the other three components (Baddeley, 1986). As executive WM functions decline among older adults, susceptibility to interference increases and WM performance suffers (Hedden & Yoon, 2006).

With increasing age, executive WM becomes more strongly associated with verbal WM and less connected with visual-spatial functioning. Also, phonological STM is the least associated with executive WM, as phonological capacity will increase even without concomitant growth in executive WM (Gathercole & Baddeley, 1993).

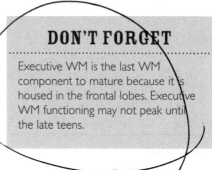

DON'T FORGET

Executive WM is the last WM component to mature because it is housed in the frontal lobes. Executive WM functioning may not peak until the late teens.

WM Strategies

Increased use of strategies, such as subvocal rehearsal, chunking, switching, visualization, and organization, is also partially responsible for developmental changes in WM performance (Minear & Shah, 2006). Strategies develop and become more sophisticated with age, leading to better retention and more efficient WM processing. Strategy use and WM span are positively correlated; higher-span individuals are more likely to use strategies, such as chunking, imagery, and elaboration (St. Clair-Thompson, 2007).

Rehearsal. Rehearsal consists of vocal and subvocal repetition of phonological or verbal information. Subvocal rehearsal most likely develops from overt speech, becoming internalized and automatized during early childhood. Whereas rehearsal in STM tends to be automated and subvocal, in verbal WM it is usually conscious and effortful and occurs only when the focus of attention switches from processing to rehearsal.

Rehearsal in verbal WM is likely to develop later than STM rehearsal. Although many children begin using a simple STM rehearsal strategy around 5 years of age, verbal rehearsal strategies, such as chunking items before rehearsing them, may not occur until the age of 10 (Gill, Klecan-Aker, Roberts, & Fredenburg, 2003). The development and increased use of verbal rehearsal strategies are thought to be at least partially responsible for the sizable growth in memory capacity, especially for the increase in span after 6 years of age (Gathercole et al., 2004; Minear & Shah, 2006).

Children with disabilities often fail to independently develop or utilize rehearsal strategies. Several studies have found explicit rehearsal training to significantly improve the STM and WM performance of children, with and without disabilities (Comblain, 1994; Conners et al., 2001). Adults with low WM spans have also shown improvement after training in simple rote rehearsal strategies (McNamara & Scott, 2001; Turley-Ames & Whitfield, 2003).

Chunking. Although less is known about its developmental progression, the strategy of chunking has also been hypothesized to contribute to the growth in memory span. Chunking, the grouping or clustering of discrete items into larger units, appears to be a naturally occurring process, much like blending phonemes into a word. Although adults can typically remember a sequence of only five or six unrelated words, chunking allows them to recall sentences of about 15 words. Chunking may also improve WM performance indirectly, through enhancing the organization of items encoded into LTM (Richardson, 1996).

METAMEMORY DEVELOPMENT

During the preschool years a child's understanding of memory develops by leaps and bounds. Although few 3-year-olds have any concept of memory, most 4- or 5-year-olds have a theory of memory and understand the concept of forgetting over time. Also, 4-year-old children have some idea that memorization is an active process requiring deliberate effort. However, most preschoolers and young school-age children have misconceptions about memory, such as believing that simply wanting to remember something will improve recall.

By age 8, children are more realistic about their memory capabilities; for example, they accurately predict that their forgetting will increase as the retention interval increases. By middle school, children have a more in-depth understanding of the intricacies of memory (O'Sullivan & Howe, 1998). For example, they are aware that memory performance varies across occasions, types of material, and individuals. Although 18-year-olds know more about memory and memory strategies than children, they typically enter adulthood possessing only a fraction of the strategies and metamemory they could possess.

Most of the research on metamemory development pertains to LTM (Dunlosky & Bjork, 2008). Nonetheless, it is safe to assume that knowledge about STM and WM generally lags behind knowledge regarding LTM. Although children eventually realize that there is an STM and an LTM, they have very minimal understanding of STM. Mainly, they don't recognize how limited STM is in span and duration, many believing that STM lasts as long as a day. Conscious awareness of WM and how it functions probably occurs only as a result of direct instruction. Even very few adults are aware of the concept and functions of WM, although the majority can report experiencing the limitations of WM.

> **DON'T FORGET**
> ···
> Metamemory includes understanding how memory works, knowing one's memory strengths and weakness, consciously regulating memory, and knowing how, why, and when to use memory strategies.

LONG-TERM MEMORY DEVELOPMENT

Regarding LTM, there are consistent improvements in the amount retained from early childhood through the adolescent years. Like STM and WM, adult-like LTM brain structures and functions are in place at age 6. The causes of LTM improvement after the age of 6 are mainly quicker retrieval, more effective encoding, an expanding knowledge base, and greater ability to store information for longer periods of time. Six-year-olds have difficulty retrieving stored information without prompting. Thus, between the ages of 6 and 12, improved memory performance mainly results from more efficient retrieval processes (Wright & Limond, 2004). Continued improvement after the age of 12 is attributed to greater ability to encode more and more features of the incoming information. More effective encoding underlies concurrent improvements in consolidation and storage. Although more efficient and effective LTM processing naturally unfolds with age, development of metamemory and strategies also plays a crucial role. Unlike STM and WM, the development of LTM is less about growth in basic capacities than about enhancement of memory processes through the use of effective strategies. Improved LTM performance is also related to growth in the amount of stored knowledge. (For more details on LTM development, see Dehn, 2008.)

THE NEUROANATOMY OF WORKING MEMORY

Brain imaging research has identified the neural basis of WM and has provided support for Baddeley's model and the integrated model of WM. Models of memory attempt to represent the functional rather than the structural properties. Therefore, the theoretical division of WM into broad functions does not mean there are distinct brain locations corresponding to different WM components.

Nevertheless, recent neuroimaging research has found activation of distinct brain regions during different WM activities. However, there is still much to be learned about the neuroanatomy of WM. (For definitions and locations of the brain structures mentioned in this section see the online resources.)

STM and WM depend on a different set of neural structures than those associated with LTM. Depending on the STM or WM task, several brain regions may be activated simultaneously, including locations in the frontal, parietal, and temporal lobes (see Rapid Reference 3.2). Whereas the frontal lobes may control WM and STM functions, the parietal and temporal lobes are involved in further processing and in the retention of modality-specific information. Cowan (1995) suggests that the frontal lobes keep active the appropriate neural systems in other parts of the brain so as to maintain representation of the stimuli. Therefore, executive WM processing is not confined to the frontal lobes. From a neurological perspective, WM capacity might depend on how many brain areas the frontal lobes can simultaneously involve in WM processing.

Despite widespread activation during WM tasks, neuroimaging of short-term storage tasks reveals that brain activation is restricted primarily to the areas related

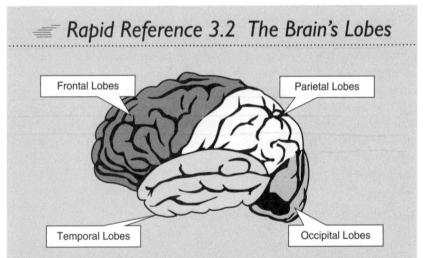

≡ Rapid Reference 3.2 The Brain's Lobes

Frontal Lobes

Parietal Lobes

Temporal Lobes

Occipital Lobes

Figure 3.1 The Brain's Lobes

From *Long-Term Memory Problems in Children and Adolescents: Assessment, Intervention, and Effective Instruction*, by Milton J. Dehn, 2010, Hoboken, NJ: Wiley. Copyright 2010 John Wiley & Sons. Reprinted with permission.

to the modality of the content (Prabhakaran, Narayanan, Zhao, & Gabrieli, 2000). Accordingly, phonological short-term storage is generally associated with the left hemisphere, whereas visual-spatial storage is generally associated with the right hemisphere. Specific areas in the parietal and temporal lobes are involved either in phonological or visual-spatial STM (Hedden & Yoon, 2006; Smith & Jonides, 1997). Thus, the different activation sites reflect the neural separation of short-term storage for phonological versus visual-spatial information, as well as the neural separation of WM from the domain-specific STM subsystem (see Rapid Reference 3.3).

To a lesser degree, the frontal lobe is also involved with retention and processing of visual-spatial and verbal material. The left prefrontal region (Broca's area) is activated when verbal material is being processed. In contrast, the right prefrontal region processes both verbal and visual-spatial information (Prabhakaran

≡ Rapid Reference 3.3 Brain Regions With Reported Activation During Working Memory Processes*

WM Process	Hemisphere	Cortical Area
Phonological STM storage	Left	Posterior parietal Inferior parietal Brodmann's area 40 Supramarginal gyrus
Phonological STM rehearsal	Left	Broca's area Anterior temporal frontal
Visuospatial STM/WM	Right	Occipital Premotor cortex Inferior frontal Superior frontal sulcus Intraparietal sulcus
Visual only	Right	Occipital
Spatial only	Right	Parietal
Executive WM	Bilateral	Dorsolateral prefrontal
General WM		Anterior cingulate Striatum

*This table is also in the online resources.

et al., 2000). However, activation of the prefrontal cortex is more likely to occur when both verbal and visual-spatial information are being processed. Hence, complex WM activities (storage-plus-processing tasks) reveal content-specific activation but also more general activation of the dorsolateral prefrontal cortex (dPFC) and anterior cingulate (Jonides, Smith, Marshuetz, & Koeppe, 1998).

Interconnectivity Determines Capacity

Although specific WM functions and components have been mapped onto specific brain structures and regions, the overall functioning and capacity of the WM system seem to depend primarily on the extent of connectivity between the WM executive center in the prefrontal cortex and the WM processing and storage areas distributed throughout the brain. Individual differences in WM capacity are correlated with the extent of white matter connecting the executive WM network with domain-general regions (Klingberg, 2010). The white matter consists of myelinated axons that connect brain networks and individual neurons.

DON'T FORGET

....

The capacity and successful functioning of working memory depend on the extent of white matter that connects the prefrontal cortex with working memory processing and storage areas that are distributed throughout the brain. As working memory improves during training, there is a measureable increase in the brain's white matter.

Thus, WM capacity is a property of the neurological and functional interactions between the prefrontal cortex and the rest of the brain (D'Esposito, 2007; Linden, 2007). The strongest evidence for this claim comes from a WM training study by Tageuchi et al. (2010). They discovered that the extent of training and the amount of improved WM performance were correlated with measureable growth in the brain's white matter. The majority of the increased connectivity was within the parietal cortex and adjacent to an area of the corpus callosum closely linked with the prefrontal cortex. There was also increased connectivity between the parietal region and the dPFC.

Phonological STM

Neuroimaging studies reveal that phonological STM and its rehearsal process operate in the left hemisphere. Specifically, Brodmann's area 40 is associated with storage and Broca's area is associated with subvocal rehearsal (Baddeley, 2003a). Some studies have found broader areas serving phonological storage and rehearsal.

Gathercole et al. (2004) reported that inferior parietal areas in the left hemisphere briefly store phonological information while the anterior temporal frontal area is involved with rehearsal. Also, Baldo and Dronkers (2006) reported that the supramarginal gyrus subserves phonological storage. Despite the somewhat different mapping, there is neurological evidence supporting the division of phonological STM into a passive storage subcomponent and a rehearsal subcomponent.

Visual-Spatial STM and WM

Neuroscientific research has discovered that visual-spatial STM and WM are principally, but not entirely, localized in the right hemisphere of the brain (Baddeley, 2003a), especially in the occipital and inferior frontal areas. Also, the superior frontal sulcus and intraparietal sulcus have been identified as contributing to visual-spatial WM functioning (Bunge & Wright, 2007). Neuroimaging studies provide evidence of separate neural systems serving the two visual-spatial subcomponents of storage and rehearsal (Smith & Jonides, 1997). Also, the visual and spatial components function separately, with visual processing and storage located in the occipital lobes and the spatial aspect in the parietal lobes.

Executive WM

The functioning of executive WM is thought to originate from the dPFC (Rypma & D'Esposito, 1999). Activation in this structure is observed whenever inhibiting, updating, shifting, and refreshing occur, such as when an individual is processing information while trying to maintain items in STM storage (Kane & Engle, 2002). The prefrontal areas seem to have a special role in integrating different types of information in WM, such as when both verbal and visual-spatial information is being integrated. As the demands on executive WM increase, there is greater activation in the dPFC. However, the level of dPFC activation varies depending on the type of WM processes that are engaged. Specifically a simple, passive STM task does not engage the dPFC, whereas manipulating, encoding, and retrieving the STM content does (Prabhakaran et al., 2000). Even this division does not account for the considerable variability across individuals. In some instances requiring executive WM processes, other brain regions are more active than the dPFC. This variability may reflect different levels of expertise or the use of strategies (D'Esposito et al., 1995).

Despite inconsistent findings, several conclusions can be drawn about the role of the dPFC in WM functioning: (a) the dPFC plays the primary role in executive WM; (b) individual differences in WM capacity are mediated by individual differences in the dPFC; (c) the dPFC is a necessary but insufficient structure for WM functions (other neurological structures are also necessary); (d) the primary role of the dPFC is to actively maintain information in the presence of interference; and (e) distinct STM systems in the posterior regions are connected with the dPFC.

THE NEUROANATOMY OF LONG-TERM MEMORY

There are several identifiable brain structures involved in the encoding, temporary storage, and retrieval of long-term memories. However, the permanent storage of specific memories is spread throughout all but the frontal lobes. Verbal and visual-spatial memories end up being stored in the same cortical regions where the information was originally processed (Milner, Squire, & Kandel, 1998). That is, visual-spatial memories are stored in visual-spatial processing areas, and verbal memories are stored in language processing areas.

The Medial Temporal Lobe

The medial temporal lobe is responsible for the formation, maintenance, retrieval, and reintegration of long-term memories (Broadbent, Clark, Zola, & Squire, 2002). It is a large region that contains the hippocampus, amygdala, fornix, and the entorhinal, perirhinal, and parahippocampal cortices. The complex processing and interrelationships among these different structures are not yet fully understood, but it is believed that each has specialized functions in memory encoding and storage and that each processes different aspects of acquired information.

These medial temporal lobe structures are involved in various aspects of memory processing, from encoding to retrieval. Encoding is initiated when the medial temporal lobe receives information from sensory integration areas (Simons & Spiers, 2003). Following encoding, the lengthy process of consolidation is orchestrated by the medial temporal lobe, especially the hippocampus. Although some consolidated memories are permanently stored in the medial temporal lobe (Moscovitch, Nadel, Winocur, Gilboa, & Rosenbaum, 2006), it appears that most memories are ultimately stored in cortical networks outside the medial temporal region (Schacter, 1996). Also, the medial temporal region is involved in retrieval.

The Hippocampus

The hippocampus is a seahorse-shaped structure that lies deep within the medial region of the temporal lobes (Giap, Jong, Ricker, Cullen, & Zafonte, 2000). Of all the medial temporal lobe formations, the hippocampus is the most directly responsible for the majority of memory processes: encoding, consolidation, storage, and retrieval. Although the hippocampus may permanently store some memories, the majority of new memories are stored only temporarily until the process of consolidation transfers them to cortical regions.

During retrieval the hippocampus binds together the multiple features of a memory that are retrieved from different cortical regions. The hippocampus seems to be involved primarily with the automatic retrieval that occurs when a cue immediately triggers an associated memory, whereas conscious, effortful, and strategic retrieval seems to be more a function of WM in the prefrontal cortex.

> **DON'T FORGET**
> ....
> The hippocampus is the most important memory structure in the brain. It is responsible for encoding, consolidation, and retrieval, as well as some storage of long-term memories.

The hippocampus may also function as the interface between WM and LTM. The associative functions attributed to Baddeley's episodic buffer probably occur within the hippocampus. Furthermore, the hippocampus probably holds the recently activated LTM representations that are currently being utilized by WM processes. In this sense, the hippocampus is the recently activated region of LTM with which WM is interacting.

Hippocampal Related Structures

The entorhinal, perirhinal, and parahippocampal cortices surround the hippocampus and are interconnected with it. Visual and auditory input passes through the entorhinal cortex on its way to the hippocampus. The perirhinal cortex is thought to serve as the interface between visual perception and memory and to play an important role in factual memory (Broadbent et al., 2002). The parahippocampal cortex is thought to be involved in spatial and topographic memory. These integrated memory structures may support encoding when the hippocampus itself is severely damaged.

Amygdala

The amygdala, an almond-shaped structure that sits just behind the hippocampus, is known for emotional learning in humans. In particular, emotional conditioning and fear conditioning, both types of classical conditioning, depend on the amygdala. The amygdala is also known as the brain area where the perception of stimuli is matched to information about its biological significance, such as whether the stimulus is a threat (Pliszka, 2003). It also has been reported that the amygdala is involved with the hippocampus when cross-modal associations are required (Nelson, 1995).

Thalamus

The thalamus, an egg-like structure that also lies near the hippocampus, functions as a relay station through which all sensory information, except smell, passes on its way from the back of the brain to the frontal lobes. The thalamus is an essential memory structure, as damage to the thalamus can produce amnesia (Schacter, 1996).

RISK FACTORS FOR WORKING MEMORY IMPAIRMENTS

Approximately 10% of the school-aged population suffers from deficits in STM or WM (Alloway & Gathercole, 2006). There are numerous behaviors, injuries, medical conditions, and mental disorders that cause or put individuals at risk for WM problems, if not actual WM impairments. Although specific risk factors for WM and LTM have been identified, it's not necessary to know all of them. In general, anything that is detrimental to the brain and cognitive functioning is very likely to have deleterious effects on WM. The reason is that WM is a vulnerable brain function, most likely because it depends on good interconnectivity between the prefrontal cortex and the other brain regions involved in STM and WM processing.

> **DON'T FORGET**
> ....
> The brain's memory structures are very vulnerable. Any acquired brain injury is likely to damage the hippocampus and the prefrontal cortex, as well as the interconnectivity that working memory functioning depends on.

Memory impairments can be developmental or acquired and temporary or permanent (Temple, 2004). Developmental impairments are thought to be present from birth. In such cases, the child has never developed average WM abilities but the impairment may not become apparent until learning and memory challenges arise. Acquired impairments occur in an infant, child, or adolescent who has had normally developing memory skills until an injury, disease, or some other medical condition affects memory development or functioning. Acquired WM problems are caused by damage to the prefrontal cortex, the other structures involved in STM and WM (see previous section in this chapter), or the connections between the prefrontal cortex and other involved structures. In most cases of acquired impairment, WM will spontaneously recover over a period of time.

Concussions and Traumatic Brain Injuries

A traumatic brain injury (TBI) occurs when external mechanical forces cause damage to brain tissue. A concussion can be considered a mild form of acquired brain injury. A TBI or concussion can cause a broad spectrum of cognitive problems, with WM, LTM, and executive dysfunctions among the most frequently reported, probably because the frontal and temporal lobes are the most frequently damaged brain regions. Because these memory and executive systems are integrated, injury to the structures of one will impact the functioning of the others.

The extent, severity, and chronicity of memory impairments depend mainly on the severity of the injury. With severe TBI, persistent LTM deficits are well documented. An estimated 54% to 84% of these cases (across all age groups) experience significant LTM difficulties, known as posttraumatic amnesia (DeLuca, Schultheis, Madigan, Christodoulou, & Averill, 2000). Of these, 36% to 79% may suffer persistent impairments (7 years or longer) in LTM (B. Wilson, 2009; Zec et al., 2001). With moderate injuries, verbal LTM impairments frequently persist beyond 2 years.

When acquired brain injuries are mild, and 85% of them are, the likelihood of persistent memory impairments is minimal. Roman et al. (1998) found that at 1 month post-injury, children with mild TBI did not have a higher incidence rate of memory impairment than control subjects. Of those who still have a problem after 1 month, nearly all will completely recover within 2 years (Babikian & Asarnow, 2009).

Although TBI can impact nearly every aspect of LTM, some memory types and processes fare better than others. In adults, verbal memory functions tend to be more affected than visual-spatial. In contrast, children and adolescents with severe TBI suffer impairments in both verbal and visual-spatial LTM (Levin, Fletcher, Kusnerik, & Kufera, 1996). Even when WM and other cognitive functions recover, LTM functioning may not.

When there is damage to the frontal lobes, executive functions, attentional control, and WM will certainly be affected. Older children with frontal lobe damage usually experience metamemory problems, even when memory performance appears relatively intact (Hanten, Bartha, & Levin, 2001). Metamemory deficiencies will result in less application of strategies, leading to more immediate forgetting, less effective encoding into LTM, and LTM retrieval difficulties (Ranganath, Johnson, & D'Esposito, 2003). For example, older children with TBI underutilize semantic clustering and even have difficulties performing and modifying basic rehearsal strategies (J. Harris, 1996). Fortunately, Gershberg and Shimamura (1995) found that patients with frontal lobe lesions benefit from strategy instruction. Victims with frontal lobe injuries also have more difficulty organizing thoughts, focusing attention, and inhibiting interference, all of which will have a detrimental impact on executive WM functioning.

When a brain injury impacts WM, the capacity of WM will be affected. The individual will be able to handle less cognitive load, processing will take longer, less information will be maintained in WM, and generally all aspects of WM functioning, especially executive operations, will suffer. However, the passive STM stores themselves may not be as affected, especially visual-spatial. A meta-analysis by Babikian and Asarnow (2009) found that of the WM components, visual-spatial STM is the most resistant to head injury.

The good news is that WM functioning usually recovers well following a mild to moderate injury or concussion. Individuals with persistent problems usually report difficulties with attention. In such cases, treatment with methylphenidate may improve WM functioning (Metha et al., 2000).

Postconcussion symptoms, such as headaches, usually clear up within a few days or within a month, but sometimes they persist for longer intervals. Chronicity of symptoms is an indication of impairments in neurocognitive functioning. Some studies of patients with persistent symptoms have found deficits in attention and memory at 6 to 18 months postconcussion (reviewed in L. Ryan & Warden, 2003). Multiple concussions or suffering a second concussion while recovering from an initial one increases the risk of enduring consequences.

Extreme Prematurity

Advancements in medical technology now allow very premature babies to survive. After extended stays in intensive care units, the majority of these infants go home with no apparent physical limitations and later reach developmental milestones normally. Nevertheless, they are still at risk for learning and memory problems, as their increased incidence rate of learning difficulties attests to. Those who are born at less than 32 weeks of gestation have the highest risks for WM and LTM impairments. LTM deficits into adolescence are well documented with this population. The cause is a smaller hippocampus, probably due to neonatal respiratory problems that caused oxygen deprivation in the brain.

Extreme prematurity is also associated with weak WM functioning (Briscoe, Gathercole, & Marlow, 2001; Pascoe et al., 2013). The cause may be poor myelination, something that these children are at risk for. Myelination, the coating on the brain's axons, facilitates fast and efficient communication in the brain. Because WM functioning depends on good connectivity and speed, a lack of myelination can diminish WM performance.

Childhood Diabetes

Type 1 diabetes mellitus (T1DM) is one of the most common chronic diseases of childhood, affecting as many as 1 in 60 children under the age of 18 (Wolters, Yu, Hagen, & Kail, 1996). Children with T1DM typically score within the average range on measures of intelligence but may acquire memory problems over time, typically within 1 to 3 years following the onset of diabetes. Memory dysfunctions have been implicated in STM, WM, and both verbal and visual-spatial LTM (Desrocher & Rovet, 2004). Diabetic children are frequently deficient in phonological STM and the use of strategies to organize and recall information (Wolters et al., 1996). For example, such children do not utilize rehearsal strategies as frequently as controls, and even when they do, their recall remains poor (Wolters et al., 1996). The extent of LTM and WM impairments seems to depend on how well glucose level is regulated (Hershey, Lillie, Sadler, & White, 2003). In adult subjects with Type II diabetes, cognitive function is improved following treatments that improve glucose regulation, and this cognitive improvement is particularly significant for tasks that involve WM (C. Ryan et al., 2006).

Dopamine Deficiency

WM also depends on neurochemical balance in the brain. Dopamine is an important neurotransmitter that is known to regulate cell activity associated with WM (Goldman-Rakic, 1992). Strong links between dopamine level and WM performance have been documented (Backman & Nyberg, 2013). A deficiency in dopamine in the prefrontal cortex can impair WM performance (Soderqvist et al., 2011). Medications that act on the dopamine system, such as methylphenidate, can improve WM performance (Backman & Nyberg, 2013).

Depression

It is well known that adults with depression exhibit impaired functioning in several types of memory. Although very little research on depression and memory has been conducted with school-age populations, it is relatively safe to assume that depression affects memory functioning in children and adolescents much the same as it does in adults (Lauer et al., 1994). Memory deficits in adults and youth with a history of depression have been reported in metamemory, STM, WM, and LTM. Within LTM, both the verbal and visual-spatial domains are affected, along with encoding and consolidation (Watts, Morris, & MacLeod, 1987). Depression affects WM because it limits the attentional resources that can be devoted to memory functions.

Anxiety

Anxiety seems to adversely impact WM and STM more than LTM. Mostly, anxiety affects verbal and executive WM. In a study by Ashcraft and Kirk (2001), high-anxiety children performed worse than low-anxiety children on verbal but not visual-spatial WM tasks. The explanation for this pattern is that worries tend to be in verbal form. As anxious individuals obsess with processing their task-irrelevant worries, they add to their cognitive load in executive WM. This results in difficulty inhibiting irrelevant information, difficulty focusing attention, difficulty shifting and updating, and taking longer to complete processing tasks (Visu-Petra, Cheie, & Miu, 2013).

Stress

Similar to depression and anxiety, chronic or intermittent everyday stress can significantly affect memory functioning, especially verbal STM and LTM (Yasik, Saigh, Oberfield, & Halamandaris, 2007). Victims of abuse or those diagnosed with post-traumatic stress disorder (PTSD) are likely to have even more serious memory problems. PTSD, chronic, and event-based stress cause the release of cortisol. Chronic exposure to cortisol destroys hippocampal neurons (D. Siegel, 1999). Accordingly, adults and youth who live with chronic stress are known to have persistent LTM impairments (Elzinga, Bakker, & Bremner, 2005). Stress especially seems to impair retrieval of personal memories (Schwabe, Bohringer, & Wolf, 2009).

However, even temporary, above normal secretions of cortisol, induced by everyday stressful events, may impact recall of information learned during or shortly after the interval of elevated cortisol. Encoding and consolidation of verbal and visual-spatial information are negatively correlated with cortisol levels (Elzinga et al., 2005).

TEST YOURSELF

1. **Which WM component is the last to mature?**

   (a) Phonological STM
   (b) Visual-spatial WM
   (c) Verbal WM
   (d) Executive WM

2. **Someone who does not understand how to effectively apply a basic memory strategy is most likely lacking in**

   (a) Motivation
   (b) Metamemory
   (c) Verbal WM
   (d) Retrieval

3. **Which neurological change in the brain corresponds with improved WM performance?**

   (a) Increased white matter
   (b) A larger prefrontal cortex
   (c) A larger hippocampus
   (d) Higher levels of cortisol

4. **In cases of extreme prematurity what accounts for weak WM?**

   (a) A smaller hippocampus
   (b) Less dopamine
   (c) Poor myelination
   (d) A smaller prefrontal cortex

5. **Injuries to the frontal lobe will affect WM but will also affect LTM functioning because the individual**

   (a) Has difficulty focusing
   (b) Has weaker STM
   (c) Has less dopamine
   (d) Is less strategic

Answers: 1. d; 2. b; 3. a; 4. c; 5. d

Four

WORKING MEMORY'S INFLUENCE ON ACADEMIC LEARNING AND PERFORMANCE

Students with higher WM capacity do better in school than students with lower WM capacity. Successful acquisition of academic skills and the performance of those skills rely heavily on WM. Of all the cognitive and metacognitive abilities involved in academic learning and performance, WM plays a very central role. The strong relations between specific areas of academic achievement and WM components are well established (e.g., Swanson, 2000; Swanson & Berninger, 1996). Overall, correlations between WM measures and achievement range as high as .55 to .92. In Rapid Reference 4.1 correlations from the Woodcock-Johnson IV (WJ IV; McGrew, LaForte, & Schrank, 2014) are used to illustrate the strong correlations between WM and achievement.

WM is an excellent predictor of achievement, perhaps a better predictor than IQ (Alloway & Alloway, 2010). Gathercole and Alloway (2008) found that 80% of students who had WM scores at the 10th percentile or lower experienced significant academic learning difficulties or learning disabilities (LD). As reported by H. L. Swanson in dozens of studies, WM deficits are a primary "cause" of all types of specific learning disabilities (SLD).

This chapter details the relations between each type of educational SLD and the five WM components. Students with literacy types of SLD tend to have deficits in verbal and executive WM, whereas those with mathematics disabilities usually have significant deficits in visual-spatial and executive WM. The more severe the WM weaknesses are, the more severe the SLD and the greater the likelihood of co-morbid SLDs. Overall, executive WM has the strongest influence on academic learning and performance. Understanding these relations is important not only for teachers but also for those who evaluate students for a possible SLD. (For a table that identifies other cognitive processes that are highly related with specific academic skills, see the online resources.)

≡ *Rapid Reference 4.1 Correlations Between the WJ IV Working Memory Cluster and Achievement Clusters, Ages 6 Through 8*

Basic reading skills	.49
Reading comprehension	.46
Math calculation skills	.48
Math problem solving	.53
Basic writing skills	.59
Written expression	.49
Oral expression	.40
Listening comprehension	.53
Academic skills	.53
Academic fluency	.50
Academic applications	.51
Broad achievement	.55

WORKING MEMORY AND CLASSROOM LEARNING

WM clearly plays a critical role in all aspects of academic learning (see Rapid Reference 4.2; Engle, 1996; Engle, Tuholski, et al., 1999). WM is necessary for learning and academic performance because they require manipulation of information, interaction with long-term memory (LTM), and simultaneous retention and processing of information. LTM, the storehouse of knowledge and experience, is able to acquire very little knowledge and few skills without support from WM. New learning is encoded into LTM after WM constructs, modifies, and associates new information. Nearly all of what must be learned and recalled must pass through WM. Hence, the capacity and effective functioning of WM strongly influence the rate and extent of learning.

In the typical classroom learning environment, continuous, heavy demands are placed on WM. Common classroom activities that impose simultaneous demands on storage and processing include: listening to a speaker while taking notes, following complex instructions, decoding unfamiliar words, writing sentences from memory, and mental arithmetic. In each case, the learner must process new information and integrate it with previously stored knowledge or with information that was just recently encountered.

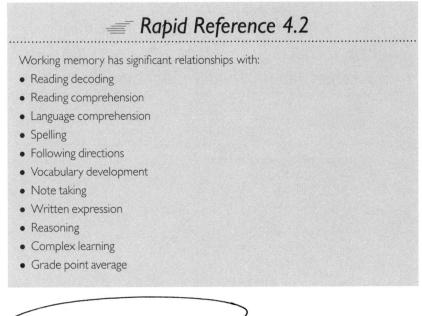

≡ *Rapid Reference 4.2*

Working memory has significant relationships with:

- Reading decoding
- Reading comprehension
- Language comprehension
- Spelling
- Following directions
- Vocabulary development
- Note taking
- Written expression
- Reasoning
- Complex learning
- Grade point average

COGNITIVE LOAD IN THE CLASSROOM

Cognitive load is the processing dimension of WM. When cognitive load is too high, the amount of information retained in WM is reduced, leading to less information being encoded into LTM. Consequently, learning and performance are reduced, or at least slowed, when students experience too much cognitive load. Even for learners with normal WM capacity and functioning, typical classroom instruction and learning activities can overwhelm WM many times during the course of a day. For example, Reber and Kotovsky (1997) found that additional cognitive load interfered with learning to solve a novel problem and that the impairment was proportional to the degree of cognitive load. For those with weak WM functions or capacity, highly demanding WM requirements can make learning and performance difficult. For example, children with poor WM often lose track of their place in a complex task, require frequent repetitions of directions, skip procedural steps, and often abandon a task before completing it (Alloway, Gathercole, Adams, & Willis, 2005).

Students with an SLD, because they are likely to have a WM deficit, have a low tolerance for normal cognitive load. In one study with a sample of 11- to 12-year-old children, Henry (2001) determined that children with a moderate LD could retain verbal instructions that contained up to three units of information, whereas non-LD children could manage five units of information.

When students were required to process other information while retaining verbal instructions (a typical classroom situation), those with LD could comfortably maintain only one item of information, whereas nondisabled students could handle an average of three units of information (Henry, 2001). A WM deficit clearly puts students with LD at a significant disadvantage in the classroom. They learn and perform best under low cognitive load conditions.

In the classroom, the degree of cognitive load is determined by the teacher's instructional methods, the learner's internal processes, and the nature and structure of the content and materials (van Gog, Ericsson, Rikers, & Paas, 2005). Recommendations for reducing cognitive load can be found in Chapter 8.

Instructional Variables

The amount of cognitive load arising from the type of instruction and from teacher behaviors is determined by:

- The instructor's language and verbosity. Wordiness and complex language add to processing load. Simple, concise, consistent wording allows the learner to focus on the required processing (Gathercole & Alloway, 2008).
- The length of the lesson. Lengthy lessons create more proactive and retroactive interference as more and more information is added. Both interference and inhibiting interference add to cognitive load.
- The organization of the lesson. Well-organized instruction makes fewer demands on the learner's processing.
- How well the teacher elaborates. Elaboration is the process of explicitly linking new information to prior knowledge in a manner that helps the learner understand the relations.
- How much secondary processing is required. For example, a student listening to a lecture is processing the information in order to comprehend it and associate it with related knowledge. The requirement to take notes while listening is secondary processing that adds to the cognitive load.

Internal Processing Variables

The amount of cognitive load resulting from the learner's internal processing is determined by:

- How much internally generated interference, such as an irrelevant thought, needs to be inhibited. Dealing with irrelevant thoughts adds to cognitive load, as does the process of inhibition itself. For example, cognitive load in learners with attention problems or obsessive thought patterns may be increased by the presence of distracting or intrusive thoughts.

- The learner's levels of mastery, automaticity, expertise, and prior knowledge. The less developed these are, the greater the amount of processing required.
- Other cognitive factors related to working memory performance (see Chapter 2). For example, slow processing speed will increase cognitive load and decrease short-term retention because rehearsal cannot occur frequently enough.
- The use of well-developed memory strategies, such as chunking. Strategies that are mastered and automated can function effectively without creating significant processing demands.
- The level of metamemory development (see Chapter 3). Learners with advanced understanding of memory functions and their personal memory weaknesses can make informed decisions and selections to regulate the type and amount of processing they engage in during learning.

Content Variables

The amount of cognitive load caused by the nature of the content and materials is determined by:

- The amount of material and the difficulty and complexity of the subject matter. Smaller units of information require less integration and relational processing, and there also is less information to maintain while processing. More difficult and complex material requires more resources to process.
- The sequencing of the material. Material sequenced from simple to complex minimizes load.
- The novelty of the subject matter. The less prior knowledge the learner has, the greater the load.
- The organization of the materials. Requiring the learner to integrate disorganized materials will add significantly to the load. For example, simply presenting the information on multiple sheets of paper increases processing demands because the learner must combine several sources of information (Jang, Schunn, & Nokes, 2011).
- Whether the information to be processed and the information to be remembered are the same or different. For instance, the learning objective may be to recall the capital of each state, but the materials may require the student to locate each capital on a map.

WORKING MEMORY AND BASIC READING SKILLS

Basic reading skills, also referred to as reading decoding skills, are primarily dependent on phonological processing—the ability to detect and manipulate the phonemes used to construct words. It is well established (National Reading Panel, 2000; Torgesen, 1996) that reading decoding problems, reading disabilities, and dyslexia are primarily caused by deficiencies in phonemic awareness and phonological processing.

Phonological processing and phonetic decoding depend on phonological STM because phonemes must be temporarily stored while being processed. To decode, beginning readers must convert printed letters into phonemes that must be held in the correct sequence until the last letter is converted and the full sequence of phonemes can be blended into a complete word (Palmer, 2000). Consequently, phonological processing and phonological STM are highly interrelated (Prebler, Krajewski, & Hasselhorn, 2013). For example, the growth of phonological awareness skills seems to depend on phonological STM (Torgesen, 1996). It has also been proposed that phonological STM shares a common underlying ability with phonological processing and that this common underlying ability accounts for the close association that phonological STM has with reading decoding (P. De Jong, 2006).

Individuals with normal phonemic awareness or phonological processing test scores may still have serious decoding problems if they have deficiencies in phonological STM. When phonological processing skills are normal, poor readers probably have a diminished phonological STM capacity. On the other hand, a deficit in phonological processing can account for poor performance on phonological STM tasks. Readers who have both a phonological processing deficit and a phonological STM deficit will experience more severe decoding problems than readers with a weakness in just one of these cognitive processes.

Articulation speed and verbal rehearsal are also associated with the degree of influence phonological STM has on reading decoding. Because effective utilization of phonological STM depends on articulation speed, it is not surprising that articulation speed can distinguish between weak and strong readers (Baddeley, 1986). Although speech rate seems to have little relationship with individual differences among normal readers, it does seem to account for part of the STM impairment in children with a reading disability.

Also, poor readers may not be spontaneously using verbal rehearsal strategies to the same extent as normal readers (Torgesen & Goldman, 1977). O'Shaughnessy and Swanson (1998) concluded that children with a reading disability use phonological rehearsal processes inconsistently. Without rehearsal, the sequence of decoded phonemes will not be maintained long enough to complete the decoding process or enable the encoding of the phonetic sequence into LTM.

Reading decoding involves more than simple storage of phonological sequences in STM. Blending of phonemes into a word requires processing of sequential information, thereby requiring a contribution from WM, particularly verbal and executive WM. Children with reading disabilities have been found to have a core deficit in executive WM (L. Siegel & Ryan, 1989; Wang & Gathercole, 2013). Specifically, there is strong evidence that updating of verbal information is essential for reading decoding (P. De Jong, 2006). A deficit in updating seems to be independent of the length of phonological STM or verbal WM spans.

Some studies have also discovered a role for inhibitory functions during reading. For instance, Palmer (2000) found that good readers were able to better inhibit visual representations of words and focus on the phonological representation. This finding indicates that poor readers may continue to focus on visual encoding of graphemes when it would be more productive to recode phonologically. Palmer postulates that a delay in inhibiting the disruptive visual representations contributes to dyslexia.

Another role of executive and verbal WM during reading decoding is to coordinate phonological processing with word-level analysis and semantic processing (Palmer, 2000). Wang and Gathercole found that poor readers had a poor ability to coordinate such processes.

To convert text into phonemes, phonological processing also depends on visual-spatial STM. The influence of visual-spatial STM is unclear because research results have been equivocal. The decoding process involves accessing learned phonetic codes for visually presented letters and words (graphemes). Readers must phonologically recode visual stimuli by matching graphemes with corresponding phonemes, a process that involves LTM. With beginning readers, visual-spatial STM must maintain the grapheme long enough for the match to be found. A recent, well-designed study by Wang and Gathercole (2013) concluded that visual-spatial retention does play a significant role in reading decoding. However, a meta-analysis of 88 studies by Swanson, Zheng, and Jerman (2009) found that the significant relation between visual-spatial STM and reading decoding disappeared when IQ was controlled for.

In summary, all five WM components are involved in reading decoding (Swanson et al., 2009). Despite extensive research, it remains unclear whether phonological STM or a combination of verbal and executive WM

plays the greater role (Swanson & Jerman, 2007; Wang & Gathercole, 2013). What is clear is that once a reader becomes fluent and basic reading decoding becomes automated, STM and WM play a less critical role in reading decoding, while LTM becomes more influential.

> **DON'T FORGET**
> ....
> All five WM components play a role in reading decoding. However, poor readers are more likely to have deficits in phonological STM, verbal WM, and executive WM than in the visual-spatial components.

Case Illustration

A case study illustrates the relations between WM components and basic reading skills. An 8-year old, second-grade child was struggling with the acquisition of basic reading skills and was being considered for educational placement as a child with a reading disability. His history included the WM risk factor of being born 8 weeks premature. When evaluated, his phonological STM was at the 14th percentile, his executive WM at the 24th percentile, and his visual-spatial STM and WM subtest scores ranged from the 50th to 95th percentiles. His initial reading decoding skills score was at the 2nd percentile, while his reading comprehension level was at the 8th percentile. He did not have any other significant cognitive processing deficits that could account for his reading difficulties. For example, his phonological processing score was at the 50th percentile. After tutoring in reading for 2 hours per week and undergoing face-to-face WM exercises on a regular basis for 12 weeks, his executive WM score improved to the 48th percentile and his phonological STM score improved to the 26th percentile. At the same time, his reading decoding skills and comprehension skills improved significantly. In sum, the combination of a working memory intervention and direct supplementary reading instruction resulted in significant growth in both his working memory and his reading skills.

Reading Fluency

With practice, readers begin to automatically recognize graphemes, syllables, and words, thereby reducing the need to engage phonological processing. Once decoding proceeds smoothly, quickly, and effortlessly, reading is considered to be "automatized" or fluent. Reading fluency is usually assessed with a test that measures the number of correct words read per minute. A high level of fluency is an indication that reading decoding has become automated. The development of automaticity facilitates reading comprehension by reducing the WM resources necessary for decoding words. Poor readers who continue to struggle with reading decoding have fewer residual WM resources for comprehension. Readers with high WM capacity have an advantage. Even before they achieve fluency, they have more WM resources to devote to comprehension than low WM capacity readers.

Even with normal phonological STM, verbal WM, and executive WM, inadequate reading speed may hinder comprehension because information will be lost before it is fully processed and integrated with a prior knowledge. It's well known that level of reading fluency is the foremost predictor of reading comprehension. However, it's important to realize that the reader's level of WM also influences reading comprehension (Seigneuric & Ehrlich, 2005).

WORKING MEMORY AND READING COMPREHENSION

To comprehend text, a reader must store recently decoded words while complex processes construct meaning (De Beni, Borella, & Carretti, 2007). Reading comprehension includes several skills and abilities that involve WM: accessing word meanings from LTM, assembling word meanings into larger information units, integrating information across phrases and sentences, focusing attention on the main ideas, creating visual images, forming new knowledge representations, drawing plausible inferences, monitoring the understanding of text as reading progresses, and associating and integrating information with prior knowledge stored in LTM. Most of these comprehension components make exceptionally heavy demands on both the storage and processing functions of WM.

To add to the challenge, the executive WM functions of switching, updating, and inhibition are continually required (Carretti, Borella, Cornoldi, & De Beni, 2009). Switching occurs when the reader switches back and forth between pieces of information. Updating replaces old, no longer relevant content with newer, more relevant content. Inhibition prevents the intrusion of irrelevant information.

After reading fluency and vocabulary level, WM capacity is the next highest predictor of reading comprehension in children, adults, and students with a reading disability (Seigneuric, Ehrlich, Oakhill, & Yuill, 2000). Numerous studies have uncovered a moderate to strong relationship between WM capacity and reading comprehension, with correlations typically around .50 (Daneman & Carpenter, 1980; Seigneuric et al., 2000). In a meta-analysis of 77 studies by Daneman and Merikle (1996), the average correlation between reading comprehension and verbal WM tasks was .41. For readers with normal word decoding skills, specific reading comprehension deficiencies are frequently associated with WM deficits (Cain, Oakhill, & Bryant, 2004; Goff, Pratt, & Ong, 2005).

The Role of Verbal WM

The role each WM component plays in reading comprehension differs from its role in reading decoding. There is a much stronger relationship between verbal WM and reading comprehension than between phonological STM and reading comprehension (Engle, Carullo, & Collins, 1991). Leather and Henry (1994) found that phonological STM accounted for only 5% of the variance in 7-year-olds' reading comprehension level, whereas verbal WM explained an additional 33% of the variance.

Verbal WM facilitates reading comprehension by holding words and sentences in consciousness until there is enough information to complete an idea. The number of sentences that can be held in verbal WM is related to reading comprehension (Daneman & Carpenter, 1980). The holding process involves subvocalization, an important form of inner speech in reading. The demands of reading comprehension typically exceed the normal storage capacity of verbal WM. Consequently, readers must form a new LTM representation of the text or combine the information in WM with existing LTM representations. Presumably, this type of interaction takes place in what Baddeley (2000) refers to as the episodic buffer.

The Role of Executive WM

Executive WM is another primary determinant of successful comprehension. Research has repeatedly confirmed this relationship; for example, Swanson et al. (2006) concluded that the functioning of executive WM, not phonological STM, discriminates between skilled comprehenders and those with comprehension deficits. Executive WM must coordinate many diverse processes, especially those that culminate in the integration of new information with an existing mental model. Of the specific executive functions, inhibition is one that has been directly linked with reading comprehension (Savage, Cornish, Manly, & Hollis, 2006; Savage, Lavers, & Pillay, 2007). Discarding information that is no longer relevant and preventing the intrusion of unnecessary or irrelevant information are crucial for comprehension (De Beni & Palladino, 2000). Ineffective inhibitory control during reading overloads WM, causing comprehension problems. Adults and children with deficient inhibitory processes are more likely to remember irrelevant words and information, resulting in weak reading comprehension (De Beni & Palladino, 2000).

The Role of Visual-Spatial Working Memory

Visual-spatial WM seems to have a minimal relationship with reading comprehension (Seigneuric et al., 2000; Swanson & Berninger, 1995). Daneman and Tardiff (1987) reported no correlation between visual-spatial measures and reading comprehension. Swanson and Berninger (1995) found that, although visual-spatial WM is correlated with reading comprehension, visual-spatial performance does not differentiate between good and poor comprehenders. If visual-spatial WM has any influence, it is likely to be during the early stages of reading development and also when readers create visual images of what they are reading about (Goff et al., 2005).

> **DON'T FORGET**
> ....
> Successful reading comprehension depends primarily on verbal and executive WM. The other three WM components have minimal influence on comprehension. Of the executive WM processes, switching, updating, and inhibition are the most important.

Related Cognitive Processes

Other cognitive processes and abilities that specifically facilitate reading comprehension include fluid reasoning, executive processing, processing speed, vocabulary development, verbal abilities, and LTM (Was & Woltz, 2006). Also, the application of effective reading comprehension strategies enhances reading comprehension, mostly because these strategies support the effective operation of WM and LTM processes. Interestingly, less skilled readers and those with a disability try to compensate for low WM capacity by rereading text (Linderholm & Van Den Broek, 2002), a basic reading comprehension strategy.

Case Illustration

The case of a seventh-grade reader illustrates the relationship between reading comprehension and WM. By seventh grade, the student's reading comprehension level was low enough to qualify for a disability in reading comprehension. When interviewed, the student attributed his low comprehension test scores to the fact that he never read, even though he could read just fine if he wanted to. The results of his evaluation revealed that he had average reading decoding skills and that he had average cognitive aptitudes for reading comprehension, including average WM and fluid reasoning scores. After several weeks of tutoring in reading comprehension strategies, his comprehension test scores improved significantly, eliminating his achievement deficiency. Presumably, his rapid improvement was due to the fact that he possessed sufficient WM resources for reading comprehension. He just needed to apply those abilities and utilize some effective comprehension strategies.

Summary

Calo's primary difficulty?

In summary, reading comprehension performance depends heavily on WM, especially on the executive and verbal WM components. Of the executive WM processes, switching, updating, and inhibition play crucial roles. Unlike reading decoding, reading comprehension processes are so complex and challenging that comprehension never reaches the level of automaticity that can be attained with reading decoding. Consequently, comprehension places a significant load on WM, even among good readers with normal WM capacity, but readers with higher WM abilities will find it easier to comprehend text than those with lower WM abilities. Comprehension differences between good and poor readers may be primarily attributed to differences in WM capacity.

larger than area for comprehension -

WORKING MEMORY AND MATHEMATICS

Mathematics skills are usually divided into two types—basic arithmetic calculation and mathematics problem solving. To varying degrees, both types of mathematics skills involve all five WM components. Research has documented strong relations between mathematics performance and measures of WM (Carmen, 2012; David, 2012). Examples of the findings include: Hutton and Towse (2001) reported a correlation of .45 between digit span and performance on mathematical tests; Swanson and Beebe-Frankenberger (2004) reported a correlation of .54 between WM and mathematics problem solving; and LeBlanc and Weber-Russell (1996) found that WM variables accounted for up to 57% of the variance in children's word-problem solutions.

With mathematics, the utilization of specific storage and processing components varies as a function of age more than by type of math skill involved (see Rapid Reference 4.3, which is also in the online resources). Age-related changes in mathematics functioning determine which WM components are relied on the most (Swanson, 2006). Preschool and early elementary children, for whom arithmetic is primarily a visual-spatial task, rely primarily on visual-spatial STM. As mathematics operations become more verbal and abstract, children depend more on verbal and executive WM. By the age of 8, children seem to rely on both visual-spatial and verbal WM during mathematical calculation. By 9 to 10 years of age, children depend primarily on phonological STM and verbal WM for

Rapid Reference 4.3 Working Memory Components Most Highly Related With Specific Academic Skills by Age

	Basic Reading Skills	Reading Comprehension	Mathematics Calculation	Mathematics Problem Solving	Written Expression	Listening Comprehension	Oral Expression
Younger Students*	Phonological STM; visual-spatial STM; verbal WM; executive WM	Verbal WM; executive WM	Phonological STM; visual-spatial STM; visual-spatial WM; executive WM	Visual-spatial STM; visual-spatial WM; verbal WM; executive WM	Phonological STM; visual-spatial STM; visual-spatial WM; verbal WM; executive WM	Phonological STM; verbal WM; executive WM	Phonological STM; verbal WM; executive WM
Older Students	Phonological STM; verbal WM; executive WM	Verbal WM; executive WM	Phonological STM; verbal WM; executive WM	Phonological STM; verbal WM; executive WM	Verbal WM; executive WM	Verbal WM; executive WM	Verbal WM; executive WM

*There is no clear age division that can be identified from the research; however, 8 years of age is probably the best dividing point for students with normal WM abilities.

the solution of mathematical problems (Holmes & Adams, 2006). At any age, word problems require executive WM to integrate the information and processes involved. In adolescence and adulthood, when mathematics algorithms are firmly represented in LTM storage, executive processes play the primary role.

The demands on WM components are also determined by the level of mastery. WM resources are needed most during the initial phases of mathematics skills acquisition, and fewer WM resources are needed as knowledge and skills grow (Imbo & Vandierendonck, 2007). Once basic mathematics facts and procedures have been mastered, solutions to simple forms of mental arithmetic can be retrieved from LTM, thereby freeing up WM resources. The demands on WM are higher when the problem is novel. Once the individual has learned to solve a particular type of problem, less WM capacity is required (Reber & Kotovsky, 1997). Consequently, the relations between WM and mathematics performance are stronger in children than in adults (K. Wilson & Swanson, 2001). Therefore, WM capacity places greater limits on the mathematics performance in children than in adults.

Even simple mathematics calculation involves all WM components to varying degrees (Frisco-van den Bos, van der Ven, Kroesbergen, & van Luit, 2013; Tronsky, 2005). The WM components that best predict mathematics calculation are visual-spatial (Swanson, 2006) and executive (Gathercole & Pickering, 2000). Compared with calculation, strategy-based problem solving and mathematics reasoning place a greater load on executive WM. According to Swanson (2006, 2011), the WM component that best predicts mathematics problem solving is the executive. When solving word problems, individuals must mentally construct an adequate problem representation—a process that depends heavily on executive WM. Completing a story problem also requires executive WM involvement in: (a) keeping track of incoming information; (b) integrating information; (c) retrieving mathematics facts and procedures from LTM; (d) matching the correct algorithm to the problem at hand; (e) updating the contents of WM; (f) making mental arithmetic calculations; (g) monitoring the computational process; and (h) evaluating the solution (Swanson & Beebe-Frankenberger, 2004).

The Role of Visual-Spatial STM and WM

The role of visual-spatial STM and WM in mathematics learning and performance seems to change significantly during childhood development. They play a prominent role during the preschool years, when the child's arithmetic mental model is primarily visual-spatial. Hitch, Halliday, Schaafstal, and Schraagen (1988) found that preschool children rely on visual-spatial STM and WM more than older children do, and Rasmussen and Bisanz (2005) found visual-spatial STM and WM to be the best predictors of preschool performance on standard nonverbal arithmetic problems.

The prominence of visual-spatial STM and WM in arithmetic computation is short-lived. By the end of first grade, verbal WM has become the best predictor of arithmetic performance. Even when older children are presented with a visual arithmetic problem, they tend to recode the visual information into a verbal code that passes through phonological STM (Rasmussen & Bisanz, 2005). Recoding allows children to manage greater quantities, as the number of items that can be manipulated in a visual mental model is relatively small. By the time children reach middle elementary years, visual-spatial WM plays only a minor role in arithmetic calculation (Imbo, Vandierendonck, & Vergauwe, 2007).

The Role of Phonological STM

Individual differences in mathematical problem solving can partially be attributed to phonological STM (Swanson & Sachse-Lee, 2001). Because numbers are words, phonological storage and processing are involved in both basic arithmetic calculation and the solution of story problems. At least in the initial stage, the solution of a mathematical word problem relies heavily on phonological processing. If phonological STM is deficient in capacity or inefficient in processing, it creates a bottleneck that constricts the flow of information to the higher levels of processing, including verbal WM, that are necessary for mathematical problem solving (Swanson & Beebe-Frankenberger, 2004). Accordingly, children with specific mathematics disabilities have been found to suffer deficits in short-term retention of verbal information (Swanson & Beebe-Frankenberger, 2004). Inefficient utilization of the phonological rehearsal process may also play a role.

The involvement of phonological STM changes with age and with the development of arithmetic skills. In general, older children utilize phonological STM more than younger children (Holmes & Adams, 2006). Older children also tend to use more subvocal rehearsal to retain mathematics problem information. The utilization of phonological STM is also determined by the level of mastery. Phonological STM is most related to arithmetic during the learning of basic mathematics facts and concepts. Although preschool children rely heavily on visual-spatial WM for mathematical operations, phonological STM is thought to be very important for learning numerals, number sequencing, and number facts in early childhood (Holmes & Adams; Prebler et al., 2013). When phonological memory span is inadequate, some of the numbers are lost before they can be associated and encoded together in long-term storage.

The Role of Verbal WM

Verbal WM is also involved in mathematical computation, especially during complex mental arithmetic calculations. It seems that verbal WM storage is most in demand when digits must be temporarily stored during multistep procedures. For example, verbal WM is required during complex subtraction where there is borrowing (Imbo et al., 2007). In contrast, simple multiplication places fewer demands on verbal WM because multiplication relies predominantly on long-term retrieval. K. Wilson and Swanson (2001) concluded that verbal WM is a better predictor of mathematical computation than visual-spatial WM.

The Role of Executive WM

Of the five WM components, executive WM plays an indispensable role during all types of mathematical computation and reasoning tasks (Andersson & Lyxell, 2007; Carmen, 2012; Imbo & Vandierendonck, 2007). Executive WM appears to be responsible for coordinating, monitoring, and sequencing all of the processing steps involved in mathematical procedures. Specifically, executive WM is necessary for estimating, counting, maintaining order of information, keeping track of information in multistep procedures, and selecting and executing problem-solving strategies (Imbo et al., 2007). Passolunghi and Siegel (2004) found that children who were poor at mathematics problem solving had significant difficulty with tests of executive WM. Limited executive WM capacity or high demands on WM resources result in slower calculation and more errors, even after mathematics facts have been mastered.

The three key executive WM processes of switching, updating, and inhibiting each make an important contribution to mathematics problem solving (Frisco-van den Bos et al., 2013). For example, switching is required when a problem requires both addition and multiplication. Updating, both verbal and visual-spatial, is involved in the storage and retrieval of partial results. Inhibition is necessary to prevent irrelevant information

> **DON'T FORGET**
>
> All five WM components are involved in mathematics learning and performance. However, the relative influence of each varies, depending on the type of math, the age of the learner, and the learner's mastery of mathematics facts, concepts, and procedures.

from entering or remaining in WM during the processing of targeted information (Passolunghi & Siegel, 2001). Good problem solvers are better able to inhibit irrelevant information (Swanson, 2011). For example, children with ADHD make more errors when problems contain irrelevant numeric or verbal information (Bull & Espy, 2006).

Other Cognitive Factors

WM is not the sole cognitive processing contributor to mathematics performance. Processing speed is another indispensable cognitive process that also underlies mathematics performance (Bull & Johnston, 1997). Other cognitive processes that play a significant role in mathematics learning and performance are attention (Kroesbergen, Van Luit, & Naglieri, 2003), executive functions (Naglieri & Gottling, 1997), fluid reasoning (McGrew & Wendling, 2010), and visual-spatial processing (Geary, 2011).

Case Illustration

A 15-year-old 10th grader who was struggling with mathematics learning and performance illustrates the relations between WM and mathematics. He had a history of struggling with math, including difficulty learning arithmetic facts and relying on finger counting. When evaluated, his Woodcock-Johnson III Working Memory (mainly a measure of executive WM) standard score was a below average 88. His processing speed and visual-spatial scores were in the average range, but his Fluid Reasoning score was below average at 85. There was nothing in his history or behavior to indicate any problems with attention, executive functions, motivation, or study skills. Over the course of a summer, this student completed online Cogmed working memory training (see Chapter 7). He followed the training regimen seriously, and by the end of the training had improved significantly on Cogmed's measures. The WM performance gains apparently transferred to improved mathematics performance. In the fall, during his first meeting with his ongoing math tutor, the student's math tutor was very impressed with the student's improved math calculation and reasoning skills. The tutor was certain the student had received tutoring in math over the summer. In fact, there had been no math tutoring over the summer—only working memory training.

Summary

To varying degrees, each STM and WM component and process is involved in each type of mathematics operation. The nature of the relationships is dependent not only on specific features of the task but also on the learner's age and on the developmental levels of both WM and mathematical skills.

WORKING MEMORY AND WRITTEN EXPRESSION

Written expression is a complex cognitive activity that requires the integration of several cognitive processes and memory components. The three main components of written expression are planning, writing, and revising. After generating ideas during the planning state, the writer must translate the ideas into words and construct grammatically correct sentences. During revising the writer compares the text with the intended meaning and checks for writing errors.

Regardless of the type of writing, all of these steps place very heavy demands on WM, especially on the executive and verbal components. Phonological STM contributes by briefly storing the words or sentence under construction. The visual-spatial components are also involved, especially during planning, when the writer may be using imagery (Kellogg, Olive, & Piolat, 2007). However, executive WM seems to be the most essential ability for translating ideas into writing. Executive WM has been found to significantly predict planning, writing, and revision, as well as the majority of skills used in writing, such as punctuation, grammar, and vocabulary (Vanderberg & Swanson, 2007).

DON'T FORGET

Once basic writing skills are automatized, executive WM is the primary component involved in written expression.

Automaticity of Basic Writing Skills

Similar to the relationship between reading fluency and reading comprehension, it appears that automaticity of basic writing skills, such as punctuation, spelling, and transcribing, frees up more WM capacity for the higher-level writing processes of generating, organizing, and revising (Swanson & Berninger, 1996). Automaticity of basic writing skills seems to reduce the influence of the phonological and visual-spatial STM components. For example, Vanderberg and Swanson (2007) reported that, with high school students, these two storage components did not predict any writing skills. Presumably, the lack of significant relations was due to mastery of basic writing skills in this high school sample. Similarly, adults require fewer WM resources during written expression than do children (Vanderberg & Swanson, 2007). Nonetheless, even with well-developed written language skills, written expression will always place extensive demands on WM because processes such as constructing ideas can never become fully automatized.

Case Illustration

The case of a middle school student with slow processing speed and below average WM illustrates how important adequate WM capacity is for written expression. The student's processing speed was below the 10th percentile, and his WM was below average. Despite his mid-average IQ, he had a history of struggling in literacy areas and had been identified as having a reading disability. By middle school, written expression had become his main problem. The student was mostly unable to get his thoughts and ideas onto paper. At home, his mother functioned as his scribe, writing as he dictated. He was also unable to take notes while listening in class. As part of his WM intervention, he learned to use basic shorthand for taking notes and for getting his ideas initially into writing. After the intervention, which included WM exercises, he became independent at note taking and written expression.

WORKING MEMORY AND ORAL LANGUAGE

The development and processing of oral language are highly related with WM capacity. Correlations between WM and oral language development as high as .70 to .90 have been documented in several studies (e.g., Crain, Shankweiler, Macaruso, & Bar-Shalom, 1990). Language learning, listening comprehension, and oral expression all depend on WM components, especially phonological STM, verbal WM, and executive WM.

Phonological STM plays a prominent role in the language development and language processing of young children. Poor language development seems to be directly connected with impaired functioning of phonological STM (Baddeley, 1996a). In particular, vocabulary learning has been directly linked with phonological STM capacity (Gathercole & Baddeley, 1990). If children are unable to retain the phonological sequence that makes up a new word, they will probably require repeated exposures to the word before they retain its phonetic representation (Leonard et al., 2007). Verbal WM is also necessary for the acquisition of new vocabulary, as it links the correct pronunciation with a semantic representation.

In oral language comprehension, WM plays the critical role of constructing and integrating ideas from a stream of successive words (Just & Carpenter, 1992). To understand the meaning of a sentence, an individual must remember previous words in order to relate them to later occurring words. During this complex process WM must also store the partial results of comprehension, as well as encode some items for later retrieval. Difficulties in processing individual sentences have been associated with deficiencies in verbal and executive WM (Moser, Fridriksson, & Healy, 2007).

Oral expression also places continual demands on verbal and executive WM, especially during the conceptualizing and sentence formulation stages. The speaker must not only retrieve words that convey the intended meaning, but also must plan for correct syntax. For example, accurate production of subject-verb agreement depends on verbal WM

> **DON'T FORGET**
> ....
> The development of language, especially vocabulary, relies primarily on phonological STM. In contrast, listening comprehension and oral expression mostly depend on verbal and executive WM.

processes. Even for individuals with normal language development, sentence planning is hindered when speakers have insufficient verbal WM capacity (Hartsuiker & Barkuysen, 2006).

Case Illustration

The case of a young child with an oral language disorder illustrates the connection between oral language and WM. This child was slow to develop speech and language. Consequently, he was evaluated and received early childhood special education for a delay in speech and language development. School-based speech and language therapy continued when he entered elementary school. At 7 years of age he was still struggling with acquiring new vocabulary, word retrieval, and expressive language. For example, he would often use incorrect verb tenses or have difficulty with subject-verb agreement. Although he had obtained an IQ of 105 when tested, his phonological STM span was below average. It was also discovered that he had a problem with maintaining rehearsal, even at the span level he tested at. That is, after the initial response, he could not maintain a sequence of words for more than one or two repetitions. After he began an intervention that included face-to-face WM exercises with an emphasis on rehearsal practice, he was able to maintain items during rehearsal. Following the WM training, he was dismissed from speech and language therapy because he no longer qualified.

Working Memory, Second Language Acquisition, and Bilingualism

With the growing population of English language learners in the United States there is interest in how WM components relate to the learning of a second language. It is already known that phonological STM is essential for learning the first language. It has recently been confirmed that phonological STM also makes a significant contribution to learning a second language (Swanson, Orosco, Lussier, Gerber, & Guzman-Orth, 2011). Earlier, Service (1992) reported that verbal

WM accounted for 47% of the variance in learning a second language. Also, Swanson et al. (2011) found that executive WM contributes unique variance in learning English as a second language.

> ## CAUTION
> ....
> English language learners may struggle to acquire a second language or master either language because they have underlying WM deficiencies in the phonological, verbal, and/or executive components. However, language-based tests of WM (in either language) may not be valid measures of WM for this population.

Therefore, second language learners who struggle to learn English may have an underlying deficiency in WM. Those who lack proficiency in both languages have an even greater likelihood of deficiencies in one or more WM components. Testing these hypotheses during an individual evaluation is challenging because an individual's performance on measures of WM will be influenced by the individual's proficiency with the language used on the WM measures (Swanson et al., 2011). For phonological STM assessment, using phonemes or nonwords, especially items that are nonwords in both languages, may be a solution. Morales, Calvo, and Bialystok (2013) reported that nonword recall is a good predictor of second language learning.

Despite the influence that WM capacity has on second language learning, acquiring a second language and becoming bilingual does not seem to have a reciprocal effect on WM strength. It has frequently been proposed that becoming bilingual strengthens WM because of the demands placed on WM by the processing of two languages. However, recent studies have found that being bilingual has very little effect on the development of WM (de Abreu & Pascale, 2011). Recently, Morales et al. (2013) found that bilingual students were stronger in the executive WM functions of inhibition and shifting, but otherwise did not outperform monolingual students. In fact, there are some indications that being bilingual actually reduces performance on language-based measures of WM. For instance, Morales et al. discovered that bilingual students outperformed monolingual students on visual-spatial measures but not verbal measures.

WORKING MEMORY AND SCHOLASTIC PERFORMANCE

Several years ago, educational researchers in the United Kingdom received a grant that allowed them to observe how students with WM deficits function in the classroom (Gathercole & Alloway, 2004). Their number one observation was that these students failed to complete assigned work and activities. Interestingly, this behavior is also typical of children with ADHD and executive dysfunctions. Not surprisingly, these researchers also discovered that teachers frequently described WM deficient learners as having an attention deficit, not a WM problem.

The teacher assessments were actually appropriate. As the cognitive load on WM increases, the executive control of attention is reduced (Hester & Garavan, 2005), resulting in a diminished ability to exert inhibitory control over extraneous, irrelevant processing and information. Consequently, focus is lost, students lose their place, and the task is abandoned (Gathercole & Alloway, 2008). Furthermore, diminished control of attention also makes switching and updating difficult, causing loss of information. Compared with individuals with high WM spans, the recall of individuals with low spans suffers more from high cognitive load processing tasks (Kane & Engle, 2000).

Normand and Tannock (2014) identified other classroom behaviors typical of students with WM impairments. The top five behaviors were: abandons activities before completion; benefits from continued teacher support during lengthy activities; does not follow classroom instructions

DON'T FORGET

Scholastic performance deficiencies in students with average academic skills may be due to a WM deficit, especially in executive WM.

accurately; is making poor progress in literacy and math; and depends on neighbor to remind them of the current task. What these behaviors have in common is that they interfere with effective productivity or performance. Consequently, classroom productivity problems may be due to a WM deficit, especially a deficit in executive WM.

Some learners with a WM deficit may, through effort and opportunities to learn under low cognitive load conditions, acquire average academic skills in all areas. However, they may still exhibit an academic production deficiency. That is, they have the general cognitive ability and academic skills to accomplish tasks and achieve normally, but fail to do so. Production deficiencies are usually reflected by slow or poor assignment completion and poor grades. Because these individuals typically are not identified as having an academic deficiency and are not considered LD, the basis of their performance problems is usually misunderstood. Frequent, but incorrect, attributions might be low motivation, limited effort, poor organization, inattentiveness, and lack of learning support in the home environment. However, the actual cause of the performance problem may be an underlying deficit in one or more WM components.

WORKING MEMORY AND LD

Research (e.g., Swanson & Berninger, 1996) has consistently found children with all types of LD and difficulties to display poor WM performance. When children with LD are matched with controls who have the same IQ, the LD group displays within-child deficits in specific aspects of WM (Swanson & Alexander, 1997). It is the within-child or "intra-individual" weakness that sets children with LD apart from other learners. For example, a student with low cognitive abilities overall will also have below average WM, but the WM level will be commensurate with the student's other cognitive abilities. Such students are usually considered to be slow learners and are not classified as LD. Although slow learners will have academic deficiencies similar to the levels of students with LD, their academic deficiencies cannot be attributed specifically to WM or other cognitive processes because all of their other cognitive abilities are also low. It is the combination of all these low abilities that results in lower achievement.

Students with a general LD or multiple SLDs perform poorly in all aspects of WM. In contrast, children with only one SLD demonstrate fairly distinctive WM profiles, with deficits limited to one or two components (see Rapid Reference 4.3). For example, children with a specific reading disability frequently have impairments in phonological STM and verbal WM (Pickering & Gathercole, 2004), whereas young children with a specific mathematics disability tend to have deficits in visual-spatial and executive WM.

Research has consistently found students with SLD to be the most deficient in the executive processing component of WM (Swanson, Cochran, & Ewers, 1990). Executive WM serves a governing function, controlling and regulating memory subsystems. Executive-loaded WM tasks, such as digits backward, provide the best discrimination between children with and without LD (Gathercole & Pickering, 2000; Henry, 2001). Also, individuals with limited executive processing often fail to spontaneously use rehearsal, organization, and other executive-dependent strategies that allow effective and efficient use of WM resources.

Reading Disabilities

Since the early 1960s, a large number of studies (cited in Torgesen, 1996) have reported that poor performance on STM tests is one of the most common characteristics of children with reading disabilities and dyslexia (Smith-Spark & Fisk, 2007). For example, Speece (1987) found that 15% to 20% of these children displayed serious difficulties on digit span tasks. Their reduced ability to temporarily maintain phonological memory codes reduces recall and impairs reading decoding. Among children with reading disabilities, impairment in phonological STM seems to be a constant research finding (for a review, see Masoura, 2006).

Deficits in verbal and executive WM may also be responsible for reading decoding problems (Swanson & Jerman, 2007). There is considerable evidence that individuals with reading disabilities have impaired verbal WM (e.g., P. De Jong, 1998). Children with a reading disability also have significant difficulty with the simultaneous storage and processing of information, the hallmark of executive WM (Van Der Sluis, Van Der Leij, & De Jong, 2005).

Longitudinal studies have also provided convincing evidence that deficient reading skills can be attributed to phonological STM and verbal WM impairments. For example, early childhood phonological STM scores have been found to be valid predictors of later performance on reading tasks (Gathercole & Baddeley, 1989). Thus, it appears that less skilled readers have a smaller short-term and WM capacity and that this capacity is independent of their reading skills (M. Turner & Engle, 1989). Nevertheless, the influence of other memory stores and cognitive processes cannot be ruled out; for example, inadequate representations of phonological units in LTM or difficulty retrieving phonological units may also be detrimental to reading decoding (Torgesen, 1996).

Mathematics Disabilities

Approximately 3% to 6% of school-age children have mathematics disabilities, and many more children struggle with mathematics. Empirical investigations have consistently implicated WM as a central deficit in children with mathematical disabilities (for a review, see Passolunghi & Siegel, 2004). Compared to their same-age peers, children with a specific mathematics disability have been found to be deficient in verbal WM, visual-spatial WM, executive WM, and WM in general (Swanson & Sachse-Lee, 2001). Also, children with a mathematics disability frequently display an intra-individual deficiency in the short-term storage of phonological information, especially when they possess comorbid reading and written language disabilities (L. Siegel & Ryan, 1989).

Some studies (e.g., L. Siegel & Ryan, 1989) have found children with mathematics disabilities to demonstrate poorer performance on visual-spatial WM than verbal WM, whereas others report poor ability in both verbal and visual-spatial WM. Nevertheless, executive WM is more frequently implicated than either verbal WM or visual-spatial WM (Andersson & Lyxell, 2007; Holmes & Adams, 2006). Individuals with executive WM deficits are unable to activate a sufficient amount of information from LTM and have difficulty integrating activated units with information in the verbal and visual-spatial components. Moreover, those with an executive WM deficit have difficulty inhibiting irrelevant information (Passolunghi & Siegel, 2004) and switching between operations (e.g., from addition to subtraction).

One of the first signs of a mathematics disability is difficulty learning arithmetic facts to the point where an arithmetic fact is automatically retrieved during computation. The difficulty with memorizing math facts and automatizing basic calculations has been attributed to STM storage deficits (Geary, Hoard, Byrd-Craven, & DeSoto, 2004; McLean & Hitch, 1999). Specifically, the learning of mathematics facts may be restrained by a low phonological STM capacity that results in the first number decaying before the child can encode the mathematics fact into long-term storage.

Alternatively, for some individuals with a mathematical disability, the source of the problem may be difficulty retrieving basic mathematics facts from LTM, thus creating an unnecessary load on WM (Geary et al., 2004). Children with math disabilities have difficulty using direct memory retrieval to solve arithmetic problems, even after they have acquired basic mathematics knowledge (Barrouillet & Lepine, 2005). However, low WM capacity itself may be the reason those with a disability are less likely to use long-term retrieval. That is, low WM capacity may result in slower and less efficient retrieval processes, as well as difficulty resisting the interference to which mathematics retrieval is particularly prone.

Although children with mathematics disabilities may demonstrate normal overall storage capacity in phonological STM, they typically have shorter digit spans and shorter spans on complex tasks that involve counting (L. Siegel & Ryan, 1989). Their specific storage deficit for numerical information may be a result of delayed growth in mathematical knowledge and skills. There is evidence that mastery of mathematics facts may have a reciprocal relationship with short-term numerical memory span (Andersson & Lyxell, 2007). When numerical knowledge acquisition is delayed, age-appropriate short-term retention of numerical information, such as digits, may be affected, as long-term representations are unable to make sufficient contributions during recall. Moreover, failure to master mathematics facts prevents automatization of mathematics computation, creating even more demands on an easily overloaded WM.

Compared to those with a mathematical disability only, students with comorbid mathematical and reading disabilities seem to have short-term and WM deficits that also involve storage of nonnumerical verbal information, and their executive WM is even more impaired (Andersson & Lyxell, 2007). Children with comorbid LD perform worse in mathematics that is mediated by language, such as story problems (Andersson & Lyxell). Students with comorbid learning disorders also may have difficulty recoding visual-spatial information into verbal information, resulting in continued use of less effective visual-spatial storage and processing. Similarly, those with comorbidity may struggle even more in mathematics because they cannot effectively use alternative verbal strategies to solve mathematics problems.

Oral Language Disabilities

An oral language disability or disorder refers to a condition in which a child experiences a delay in language development despite adequate progress in other cognitive areas. Research has established that individuals with language impairments perform poorly on verbal WM tasks, especially tasks involving phonological processing (for a review, see Masoura, 2006). For example, children with a language disorder typically exhibit poor performance on digit span and nonword repetition tasks (Baddeley, 2003a). Gutierrez-Clellen, Calderon, and Weismer (2004) found that children with a language impairment have word recall two standard deviations below the mean for their age. Gathercole and Baddeley (1990) reported that children with a language disability have poor phonological STM compared to controls matched on nonverbal intelligence. Children with a language disability also exhibit specific difficulties on executive WM processing tasks.

There are several contributions and reciprocal influences connected with oral language impairments: (a) the weak phonological memory performance of individuals with a language impairment may originate from their slow recognition and discrimination of speech sounds, a function of phonemic awareness (Masoura, 2006); (b) articulation rate may be a cause of a phonological STM deficit that in turn inhibits language processing; (c) slow processing speed may allow phonological traces to fade before meaning can be extracted; and (d) difficulties with word retrieval may also play a role. Overall, children with a language impairment have a limited capacity for processing and remembering verbal information (Gill, Klecan-Aker, Roberts, & Fredenburg, 2003).

THE IMPORTANCE OF AUTOMATICITY

Automaticity is attained when a skill or procedure is mastered so well that it no longer requires conscious, effortful cognitive processing. The burden on WM is greatest in the early stages of skill development (Kyllonen & Christal, 1999) when automaticity is lacking. As students master skills and develop expertise, the skills and procedures become automated and require less processing by WM. Automated processing requires only minimal WM resources, and it does not interfere with effortful conscious processing (Richardson, 1996).

Students who do not obtain automaticity at the same time as their peers have relatively fewer residual WM resources for other tasks. For example, a fifth grader still struggling with reading decoding has fewer resources to devote to comprehension. Therefore, it is crucial that basic skills be taught and practiced to a high level of mastery so that automaticity is assured and WM can focus on higher-level processing.

The principle of automaticity also applies directly to WM strategy use. More resources are freed up as WM routines and strategies, such as subvocal rehearsal and chunking, become automated. In fact, chunking (see Chapter 3) may be the primary process that underlies automaticity. Consequently, extensive opportunities to deliberately practice a WM strategy may improve WM performance without actually expanding preexisting WM capacity (MacDonald & Christiansen, 2002).

When it comes to individual differences in WM capacity, the development of automaticity may be the great equalizer. For learners with WM impairments, acquiring expertise and automaticity is more important than it is for those who have ample WM resources. As basic skills develop to the point of full automaticity, WM capacity becomes less of a factor in skill performance (A. R. A. Conway & Engle, 1994), thereby allowing students with WM deficiencies to progress academically. Automaticity essentially creates higher processing efficiency, leading to stronger WM performance, as well as better products and outcomes for the processing or learning task at hand. For students with WM deficits, reaching automaticity is crucial.

IMPLICATIONS FOR ASSESSMENT

Knowing the relationships between specific academic skills and specific WM functions is valuable information that can guide assessment, interpretation of results, and diagnosis of learning disorders. Children with different SLDs tend to demonstrate unique types of WM deficits (L. Siegel & Ryan, 1989; Swanson et al., 2006). Thus, an individual's WM profile, at least to some extent, can help to differentiate among types of SLD (see Rapid Reference 4.3). Consequently, assessment procedures that allow discrimination of WM components, such as testing all five WM components (see Chapter 5), can help to differentiate among specific academic learning dysfunctions and disabilities.

Other Cognitive Processing Deficits

The empirical evidence indicates that WM performance is an important source of data that can reliably differentiate between students with LD and those who are slow learners (Swanson et al., 1990). Of course, WM scores alone are insufficient for a diagnosis; other assessment data need to be taken into account. A WM deficit is seldom the only deficiency found within individuals with LD (see Chapter 4). For example, those with a basic reading skills disability might have coexisting deficits in phonological processing or long-term storage. Individuals with lower general cognitive ability also are likely to be low in WM. What sets those with LD apart from slow learners is that for slow learners, WM is not necessarily an intra-individual weakness.

CAUTION

Although it is central, WM is not the only cognitive process necessary for successful academic learning and performance. Consequently, not all SLDs are due to a WM deficit. Other cognitive processes highly related with specific academic skills also need to be considered during assessment.

Preschool WM Screening

Given the well-established relationship between poor WM capacity and academic failure, a WM measure would be an appropriate addition to early childhood and early elementary school screenings. WM assessments with children as young as 4 years of age can identify children at risk of future low achievement (Gathercole & Pickering, 2001). With the emphasis on early intervention, most school systems now conduct universal screening of reading and arithmetic skills. Processing assessment—namely, phonological processing—is already embedded in most reading assessments. Including a brief measure of phonological STM and verbal WM span may improve early identification of children at risk for academic failure and LD. For example, longitudinal research in England discovered that a backward digit-recall task administered at school entry is a good predictor of who will need special education 3 years later (Pickering & Gathercole, 2004).

DON'T FORGET

Preschool screening of WM ability in children as young as 4 years of age can identify children at risk for LD.

CONCLUSIONS

- There is a strong relationship between WM capacity and overall learning rate; greater capacity is related to faster learning (Radvansky & Copeland, 2006). Even basic STM functions have significant relationships with learning. For example, scores on word and nonword repetition tasks are closely linked with vocabulary learning (Gathercole & Adams, 1993).

- The primary reason that WM has such a strong influence on general learning is that adequate WM is necessary for conscious encoding of information into LTM, and WM is also involved during effortful retrieval from LTM.
- The probability of information being encoded into LTM is partly a function of the amount of time an item is maintained in STM or WM. Also, making associations that will be encoded into LTM requires adequate WM capacity for processing.
- With the exception of mathematics, academic learning and performance depend more heavily on the phonological and verbal components than on the visual-spatial components.
- WM functioning in general is most important during the initial stages of learning. It declines in importance as facts and procedures become firmly established in LTM and as procedures are performed automatically and effortlessly (Geary et al., 2004).
- The relative importance of each WM component changes during development and skill acquisition. For example, the relationship between visual-spatial WM and learning is stronger in preschool and early grades.
- Some of the relationships between academic learning and WM are reciprocal. Not only does WM capacity influence all types of learning, but also skill development influences WM development and capacity (Henry & Millar, 1993; Van Der Sluis et al., 2005).
- In general, the most influential WM component when it comes to academic learning and performance is the executive. The development, capacity, and effective use of executive WM have important consequences for academic learning and performance. SLD students are more likely to have a deficit in executive WM than in any other WM component.
- The more WM components that are deficient, the more severe the SLD and the more likely the learner will have multiple SLDs.
- Because children with different SLDs tend to demonstrate unique types of WM deficits, all five WM components should be assessed whenever a child is referred for a possible SLD.
- Classroom learning and performance are highly influenced by the degree of cognitive load experienced by the learner. Most classroom instruction and activities create too much cognitive load for students with low WM capacity.

- If students with WM deficits are to attain normal achievement, they must experience frequent learning situations that place only minimal demands on WM, thereby allowing them to attain skills and knowledge comparable to peers who possess average WM capabilities. In particular, the methods and materials used with students who have an SLD should keep WM processing demands to a minimum.

🖋 TEST YOURSELF 🖋

1. **Regardless of which specific LD a student may have, which working memory component is most likely to be deficient?**
   - (a) Phonological STM
   - (b) Visual-spatial WM
   - (c) Verbal WM
   - (d) Executive WM

2. **All of the following influence the extent to which any given WM component is related to mathematics performance *except***
   - (a) Age
   - (b) IQ
   - (c) Automaticity
   - (d) Type of math problem

3. **Which WM component has the strongest influence on vocabulary development?**
   - (a) Phonological STM
   - (b) Visual-spatial WM
   - (c) Verbal WM
   - (d) Executive WM

4. **For students with deficient executive WM, what most needs to be kept to a minimum?**
   - (a) Assignment length
   - (b) Repetition
   - (c) Cognitive load
   - (d) Visual representations

5. **Which skill is least likely to reach a high level of automaticity in any learner?**
   - (a) Reading decoding
   - (b) Mathematics calculation
   - (c) Written expression
   - (d) Listening comprehension

6. Because of the additional cognitive demands of coping with two languages, bilingual individuals have higher **WM** levels than monolingual speakers. **True or False?**

    (a) True
    (b) False

7. An academic performance deficiency may be due to low **WM** capacity even when the student has developed average academic skills. **True or False?**

    (a) True
    (b) False

Answers: 1. d; 2. b; 3. a; 4. c; 5. c; 6. False; 7. True

Five

ASSESSMENT STRATEGIES

Whenever WM is a referral concern, a comprehensive evaluation of WM should be conducted, especially when the client is a student who is experiencing academic learning problems. A comprehensive assessment means that all five WM components from the integrated model of working memory (see Chapter 1) should be directly tested with standardized measures. (The five components are listed in Rapid Reference 5.1.) A partial assessment of WM may result in a misleading impression of the examinee's WM abilities. For example, testing only the phonological and verbal aspects of WM provides no information on visual-spatial WM abilities. Also, executive WM testing is essential because of the crucial role the executive component plays in overall WM functioning. A comprehensive assessment of WM will lead to a better understanding of the cognitive, learning, and performance problems being experienced by the client. The assessment data will also be helpful in planning an

≡ Rapid Reference 5.1 The Five Working Memory Components to Assess

1. Phonological STM
2. Visual-spatial STM
3. Verbal WM
4. Visual-spatial WM
5. Executive WM

intervention that addresses the WM shortcomings. This chapter lays out the rationale and detailed procedures for accomplishing comprehensive testing of WM in
a psychometrically valid and acceptable manner.

HOW TO DETERMINE WHICH WORKING MEMORY COMPONENT A SUBTEST MEASURES

Later in this chapter there are classification tables that align subtests from cognitive and memory batteries with the five WM components from the integrated
model. In addition to the tables herein, a comprehensive list is provided in the
online resources. However, not every commercially available battery is included.
Therefore, it is important to be able to independently determine which kinds
of activities measure specific WM abilities. This section will help the reader
understand the criteria and methods used to identify measures of WM and to
determine which WM component is being assessed.

Differences Between STM Components and WM Components

Even though STM is considered part of WM, testing STM and WM separately is
important because the functions are different and because STM and WM can be
separated neurologically. When an assessment fails to include measures that isolate
STM, it can be difficult to determine where the specific WM weaknesses may
lie. Contrasting STM with WM performance can reveal whether the weakness is
primarily a storage limitation or a processing dysfunction. Unfortunately, some
test batteries do not offer measures that isolate STM.

A subtest measures STM whenever storage but no additional processing or
only minimal processing is required. A digits forward subtest is a classic example
of an STM task. An activity measures one of the WM components whenever processing occurs while simultaneously trying to maintain information. Both types
of tasks measure span—the number of items that are retained in the correct
sequence. *Simple span* activities require only the passive retention of information
and are, therefore, presumed to mainly measure STM. Examples of simple-span
tasks include the serial recall of letters, digits, words, or nonwords without any
manipulation of the information or dealing with distractors. *Complex span* activities, used to measure the specific WM components, require effortful processing
of information while trying to retain a list of items. The classic example of a
complex-span task is the reading span task in which the examinee reads a sentence, responds to a simple question about it, and then later must sequentially
recall the final word of each sentence. Rapid Reference 5.2 lists criteria for determining whether a subtest is primarily measuring STM or WM components.

≡ Rapid Reference 5.2 Criteria for Distinguishing Between STM and Working Memory

- The task is measuring STM if only passive, unchanged, serial recall of information is required.
- The task is measuring WM whenever simultaneous processing and storage are required.
- The task is measuring WM whenever any manipulation or transformation of the information is required.
- The task is measuring WM whenever a concurrent or intervening processing task designed to function as a distractor is required.
- The task is measuring WM whenever verbal information and visual-spatial information need to be integrated.

Phonological STM Tasks

To be considered a valid phonological STM measure, the task should: (a) have orally presented stimuli; (b) not require the examinee to read the stimuli; (c) allow an oral response only (no pointing to or clicking on responses); (d) require the items be repeated in the correct sequence; (e) not include an irrelevant, distracting task that creates interference; (f) allow vocal or subvocal rehearsal; (g) have all items with similar articulatory length, such as monosyllabic words; and (h) not contain any rhyming stimuli within the same item.

The use of digits as the only stimuli should be avoided with examinees who have numeracy, arithmetic, or mathematics weaknesses. Delayed arithmetic development can influence the recall of digits, producing a score that underestimates overall phonological short-term storage capacity. A forward letter span task is ideal for use with examinees who are deficient in mathematics skills.

It is acceptable for phonological STM tasks to allow support from LTM. However, the extent of LTM influence should be taken into account. Immediately recalling lists of words probably receives the highest level of support from LTM. To reduce this influence, all of the words should be unrelated so that they cannot be categorized. Letter span also keeps the processing close to the phonological level because letters activate fewer meaning-based long-term representations than words. To further reduce the influence of lexical knowledge from LTM, nonwords or just phonemes are ideal stimuli. The less support items receive from LTM, the shorter the span is likely to be.

Verbal WM Tasks

When a WM task is limited to processing verbal content and there is no irrelevant, distracting processing introduced, it is considered verbal WM, rather than executive WM. The verbal processing that is required should be task-relevant processing that would naturally take place in order to accomplish the cognitive goal, such as the verbal processing that occurs during reading comprehension. Both phonological STM and verbal LTM will play key roles in verbal WM, as both will provide temporary storage of the information being utilized.

A memory for sentences task is classified as verbal WM rather than phonological STM because sentences will invoke meaning-based processing, which will promote grouping the words into meaningful phrases. The result is several more words being recalled than the span for a series of unconnected words. Although there is some crossover with LTM encoding and recall, retelling of brief stories can also be considered a verbal WM measure. Another verbal WM task is remembering the last word in a series of sentences that are read or orally presented.

Another distinction between phonological STM and verbal WM is that WM recall need not be sequential. In the real world, retaining and processing verbal information contain a sequential element that is not always essential for effective functioning. Thus, it is valid for subtests to offer full or partial credit for words, phrases, and sentences that are out of sequence.

Visual-Spatial STM Tasks

Tasks that involve recalling stimuli or their location without any need to process the information, deal with distractors, or manipulate images are classified as visual-spatial STM measures. Although standardized tasks of this nature often include pictures of common objects, it is best to use abstract stimuli that cannot be easily named. When the stimuli can be easily named, phonological STM comes into play during recall, prohibiting a relatively pure evaluation of visual-spatial STM. Visual-spatial STM tasks may or may not require sequential recall. Classic block-tapping tasks require sequential recall, but much of real-world visual-spatial processing is not sequential in nature.

Visual-Spatial WM Tasks

A visual-spatial task graduates from STM to WM when the mental manipulation of stimuli or internally generated images is required. When irrelevant, distracting processing is introduced, the task should be considered executive WM, rather than visual-spatial WM. Task-relevant processing would include maintaining orientation during rotation, counting the number of stimuli on a sequence of cards, or reversing the sequence in a block-tapping activity.

Executive WM Tasks

In general, executive WM tasks are more challenging than either verbal or visual-spatial WM. There are four main ways that executive WM functioning can be distinguished from the more modality-specific WM components. First, the task is executive if integration of verbal and visual-spatial information is required, such as immediately recalling new symbols (rebuses) that represent words. Second, the task introduces distracting information or requires task-irrelevant processing. The third criterion is that the task requires extensive, ongoing inhibition, updating, or switching. Finally, the conscious application of a strategy other than basic rehearsal will engage executive WM. A strategy example would be visualizing words on a list. A general indication that the task is executive in nature is that the span is noticeably lower than verbal or visual-spatial WM spans, or the individual takes much longer to complete the task.

If designed correctly, executive WM tasks have good ecological validity because real-world functioning involves coping with information that is distracting and needs to be inhibited. For example, in the classroom, students must continually deal with all kinds of interference that makes immediate task completion challenging.

The ideal activity for assessing executive WM functioning is an *n-back* task. The procedure requires the examinee to identify a stimulus that was presented a predetermined number of items before. The presentation of stimuli and the response by the examinee are continuous, rather than presenting all the stimuli at once, followed by a span response. For example, in a 2-back task using numbers, the examinee needs to say the number exposed two numbers earlier. For instance, if the exposure sequence is "10," "2," "6," "8," the correct response is "10" when the "6"

DON'T FORGET

A task involves executive working memory when it requires one or more of the following:

- Integration of verbal and visual-spatial information
- Processing task-irrelevant, distracting information
- Ongoing inhibition, switching, or updating
- The conscious application of a strategy

is exposed, "2" when the "8" is exposed, and so on. The *n*-back task presents an exceptional challenge to executive WM because constant updating, switching, and inhibition are required.

Task Analysis

All cognitive and memory subtests measure multiple cognitive and memory abilities. This is not due only to the structure, content, and demands of the subtests themselves. Rather, it mainly reflects the integrated functioning of the brain. Test authors attempt to design subtests so that they primarily measure the targeted ability. The extent to which a subtest taps a particular ability more than other abilities is assessed through expert opinion, correlational studies, and factor analysis.

The results of factor analysis can be deceiving because factor analysis mainly identifies groupings of items or subtests that are measuring something in common. However, the entity they have in common is open to debate, and the name assigned to a factor may not be the best descriptor of what is actually being measured. Factor analysis can also be helpful. Sometimes, studies reveal that a subtest is primarily measuring an ability other than the one intended. For instance, a factor analysis of the Wechsler Intelligence Scale for Children, Fourth Edition (WISC-IV; Wechsler, 2003), discovered that the Arithmetic subtest was measuring fluid reasoning, even though the structure and scoring of the WISC-IV had Arithmetic as a WM measure (Keith, Fine, Taub, Reynolds, & Kranzler, 2006).

At other times, experts may dispute what is being measured. This is often based on differences of opinion regarding how the ability being measured is labeled or defined. For example, some experts might claim a subtest is measuring a cognitive "ability," whereas others would say it is measuring a cognitive "process."

Finally, a test author may use a traditional measurement paradigm to measure something else. An example of this is using a verbal span task to measure oral language. For example, the WJ IV Oral Language Battery (Schrank, Mather, & McGrew, 2014b) subtest known as *Sentence Repetition* is a classic measure of phonological STM. Yet, in the WJ IV it is categorized as a measure of oral expression.

The result of these inconsistencies is that not all official STM and WM subtests are measuring the specific WM component indicated. Also, some subtests ostensibly used to measure a non-WM ability may primarily be measuring WM. Consequently, a small percentage of the subtests listed as measures of STM and WM components in the online resources are not classified as WM measures in their respective scales or batteries.

To determine whether a subtest primarily measures WM and also identify which specific WM components it taps, a task analysis is conducted. In task analysis, subtests are analyzed to determine the primary cognitive ability or process that is needed to succeed at the task. Input, such as directions, processing, and output (responses) are all considered, but the processing required is given the most weight (Hale & Fiorello, 2004). If the task is judged to be primarily a WM task, based on the definition of the construct, then it is examined further to determine which specific WM component is primary. The criteria discussed in the previous section are used to distinguish between the five different WM components. For example, a verbal task that requires basic sequential recall without the need for any significant processing will be classified as phonological STM.

Task analysis with WM in mind will sometimes identify subtests as WM measures when they are purportedly measuring other abilities. This difference in classification often results because the task analysis applied herein emphasizes the processing involved, not the input or the output. For example, a task with verbal input and required verbal output may be used as a measure of oral language. However, the fact that oral language is involved during input and required during output does not mean that the primary cognitive processing demand is on oral language. For example, the classic digits backward task is mainly verbal from an input and output perspective. Yet, there is expert consensus that digits backward is primarily a measure of WM.

Identifying the primary process required during an evaluation task is challenging, and there will be differences of opinion. The challenge arises because several processes are involved in any cognitive task. With the digits backward task the processes that come into play include attention, auditory processing, executive functions, sequencing, processing speed, and WM. Of these, WM appears to be the primary processing demand because it appears to be indispensable for the task. The classification of digits backward is also supported by extensive validity evidence.

An example of an unexpected reclassification is the *Understanding Directions* subtest in the WJ IV Tests of Oral Language (Schrank et al., 2014b). Although the WJ IV identifies it as a test of listening comprehension, it is herein classified as an appropriate measure of executive WM because WM more than any other cognitive process seems to be necessary for successfully completing the task.

Finally, official WM subtests and those identified as primarily measuring WM are analyzed further to determine which of the five WM components they are specifically measuring. At this level of classification there is less conflict with the official structure of published scales and batteries because many of the tasks are already identified as WM subtests. Nonetheless, the majority still need to be

CAUTION

Some of the subtests classified as measures of WM components in this text are not identified as WM measures in their respective scales or batteries. These subtests have been reclassified based on factor-analytic research, task analysis, or expert opinion. The reclassifications occur when it appears that WM is the primary ability that is required to successfully complete the task.

assigned to a specific WM component. At this stage, the definition and criteria for each component are used to decide which specific WM component is primary. Some matches are easily determined, such as whether the measure is verbal or visual-spatial. However, some of the lines within modalities are fuzzy, such as deciding whether a verbal task is more WM than STM. The most difficult discriminations are those between executive WM and verbal and visual-spatial WM. Some of the subtests classified as primarily measuring verbal WM might also be considered measures of executive WM. In such instances, the experienced practitioner may use clinical judgment and interpret the task as also measuring the other closely related WM component. However, crossing over between the STM and WM components within the same modality is not recommended because the distinction between STM and WM components is well defined.

INFORMAL ASSESSMENT PROCEDURES

The consideration of informal and qualitative assessment data is good practice in any type of psychological assessment. Such data can be used to corroborate test scores and support assessment hypotheses. The sections ahead provide suggestions and structure for the informal assessment of WM.

Collecting Background Information

Gathering information about history should be the first step when evaluating a client for a potential WM impairment. Going all the way back to the individual's birth is important because it increases the odds of uncovering a potential cause of WM problems other than genetics. Interviewing, especially a parent interview, is a primary method of collecting this data. There should also be a review of available records—educational, medical, neurological, and psychological.

A main objective in collecting background information is to confirm the presence or absence of risk factors. (A short list of risk factors is provided in

≡ Rapid Reference 5.3 Risk Factors for Working Memory Impairments

- Traumatic brain injury
- Concussion
- Extreme prematurity
- Diabetes
- Dopamine deficiency
- Depression
- Anxiety
- Stress
- Anything that usually has a detrimental effect on cognitive functions

Rapid Reference 5.3.) However, any condition that is detrimental to the brain and cognitive functions is a general risk factor for WM impairments. When a risk factor is identified, it is important to find out the client's age at onset or when the incident occurred. Determining the number of recurring episodes is also helpful information.

If no risk factors are present, the odds are that the WM deficiency is developmental. When WM deficits are genetic and developmental, the first clues should emerge in early childhood. For example, a delay in speech and language development is a marker for a WM delay. ADHD-like symptoms or delays in executive functions are other clues. Any indications of memory problems, even if they are attributed to LTM, may originate with WM.

When the records are anecdotal, such as some elementary school records, the reviewer should look for reports or indications of behaviors that are associated with WM difficulties. (See Rapid Reference 5.11 for a listing of WM-related behaviors.) For instance, a teacher's comment that a fourth-grade student is still finger counting is a red flag for WM problems. Isolated reports should not be accepted as adequate documentation but rather as items needing further corroboration.

If test records are available, the results should be carefully re-examined. First, the current reviewer should identify measures that typically tap WM components. If these scores appear to be potential weaknesses or deficits and the report's interpretive section ignored these concerns, then the reviewer should re-analyze the data, following the procedures recommended later in this chapter. Previous examiners may have been uninterested or unaware of WM measures embedded in the scales they used. For example, a child may have obtained an extremely low digit span subtest score, but it was interpreted as a measure of distractibility, instead of WM. In incidences where this occurred, the evidence for a WM deficit was previously present, but was undetected or ignored. Consequently, the client and significant others have been unaware of an existing WM deficit.

The absence of any history related to WM problems does not rule out the possibility of significant WM weaknesses. Sometimes, WM deficits and the learning and performance problems associated with them will not appear until the individual reaches an environment that demands normal WM functioning.

Interviewing

Interviewing allows a more in-depth investigation of variables hypothesized to underlie the referral concerns, and interview data can be used to corroborate test results. Addressing WM functioning during an interview can be challenging because most interviewees do not know what WM is or how its deficits are manifested. For example, teachers and parents often attribute behaviors resulting from WM weaknesses to attention problems or lack of motivation. To add to the challenge, structured interview formats seldom include items specifically related to WM. Consequently, the interviewer must make a special effort to generate questions that address WM concerns. To begin the process, interview items are suggested herein. The behavior observation items provided later in this chapter can also be converted into interview items.

Teacher Interviews. In the initial part of the interview, the primary objective should be to ask about behaviors, learning problems, and cognitive processes that are related with WM deficits, without explicitly mentioning WM. For example, the interviewer might ask if the student appears to be having attention problems, processing speed problems, or difficulty following directions. If the teacher's report gives the impression of a WM deficiency, the next round of questions should attempt to identify which WM components are the sources of the problem. Such interview items might pursue: (a) whether the observed problems are primarily verbal or visual-spatial; (b) how increasing demands in a learning situation impact the student's performance; and (c) whether the student is using any memory strategies. (See Rapid Reference 5.4 for more items.) When the interviewee seems unfamiliar with the behavior in question, the interviewer should

≡ Rapid Reference 5.4 Teacher Interview Items*

- What kinds of learning activities are most difficult for the student?
- Is the student stronger in visual or auditory learning?
- Does it take the student exceptionally long to complete assignments?
- How well does the student remember directions and information?
- How often does the student ask you to repeat directions?
- How often does the student ask peers for help?
- How much repetition does the student require before learning new information?
- Does the student have difficulties memorizing information?
- Does the student have any difficulties with listening comprehension?
- How well does the student stay focused on the task at hand?
- How well can the student do two things simultaneously, such as listen and take notes?
- Is the student slow to recall information that he knows?
- Does the student have difficulty expressing ideas orally or in writing?
- How well does the student retain information during multistep operations, such as when completing a multistep arithmetic problem?
- What memory strategies, if any, have you observed the student using?
- To what do you attribute the student's learning problems?
- What signs have you observed that indicate the student might have problems with short-term memory?
- Do you believe short-term or working memory weaknesses could be the cause of the student's problems?

*This is also in the online resources.

provide examples. This part of the interview should conclude with eliciting the teacher's hypotheses regarding the potential causes of the referral concerns. That is, the teacher should be asked why she believes the student is having the referral problems. In some cases, the teacher's hypotheses may include WM functions, even when the teacher is unaware of the concept of WM.

The final part of the interview should explicitly address WM. The interviewer should begin by asking the teacher if she is familiar with WM. Regardless of whether the teacher replies in the affirmative, WM should be defined in simple terms at this point, such as stating that WM is a combination of thinking and short-term memory. The interviewer should then identify some behaviors that are indicative of WM problems and indicate which of the referral concerns could be due to a WM problem. It is important at this point to explain that WM lasts for only a few seconds so that the interviewee does not confuse it with LTM. The interviewer should then ask the teacher if she now believes that WM might be a concern, and then discuss the implications of this possibility further.

Parent Interviews. After the child's history has been collected from the parent, the structure and issues addressed during the interview should be similar to that of the teacher interview. Parents should be asked about behaviors that are associated with learning and memory problems, such as how well the child can pay attention and how long it takes to complete homework. The only difference is that the parent interview should contain home environment examples of WM problems. For example, the interviewer might ask how often the child forgets what was just said in a conversation. Like the teacher interview, parent hypotheses about the causes of the problems should be invited. Also, the interview should conclude with introducing the concept of WM and how it impacts behavior and learning, and then asking the parent if these WM problems seem to fit with what he is observing. To reduce confusion about WM, it might be best to refer to it as "short-term memory."

Client Interviews. Although child and adult clients vary widely in their ability to self-appraise, child interviews can be a valuable source of assessment data. At the very least, it is valuable to hear the individual's attributions as to the cause of his problems. Some children lack self-awareness of their problems, and some simply deny they are having any problems. To avoid biasing their attributions, it is best to ask the individual about his attributions before there is any mention of memory problems. (See the sequence of items in Rapid Reference 5.5.) Children who are middle-school age or older should be directly questioned about behaviors related to WM, and simple, age-appropriate items should also be attempted with elementary students. When it is highly likely that the individual has some kind of WM deficiency, the interview should also address metamemory development and strategy use. For details, see the sections on these assessment topics later in this chapter.

≡ Rapid Reference 5.5 Student Interview Items*

- What do you think is the cause of the learning problems you are having?
- Do you ever forget to do something? Can you give me an example? How often does this happen?
- How often do you forget what the teacher just said?
- How often do you ask the teacher to repeat directions?
- How often do you raise your hand in class and then forget what you were going to say?
- When you are writing, do you leave out letters or words without knowing that you did?
- Is it hard for you to listen and take notes at the same time?
- Do you have difficulty memorizing facts?
- Do you sometimes lose your place when reading?
- Is it hard for you to do arithmetic in your head?
- What do you do when you want to keep track of information in your head?
- Do you think memory problems might be the cause of your learning problems?

*This is also in the online resources.

Assessment of Metamemory and Strategy Use

Chapter 3 has details on the development of metamemory and strategy use. The main topics interviewees should be queried about are: (a) their knowledge and understanding of human memory functions; (b) their awareness of their personal memory strengths and weaknesses; (c) their self-regulation of memory functions; and (d) their knowledge and use of specific memory strategies. (For suggested items, see Rapid References 5.6 and 5.7.)

≡ Rapid Reference 5.6 Metamemory Interview Items*

- Tell me what you know about how memory works.
- What are some different kinds of memory that people have?

- How long does short-term memory last?
- How much do most people forget?
- What do you think makes people forget things?
- What kinds of things are easy for you to remember?
- What makes it easy for you to remember these things?
- What kinds of things are hard for you to remember?
- What makes it hard for you to remember these things?
- Do you believe it's harder for you to remember things than it is for other people your age?
- Do you have any control over how well you remember?
- What do you do when you really want to remember something?
- What do you do when you need to keep track of two things at the same time?

*This is also in the online resources.

≡ Rapid Reference 5.7 Memory Strategies Interview Items*

- Tell me what you do when you need to remember something that was just said, for at least a short period of time.
- How often do you repeat something you just heard over and over to yourself?
- What do you do when you want to remember things you just saw?
- Tell me about the methods you use when you try to memorize information.
- Which of your memorization methods work best?
- Do you ever try to group words or other information together to make it easier to remember?
- Do you ever try to picture things in your mind so that you can remember them better?
- What do you do when you need to focus on something and you are having distracting thoughts?
- Has anyone taught you methods for remembering things better? If so, what are they?

*This is also in the online resources.

Assessing Cognitive Load in the Classroom

A student's difficulty coping with the cognitive load generated in the typical learning environment is another indication of a WM deficit. As cognitive load increases, the student will experience increased difficulties with short-term storage of information. Some key manifestations of cognitive overload are that the student will take longer to complete tasks and will have more difficulty with initial learning of new material. (See Chapters 1 and 4 for more details on cognitive load.)

As part of a WM evaluation, the examiner should observe the student in his usual learning environments in order to informally assess the degree of cognitive load. First, teachers' instructional behaviors should be observed. Second, the structure and content of the learning materials should be reviewed. Teacher behaviors that increase cognitive load are presented in Rapid Reference 5.8, and structure and content variables are listed in Rapid Reference 5.9.

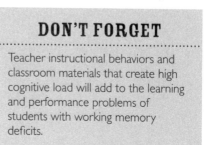

DON'T FORGET

Teacher instructional behaviors and classroom materials that create high cognitive load will add to the learning and performance problems of students with working memory deficits.

≡ Rapid Reference 5.8

Teacher Behaviors That Increase Cognitive Load*

- Long, complex, and inconsistent verbalizations
- Disorganized presentations and lessons
- Not allowing enough time for learners to process information
- Requiring students to multitask
- Not allowing students to use memory aides
- Allowing a noisy learning environment
- Presenting excessively long lessons
- Introducing procedural steps before they are needed
- Not providing visual representations

*This is also in the online resources.

≡ *Rapid Reference 5.9*

Content Variables That Increase Cognitive Load*

- Complex material
- Difficult material
- Material that requires the learner to integrate lots of information
- Material that is not broken down into small units
- Material that lacks examples and illustrations
- Material that is poorly organized
- Content for which the student lacks prior knowledge
- Assignments that require multiple tasks simultaneously

*This is also in the online resources.

Observations

Observation of behavior is a fundamental assessment method that should be included in every comprehensive evaluation of WM. To increase the validity of observations regarding WM, the observer needs to become familiar with the intricacies of WM and the behaviors that are indicative of atypical limitations. Knowledge of the relationships between academic functioning and WM processes (see Chapter 4) will also be beneficial when conducting observations. Even an observer with expertise in WM needs to be cautious about making inferences from observed behaviors, mainly due to the lack of one-to-one correspondence between behaviors and WM processes. For example, observers should not assume that failure to follow directions is due to a WM deficit. There are many reasons why students do not follow directions. Also, deficiencies in other cognitive or metacognitive processes may underlie a specific observable behavior.

Observations During Testing. Observations during one-on-one standardized testing can provide valuable clinical information about the examinee's WM strengths and weaknesses. Insights into an examinee's WM functioning can be gained from observations during any type of testing, not just during WM subtests. Familiarity with observable indicators of WM processes will increase the examiner's awareness of behaviors that are noteworthy. Many of the behaviors suggested for classroom observation can also be observed during testing. Testing behaviors indicative of WM deficits are listed in Rapid Reference 5.10. Examiners also should observe for indications of strategy use. These include

≡ Rapid Reference 5.10

Testing Behaviors Related to Working Memory Weaknesses*

- Asking for directions or items to be repeated
- Taking a long time to respond, especially on more difficult items
- Requesting supplemental materials, such as paper to write on
- Increasing frustration as the complexity of the task increases
- Difficulty expressing ideas
- Difficulty elaborating upon a response when requested to do so
- Difficulty retrieving simple information on demand
- Difficulty staying focused on the task at hand
- Not appearing to use any strategies
- Lacking confidence with or fearing memory activities

*This is also in the online resources.

thinking aloud, repeating items, and chunking or clustering information. These strategic behaviors are not signs of WM problems but rather indications of appropriate metamemory development and strategy use.

When observing during testing, it is important to note when the behaviors occurred. A convenient method of tracking behaviors is to record the behavior alongside the item or subtest where it occurred. After completing the administration, review the recorded observations and consider the demands of the task at the time each one occurred. Challenging and complex tasks increase cognitive load, making it easier to observe WM difficulties, such as making simple mistakes or not detecting errors.

Classroom Observations. Much can be learned about a referred student's WM characteristics by observing the student in the classroom. It is most productive to observe the referred pupil when he is engaged in academic areas that are challenging, because the pupil is less likely to display WM problems during simple, routine activities. Rapid Reference 5.11 provides observable behaviors, broken down by specific WM components. Although the list is not standardized, the behaviors in the list are those that have frequently been reported in research articles and published case studies. The list should be used cautiously, as other cognitive and noncognitive problems also underlie these behaviors. For example, not completing multistep directions could be due to WM limitations but could also occur because of such factors as oppositional behavior or not having the skills needed for the task. Consequently, multiple behaviors that can be associated with WM difficulties should be evident before the behaviors are attributed to a WM deficit.

≡ Rapid Reference 5.11 Classroom Behaviors Indicative of Working Memory Problems*

General Working Memory

- Has trouble remembering information for just a few seconds
- In the middle of an activity, forgets how to continue or finish it
- Has difficulty staying focused during cognitively demanding activities
- Performance is worse during challenging activities
- Prefers simple tasks over complex tasks
- Takes a long time to complete assignments
- Has difficulty retrieving information efficiently
- Has difficulty relating new information with prior knowledge
- Makes comments about having memory problems
- Has difficulty with mental arithmetic
- Has difficulty memorizing and retaining facts
- Is very slow at arithmetic computation
- Seeks assistance from peers
- Does not appear to use any memory strategies
- Misses a lot of information during instruction

Phonological Short-Term Memory

- Has difficulty repeating what was just said
- Has difficulty remembering multistep oral directions
- Has difficulty restating instructions
- Has difficulty with phonemic awareness
- Has difficulty learning new vocabulary
- Speaks mostly in very short sentences
- Does not appear to repeat information to self

Visual-Spatial Short-Term Memory

- Has difficulty remembering what he just saw
- Has difficulty learning colors, shapes, numerals, or letters
- Confuses names of shapes and symbols
- Is slow when copying
- Has difficulty copying without making errors
- Forgets where materials have just been placed
- Has difficulty putting puzzles together
- Does not seem to notice visual details

Verbal Working Memory

- Requires frequent reminders of what needs to be done
- When called on, forgets what he was planning to say
- Has difficulty understanding directions
- Has difficulty with oral comprehension
- Has difficulty with reading comprehension
- Has difficulty organizing information when writing
- Produces only short sentences during written expression
- Has subject-verb agreement errors in written expression
- Does not notice written expression errors
- Omits some of the content when writing a sentence
- Repeats words when writing a sentence
- Has difficulty blending phonemes into words when reading
- Has difficulty with phonetic recoding (spelling)
- Has difficulty paraphrasing
- Rarely contributes to class discussions

Visual-Spatial Working Memory

- Doesn't notice the signs—for example, "+"—during arithmetic calculation
- Loses place when reading, counting, or doing math
- Gets confused when something is moved or rotated
- Seems to have difficulty imaging things
- Has difficulty describing a scene
- Seems to miss or forget details when watching a video
- Is slow at video games

Executive Working Memory

- Has difficulty multitasking
- Has difficulty coping with distractions
- Has difficulty focusing attention
- Has difficulty sustaining attention
- Has difficulty dividing attention
- Answers to questions are off-topic or irrelevant
- Has difficulty switching back and forth during an activity
- Has difficulty taking notes and listening at the same time
- Does not seem to use learning or memory strategies
- Prefers to use simple instead of complex learning strategies
- Selects inefficient strategies during problem solving
- Has difficulty with planning and organization
- Has difficulty keeping up with ongoing presentation of information
- Does not like games that require planning or a strategy

*This is also in the online resources.

ASSESSING INTERACTION WITH LONG-TERM MEMORY

As discussed in Chapter 2, WM performance is influenced by LTM functions, and conversely, WM can enhance LTM processing. Even when LTM is presumed to be normal, the interaction between the two systems should be considered during a WM assessment.

Activated Long-Term Memory Items

Although recently activated LTM items contribute to WM capacity and functioning, there are currently no standardized instruments for assessing the number of such items and the speed with which they can be accessed. Nonetheless, the extent to which LTM is supporting WM functioning should be considered and assessed informally. Here is a suggested informal approach that may indicate how well the examinee can maintain and quickly access several activated LTM items:

- Use a social studies reading passage on a topic that the examinee has adequate background knowledge on. The passage can be read to examinees who lack fluency or can't read.
- Preview the topic with the examinee by looking at the title, subtitles, pictures, graphics, and information in bold print. Then ask the examinee to

tell what he already knows about this topic. If the examinee claims no prior knowledge, provide prompts to remind the examinee of basic information he probably knows about the subject. The purpose of this is to begin the activation of relevant LTM items.

- As the passage is read, have the examinee stop after each paragraph and first state a fact or idea from the paragraph that is new the examinee.
- The examinee must then say why this new fact makes sense, given what he already knows about the subject. This will require the examinee to consider background knowledge that has been activated about the subject and make some kind of association. For example, if the new fact is, "The rivers in Europe are polluted," the examinee might reply with, "They are polluted because Europe has a lot of big cities."
- It is not the accuracy of the responses that matters but the examinee's ability to quickly respond with some type of logical association between a new fact and prior knowledge. Quick responding is an indication that the retrieved information is readily accessible because it is being maintained in a pool of recently activated information from LTM. The advantage of a social studies passage is that it will have numerous new facts that will require retrieval and then repeated access to related prior knowledge items.

Another informal appraisal can be garnered from comparing performance on WM tasks that vary in the degree to which LTM can support them. This can be accomplished by comparing performance on WM tasks that have known or nameable content versus unknown or abstract content. For example, memory for words and memory for pseudowords can be compared. When LTM is supporting WM, the span for known words should be longer than for nonwords. Thus, when the score on memory for words is higher, normal support from LTM is indicated.

CAUTION

The number of recently activated long-term memory representations that can be easily and quickly accessed during working memory processing affects the capacity and functioning of working memory. However, there are no standardized procedures for assessing this aspect of working memory.

The Influence of Working Memory on Long-Term Memory

To assess the influence of WM on LTM, different types of retrieval fluency tests can be administered. Performance on tests of rapid automatic naming (RAN), where the retrieval is direct and automatic, can be contrasted with a more semantic type of retrieval, such as a task where the examinee is directed to quickly retrieve items from a particular class of items. The latter task will require a directed search supported by WM processes. When this is noticeably weaker than the RAN task, poor support from WM is indicated.

WORKING MEMORY TESTING

Because of the complexity of cognitive processing, and WM in particular, determination of WM functioning levels should never be based on informal assessment data alone. Not only is standardized testing essential, but also each of the five WM components in the integrated model of working memory should be tested as specifically as possible, regardless of the age of the examinee, the examinee's history, or the referral concerns related to WM.

There are some challenges involved in testing WM in a comprehensive fashion. Some of these challenges, such as the misuse of classic WM tests to assess other abilities, were addressed in the first section of this chapter. One of the main challenges is that there is currently no published WM "battery" available that has up-to-date U.S. norms. This reality will require examiners to draw from more than one battery in a selective-testing fashion. After multibattery testing is completed, the remaining challenge will be to analyze the scores. The second major issue is that even scales that claim to measure WM do not measure all five WM components or do not measure them in a distinct manner. For example, the subtest names in some memory batteries are misleading, such as when a classic measure of phonological STM is labeled as an "attention" subtest. Thus, examiners will need guidance on how to determine the primary ability or specific WM component that a subtest is tapping. (Some of this guidance was presented earlier in this chapter.) The final issue is that the available subtest options for some of the WM components are very limited. Recommendations for addressing all of these challenges and issues are included in this chapter and Chapters 6 and 9.

Criteria for Composite and Subtest Inclusion

Not every published standardized scale that claims to measure some aspect of WM is included in this chapter and in Chapter 6. Even when a scale or battery is acknowledged, not every subtest claimed to measure WM is recommended. On the other hand, some subtests officially classified as measuring something other than WM may be included. The criteria for inclusion are:

- The scale must have been published since January 1, 1998.
- The scale must be recognized as having met the basic standards for the development of psychological tests.

- The scoring system needs to be norm-referenced.
- Internal consistency reliability coefficients must be reported for the WM subtests and composites.
- There is evidence of validity.
- The subtest task must appear to be measuring a single primary ability, not multiple abilities that cannot be prioritized.
- When a subtest is not officially categorized as a measure of WM, task analysis indicates that some aspect of WM is the primary ability required by the task.

Selecting Composites and Subtests for Testing

Whenever feasible, each of the five WM components in the integrated model should be tested with a minimum of two subtests. In the analytical procedure described later in this chapter, the two subtest scores (if they do produce a formal composite score) will be averaged to produce a "clinical" composite that will be used to represent the level of functioning for that specific component. Whenever they are available, the use of official WM composite scores taken directly from a standardized scale is preferable to clinical composites or individual subtest scores. The main reason composites are preferred is that they are more reliable. Unfortunately, not many standardized WM composites can be recommended because many scales mix specific WM components, such as including both verbal and visual-spatial subtests in the same composite. On occasion, one subtest score for a specific WM component will suffice, especially if there is no reason to suspect a weakness in that component. Also, in some instances it may not be possible to test every WM component, especially visual-spatial WM, for which few specific measures exist.

In a multibattery assessment, the examiner should begin by noting which WM components are covered by the primary battery. If a complete cognitive scale, such as the WISC-V, is always administered, then only those WM components not assessed by the WISC-V need to be tested with other batteries. Supplemental batteries should be administered in a selective-testing manner, whereby only the desired subtests are administered and WM subtests that duplicate what has already been adequately tested are omitted. A combination of cognitive, memory, and rating scales may be used. To accomplish such multibattery testing efficiently, it is best to plan in advance, selecting scales and subtests before actual testing begins. The tables in Rapid References 5.12 and 5.13 are designed to facilitate this process.

≡ Rapid Reference 5.12

Working Memory Composites* and Subtests in Cognitive and Achievement Scales***

Working Memory Component	CAS II**	DAS-II	KABC-II	WAIS-IV	WISC-IV Integrated	WISC-V	WJ-IV COG	WJ-IV ACH and Oral	WPPSI-IV
Phonological STM	Word Series	Recall of Digits Forward	Number Recall	Digit Span Forward	Letter Span Rhyming; Letter Span Nonrhyming	Digit Span Forward	Memory for Words		
Visual-spatial STM	Figure Memory; Visual Digit Span	Recall of Designs; Recall of Objects-Immediate; Recall of Pictures	Face Recognition; Hand Movements		Spatial Span Forward; Visual Digit Span	Picture Span	Picture Recognition		WORKING MEMORY; Picture Memory; Zoo Locations
Verbal WM	Sentence Repetition; Sentence Questions						Story Recall	Reading Recall; Sentence Repetition	
Visual-spatial WM					Spatial Span Backward				
Executive WM	WORKING MEMORY; Recall of Digits Backward; Recall of Sequential Order	Word Order		Arithmetic; Digit Span Backward; Digit Span Sequencing; Letter-Number Sequencing	Letter Number Sequencing; Spatial Span Backward	Digit Span Backward; Digit Span Sequencing; Letter-Number Sequencing	SHORT-TERM WM; Numbers Reversed; Object-Number Sequencing; Verbal Attention	Understanding Directions	

*Items in upper case are the names of composites.

**CAS II = Cognitive Assessment System–Second Edition; DAS-II = Differential Ability Scales–Second Edition; KABC-II = Kaufman Assessment Battery for Children–Second Edition; WAIS-IV = Wechsler Adult Intelligence Scale–Fourth Edition; WISC-IV = Wechsler Intelligence Scale for Children–Fourth Edition; WISC-V = Wechsler Intelligence Scale for Children–Fifth Edition; WJ IV COG = Woodcock-Johnson IV Tests of Cognitive Abilities; WJ IV ACH & Oral = Woodcock-Johnson IV Tests of Achievement and Woodcock-Johnson IV Tests of Oral Language; WPPSI-IV = Wechsler Preschool and Primary Scale of Intelligence–Fourth Edition

***This table is also in the online resources.

⚟ Rapid Reference 5.13

Working Memory Composites* and Subtests in Memory, Neuropsychological, and Other Scales***

Working Memory Component	CTOPP 2**	NEPSY-II	TAPS-3	TOMAL-2	WMS-IV	WRAML2
Phonological STM	PHONOLOGICAL MEMORY; Memory for Digits; Nonword Repetition	Repetition of Nonsense Words Total Score	Number Memory Forward; Word Memory	Digits Forward; Letters Forward		Number/Letter
Visual-spatial STM		Memory for Faces Total Score		Abstract Visual Memory; Facial Memory; Manual Imitation; Memory for Location; Visual-Sequential Memory	Designs I; Visual Reproduction I	Design Memory; Finger Windows
Verbal WM		Narrative Memory Free Recall Total Score; Sentence Repetition Total Score; Word List Interference Total Score; Memory for Designs Total Score		Memory for Stories	Logical Memory I	Sentence Memory; Story Memory
Visual-spatial WM					VISUAL WM; Spatial Addition; Symbol Span	Picture Memory
Executive WM				Digits Backward; Letters Backward		Symbolic WM; Verbal WM

*Items in upper case are the names of composites.

**CTOPP-2 = Comprehensive Test of Phonological Processing, Second Edition; TAPS-3 = Test of Auditory Processing Skills, Third Edition; TOMAL-2 = Test of Memory and Learning, Second Edition; WMS-IV = Wechsler Memory Scale–Fourth Edition; WRAML2 = Wide Range Assessment of Memory and Learning, Second Edition

***This table is also in the online resources.

Cognitive Scales. For WM testing, the use of cognitive scales has some advantages over memory batteries. First, using cognitive scales can reduce costs and total testing time when the cognitive scale is already going to be administered. Second, there are fewer confounds with other memory processes. For example, some memory batteries count immediate recall during multiple-trial "learning" tests as short-term memory when the primary process is really LTM encoding. WM measures found in prominent contemporary scales are in Rapid Reference 5.12. Additional cognitive scales are listed in the online resources.

Memory, Neuropsychological, and Other Scales. The main advantage of using a general memory battery, such as the Wide Range Assessment of Memory and Learning, Second Edition (WRAML2; Adams & Sheslow, 2003), is that the examiner can more easily determine how WM performance compares with LTM. All of the general memory scales tap at least four of the five working memory components, but this is not always evident when one examines the structure of the scale and the names of the subtests. Accordingly, the classifications in Rapid Reference 5.13 should be followed.

Using Rating Scales

Another form of standardized testing applicable to WM testing is the use of rating scales. The main drawback to such scales is that they assess WM only globally. That is, none of them have any scores corresponding to the five specific WM components. Nonetheless, they can be used as screeners and for corroborating evidence regarding overall WM functioning.

It should not be assumed that direct testing of WM is more reliable and valid than scores from rating scales. In fact, it has frequently been argued and supported with evidence that ratings of executive functions, such as WM, often have more ecological validity than scores from direct testing (Gioia, Isquith, Guy, & Kenworthy, 2000). The analytical procedures and software discussed later in this chapter allow the inclusion of scores from rating scales. However, very few are suggested because they lack WM component specificity.

A brief WM teacher rating scale intended for screening purposes is the *Working Memory Rating Scale* (WMRS; Alloway, Gathercole, & Kirkwood, 2008). The WMRS was developed on the basis of interviews with teachers and consists of 22 items. Because it was normed in the United Kingdom, its scores should be interpreted with caution in the United States. However, the individual items may be used to guide interviews with teachers and might be considered during classroom observations. A study that analyzed the WMRS items has reported five key items (behaviors) that form a factor that represents the scale well (Normand & Tannock, 2014). These key behaviors are quite observable. They are:

- Abandons activities before completion.
- Benefits from continued teacher support during lengthy activities.
- Does not follow classroom instructions accurately—for example, carries out some but not all steps in an instruction.
- Is making poor progress in literacy and math.
- Depends on a peer to remind him of the current task.

A comprehensive teacher rating scale that includes a working memory subscale is the Internet-based Children's Psychological Processes Scale (CPPS; Dehn, 2012). The 15-item subscale addresses all five WM components. Rapid Reference 5.14 displays the items in developmental sequence. An advantage to the U.S. normed CPPS is that it includes 10 other cognitive processes that are closely related with WM, including LTM.

≡ *Rapid Reference 5.14*

CPPS Working Memory Items Arranged in Developmental Sequence

- Loses place when counting
- Has difficulty remembering what he just saw
- Has trouble remembering information for just a few seconds
- In the middle of an activity, forgets how to continue or finish it
- Has difficulty repeating what was just said to him
- Forgets what he/she was doing
- Forgets the necessary information before completing a mental task
- Has difficulty thinking and retaining information at the same time
- Forgets what he/she was going to say when called on in class
- Has difficulty multitasking without forgetting information
- Requires frequent repetition and reminders
- Has difficulty with mental arithmetic
- Has difficulty listening and taking notes at the same time
- Forgets some of the steps when given multistep directions
- Has difficulty organizing information when writing

General executive functions rating scales can also be used to screen WM and corroborate scores from direct testing. Examples of such scales include the *Behavior Rating Inventory of Executive Functions* (BRIEF; Gioia et al., 2000), the *Comprehensive Executive Function Inventory* (CEFI; Naglieri & Goldstein, 2013), and the *McCloskey Executive Functions Scale* (MEFS; McCloskey, 2015). They have the advantage of sampling various executive functions, thereby allowing a direct comparison of WM with other executive functions. However, these scales should be used cautiously because of the limited number of items that make up their WM subscales and because some of the WM subscales contain both WM and attention items.

TESTING RELATED COGNITIVE PROCESSES

Multibattery, selective testing for WM problems should also include assessment of related cognitive processes. Closely related cognitive processes include attention, phonological processing, processing speed, long-term retrieval, executive functions, fluid reasoning, visual-spatial processing, and auditory processing (see Chapter 2 for details). Some examinees who appear to be struggling because of WM deficiencies may actually have impairments in related processes, rather than in WM. Similarly, poorly functioning related processes may lower performance on WM, especially when a significant amount of processing is required. Conversely, poor WM ability will impact the functioning of related cognitive processes. When both WM and a closely related cognitive process are weak, the individual will face even more cognitive and learning challenges.

Not all related cognitive processes need to be assessed or considered. It depends on the specific WM deficiencies identified during the WM part of the assessment. Also, only those cognitive processes highly related with specific WM components need be tested. See Rapid Reference 5.15 for guidance. Additional information on the assessment of cognitive processes is provided in Dehn (2014b), and details on LTM assessment can be found in Dehn (2010).

ANALYZING TEST RESULTS

For most comprehensive assessments of WM, examiners will use two or more scales in a multibattery, selective testing fashion. When an entire scale, such as the WISC-V, has been administered, the results for that scale should first be analyzed separately. Although an analysis of the primary scale results may provide information on the examinee's cognitive abilities measured by the primary scale, it will not provide much information about the examinee's specific WM strengths

≡ Rapid Reference 5.15

Cognitive Processes Closely Associated With Working Memory Components

WM Component	Cognitive Processes
Phonological STM	Auditory processing; oral language; phonological processing; processing speed; sequential processing
Visual-spatial STM	Visual-spatial processing
Verbal WM	Long-term memory; oral language
Visual-spatial WM	Attention; visual-spatial processing
Executive WM	Attention; executive functions; fluid reasoning long-term memory; processing speed

and weaknesses. Consequently, practitioners should select the WM and related scores from the primary scale and combine them with the WM and LTM scores obtained from other scales. First, tables in Rapid References 5.12 and 5.13 and the complete list in the online resources should be used to identify which WM component is being measured by the completed subtests and composites. Then, the scores from various scales can be analyzed together, following the procedures suggested in this section.

The purpose of including all of the relevant scores in one analysis is to identify the examinee's strengths and weaknesses among the WM components, as well as strengths and weaknesses among related cognitive and LTM processes. A structure for conducting this analysis is the *Working Memory Analysis Worksheet*. A completed example is provided in Rapid Reference 5.16, and a blank template for the reader's use is in the online resources. Commercially available software called the *Memory Processes Analyzer* (Dehn, 2014d) can also be used to conduct this type of analysis. More information on this program is available at the end of this chapter.

The rules for using the *Working Memory Analysis Worksheet* to conduct the analysis by hand are described in this section. Examples of each step are provided in the completed worksheet

DON'T FORGET

The analysis of WM scores may be conducted as part of an overall analysis of cognitive processing strengths and weaknesses, or the analysis may be limited to memory components and processes only.

Rapid Reference 5.16 Working Memory Analysis Worksheet: Completed Example

Student's Name: _____ Date of Birth: _____

Gender: Male   Age: 8   Grade: 3   Date of Testing: _____

Memory Component or Process	Name of Scale	Names of Composites and Subtests	Obtained Standard Scores	Process or Component Score	95% Confidence Interval	IQ or Mean	Discrepancy	Normative S or W	Intra-Individual S or W	Deficit or Asset
Phonological STM	WISC-V / WJ-IV Cog	Digits Forward / Memory for Words	(7) 85 / 82	84	74–94	98	–14	W	W	D
Visual-spatial STM	WRAML2	Design Memory / Finger Windows	(10) 100 / (12) 110	105	95–115	98	+7	—	—	—
Verbal WM	WRAML2	Sentence Mem. / Story Memory	(9) 95 / (11) 105	100	90–110	98	+2	—	—	—
Visual-spatial WM	WRAML2	Picture Memory	(9) 95	95	85–105	98	–3	W	W	D
Executive WM	WJ IV	SHORT-TERM WORKING MEM.	81	81	71–91	98	–17	W	W	D
LTM encoding	WRAML2	Verbal Learning	(7) 85	85	75–95	98	–13	W	W	D
LTM retrieval fluency	WJ IV ORAL	SPEED OF LEXICAL ACCESS	96	96	86–106	98	–2	—	—	—
Processing speed	WISC-V	PROCESSING SPEED	111	111	101–119	98	+13	S	S	A
Phonological processing	WJ IV ORAL	PHONETIC CODING	89	89	79–99	98	–11	W	—	—

Pairs

Component or Process	Confidence Interval	Component or Process	Confidence Interval	Significantly Different	Relationship
Processing speed	101–119	Phonological STM	74–94	Yes	Proc. speed > phonological STM
Phonological STM	74–94	Phonological proc.	79–99	No	

in Rapid Reference 5.16. A summary of the steps is in Rapid Reference 5.18 and in the online resources. Interpretation of the WM testing results is discussed later in this chapter and in Chapter 9.

Step 1. Decide on the Components and Processes That Will Be Included

If scores for one or more WM components have not been obtained, it is still acceptable to proceed with the analysis. There are three types of analyses that might be completed. For any given case, one, two, or all three types may be conducted. The first is a within WM analysis, using only scores representing working memory components. The second type is a within memory analysis that includes LTM processes along with WM components. The third type is to include WM components, LTM processes, and related cognitive processes all in one cognitive processing analysis. The third option is the most efficient and provides the most comprehensive information.

If the mean of scores included in the analysis is being used as the predictor, then it is best to avoid the first option. For example, if all of the WM components tested have low scores, using the mean of these components is unlikely to reveal any relative strengths and weakness. However, a pattern of strengths and weaknesses may emerge when a broader range of cognitive scores are used to compute the mean, such as the third option. Another option is use an IQ score or cognitive composite in lieu of a multibattery mean to determine WM strengths and weaknesses.

The worksheet template comes with the five WM components, two suggested LTM processes, and two rows for related cognitive processes filled in. The LTM processes may be ignored and altered, and rows for more cognitive processes can be added if desired. The scores from academic achievement testing should not be included in this analysis.

Step 2. Enter the Names of the Scales, Composites, and Subtests Administered

More than one scale may be used to measure each memory component or process. In the completed example (Rapid Reference 5.16), subtests from both the WISC-V and the WJ IV were used to measure phonological STM. So, both of the battery names are entered in the Name of Scale column for phonological STM. Next, the names of the composites and subtests are entered in the third column. When composite scores are used, the name of the composite should be listed in uppercase font, such as the WJ IV's SHORT-TERM WORKING MEMORY, in the Executive WM row. If a composite score is used, the names of the individual subtests making up that composite need not be entered separately. It is best *not* to combine composite and subtest scores in the same cell or derive an average from them. Composite scores are preferred whenever possible, as they are more reliable than subtest scores. To verify that appropriate composites and subtests are being used to represent specific memory components and processes, use Rapid References 5.12 and 5.13 or the more comprehensive list in the online resources.

Step 3. Calculate and Enter Obtained Standard Scores

Using each scale's manual or scoring software, determine the norms-based, derived scores and enter them in the Obtained Standard Scores column. Any derived score that is not a standard score with a mean of 100 and standard deviation of 15 will need to be transformed. For example, scaled scores and *T*-scores require this transformation. The scores from which the standard scores are derived are displayed within parentheses. In the first row of the completed example, *Digits Forward* has a scaled score of 7, which was transformed into a standard score of 85. Memory for Words comes as a standard score of 82; so, no change is necessary. Appendix A has a table for changing scaled scores into standard scores, and Appendix B has a table for *t*-score to standard score conversion. Both appendixes are also in the online resources.

Step 4. Calculate and Enter the Component or Process Scores

The score entered as the *Component or Process Score* represents the functioning or ability level of that specific process or component. When only one obtained composite or subtest score is available, that score can be used directly. In the completed example, the only obtained score for visual-spatial WM is a standard score of 95. Thus, 95 becomes the score representing this component. When there are two or more scores available, the mean of the scores should be used as the component or process score. For phonological STM in the completed example, the scores of 85 and 82 average out to 83.5 and are rounded to 84. An averaged score from two subtests that are not officially part of any composite is considered a "clinical composite." This averaged score is then used as the best estimate of a memory component or process. When rounding averages to whole numbers, the nearest even number should be selected. For instance, 85.5 is rounded to 86, but 86.5 is also rounded to 86.

Step 5. Enter 95% Confidence Intervals

A confidence interval is a range or "band" of scores within which there is certain probability that the individual's "true score" is likely to fall. Alternatively, when the individual is retested there is a certain probability that his obtained score will fall within the confidence interval. Except for clinical composites, the confidence intervals should be taken from the scale's technical manual or scoring software. In the completed example, the WISC-V Processing Speed confidence interval of 101 to 119 is taken from the WISC-V manual. For clinical composites, a range of minus to plus 10 points should be used as the best estimate of what the 95% confidence interval might be. In the completed example, the estimated 95% confidence interval for the phonological STM component score of 84 is 74 to 94. The confidence intervals are used to evaluate pairs for significant differences (see the lower part of the completed worksheet). When used for significance testing such as this, 95% confidence intervals are better than 90% or 68% confidence intervals.

Step 6. Enter the IQ or Mean as the Predicted Score

The number entered into this column will be used as the predictor of the obtained scores. This score should represent overall cognitive ability, overall processing ability, overall memory ability, or overall WM ability (see Step 1 for more explanation). In most cases, it is best to use an IQ or similar cognitive composite if one is available. IQ and cognitive composites are appropriate predictors of WM, LTM, and individual cognitive processing scores because of the high correlations IQ has with these abilities. Not using an IQ may result in fewer weaknesses and strengths being identified. However, at times, more of a "within memory" analysis is desired, in which case the mean of the scores involved can be used as the predictor. In such cases, the mean is determined by summing all of the scores in the Process or Component Score column, dividing by the number of components and processes tested, and rounding to the nearest even number. In the completed example, an IQ score of 98 is being used.

Step 7. Compute and Enter the Discrepancy Values

The *discrepancy* is computed by subtracting the predicted score (IQ or Mean) from the *process or component score*. The value is then entered in the eighth column along with a plus or minus symbol in front of it. In the completed example, the phonological STM score of 84 is 14 points lower than the predicted score of 98, resulting in an entry of −14.

Step 8. Determine Normative Strengths and Weaknesses

In the Normative S (Strength) or W (Weakness) column, an "S" is entered when *Process or Component Score* entries are above average, a "W" is entered for below average scores, and a dash (–) or "Average" is entered for scores within the average range. For the purposes of this analysis, the average range includes any score from 90 to 109, while 89 and lower is considered below average, and 110 and higher is considered above average. For the sake of consistency and usefulness of this approach, all scores entered into the analysis should follow these guidelines, even scores from tests that officially label scores from 85 to 114 as average. The worksheet scores used to make this determination are the scores in the Process or Component Score column. In the completed example, a "W" is entered for the phonological processing score of 89 and an "S" is entered for the processing speed score of 110.

Step 9. Determine Intra-Individual Strengths and Weaknesses

From a pattern of strengths and weaknesses (PSW; Dehn, 2014b) perspective, identification of intra-individual strengths and weaknesses is the primary benefit of using this analysis worksheet. In the Intra-Individual S (Strength) or W (Weakness) column, an "S" is entered for intra-individual strengths, a "W" for intra-individual weaknesses, and a dash (—) when there is neither. Given scores that have respectable reliability coefficients (.80 or higher), a critical value of 15 is very likely to be a significant difference at approximately the .05 probability level. However, a general critical value of 12 points is recommended because requiring a 15-point discrepancy is more likely to miss genuine within-person weaknesses that are impacting functioning. The value in the Discrepancy column is used to make this determination. If the discrepancy is –12 or more points, then the process should be identified as a weakness. If the discrepancy is greater than +12 points, then it should be labeled a strength. In the completed example, the subject has three intra-individual weaknesses and one strength. When a 12-point discrepancy is used to identify intra-individual strengths and weaknesses, there should be corroborating evidence from other assessment data. For practitioners concerned about applying the same critical value to all discrepancies, the *Memory Processes Analyzer* (Dehn, 2014d) software uses equations based on reliability coefficients to statistically determine a unique critical value for each discrepancy.

Step 10. Determine Deficits and Assets

There are two different types of weaknesses: normative weaknesses and intra-individual weaknesses. When an individual has both types of weaknesses, it is considered a "deficit." A deficit is rare statistically and is a more serious problem than either a normative or intra-individual weakness alone. Also, a deficit is more likely to impair learning and memory than is either type of weakness alone. Finally, a deficit, according to this definition, is a strong indication that there is an underlying neuropsychological dysfunction (Naglieri, 1999). In contrast, an "asset" occurs when there is both a normative and intra-individual strength. In the completed example, the subject has three deficits and one asset. The phonological processing score of 89 is labeled a normative weakness but does not qualify as a deficit.

Step 11. Examine Pairs for Significance

In addition to identifying intra-individual strengths and weaknesses relative to overall cognitive and memory abilities, a pairwise analysis can be conducted (see the separate table at the bottom of the worksheet in Rapid Reference 5.16). This kind of analysis facilitates more in-depth interpretation, and the results can be used in planning interventions. First, only related pairs, not every possible combination, should be compared. "Related" pairs are those that are usually considered opposites and those that are known to be highly correlated. Rapid Reference 5.17 lists the most meaningfully related pairs among WM components, LTM processes, and cognitive processes. Second, not every listed pair needs to be entered and checked. When a cursory examination reveals that certain pairings cannot possibly be significantly different, there is no need to enter them.

The statistical procedure of comparing confidence intervals is used to determine if one of the pair is significantly different from the other. When the two confidence intervals "overlap" there is no significant difference, but there is a significant difference when they do not overlap. In the completed example, the confidence band of 101 to 119 for processing speed does not overlap with the confidence band of 74 to 94 for phonological STM. Thus, processing speed is significantly stronger than phonological STM, as is indicted in the Relationship column. In contrast, the bands for phonological STM and phonological processing do overlap, indicating no significant difference.

≡ Rapid Reference 5.17 Recommended Pairwise Comparisons

Phonological STM vs. Phonological Processing
Phonological STM vs. Visual-Spatial STM
Phonological STM vs. Verbal WM
Phonological STM vs. Executive WM
Phonological STM vs. LTM Encoding
Phonological STM vs. Processing Speed
Visual-Spatial STM vs. Visual-Spatial WM
Visual-Spatial STM vs. Executive WM
Verbal WM vs. Visual-Spatial WM
Verbal WM vs. Executive WM
Verbal WM vs. LTM Encoding
Verbal WM vs. LTM Retrieval Fluency
Verbal WM vs. Oral Language
Visual-Spatial WM vs. Executive WM
Executive WM vs. Attention
Executive WM vs. Executive Functions
Executive WM vs. LTM Encoding
Executive WM vs. LTM Retrieval Fluency

Step 12. Determine Whether Each Composite Is Unitary

After the worksheet has been completed, the subtest scores that contribute to each official and clinical composite should be examined for consistency. When the difference between the lowest and highest subtest scores used to calculate a composite or *process or component score* is greater than 22 standard score points (1.5 standard deviations), the scores lack consistency. In such instances, the composite or *process or component score* is considered "nonunitary." Scores that are nonunitary can be used in the analysis, but should be interpreted cautiously and should not be used in the pairs comparisons. There are no nonunitary examples in Rapid Reference 5.16, but if *Digits Forward* had been an 80 and *Memory for Words* a 103, then the average of these two would be considered nonunitary. Ideally, examiners should be able to explain why the two scores involved are inconsistent. If not, further testing of the component or process involved is recommended.

≡ Rapid Reference 5.18 Working Memory Analysis Worksheet Directions

1. Decide on the components and processes that will be included. The analysis can be limited to WM components only, consist of WM components and LTM processes, or include related cognitive processes in addition to the WM components and LTM processes.

2. Enter the names of the scales, composites, and subtests administered in the second and third columns. Verify the classification of composites and subtests by using the list in the online resources.

3. Calculate and enter obtained standard scores in the fourth column. As needed, transform scores into standard scores, using Appendixes A and B.

4. Calculate and enter the component or process scores in the fifth column. Use official composite scores directly or calculate clinical composites by computing the mean of the obtained scores and rounding to the nearest even number.

5. Enter 95% confidence intervals in the sixth column. Except for clinical composites, use the scale's provided confidence intervals. For clinical composites, a range of minus to plus 10 points should be used around the score in the fifth column.

6. Enter the IQ or Mean as the predicted score in the seventh column. In most cases, it is best to use an IQ or similar cognitive composite. A mean is determined by summing all of the scores in the Process or Component Score column, dividing by the number of processes tested, and rounding to the nearest even number.

7. Compute and enter the discrepancy values in the next column. The discrepancy is computed by subtracting the predicted score (IQ or mean) from the process or component score.

8. Determine normative strengths and weaknesses and enter an S, W, or dash in the next column. The average range includes any process or component score from 90 to 109, while 89 and lower is below average, and 110 and higher is above average.

9. Determine intra-individual strengths and weaknesses and enter an S, W, or dash in the next column. If the discrepancy is −12 or more points, then the process should be identified as a weakness. If the discrepancy is greater than +12 points, then it should be labeled a strength.

10. Determine deficits and assets and enter a D, A, or dash in the last column. Enter a D when both types of weaknesses are present and an A when both types of strengths are present.

11. Examine pairs for significance, using confidence intervals. The scores in a pair are significantly different when the confidence bands do not overlap.
12. Determine whether each composite is unitary by comparing each composite's subtest scores. Composites should be considered nonunitary when the subtest scores differ by 22 or more standard score points.

INTERPRETATION OF WORKING MEMORY ASSESSMENT DATA

Interpretation should be more than a discussion of WM standard scores. Data from observations, interviews, history, and other cognitive testing need to be considered and integrated with WM test results (see Chapter 9). Identification of potential WM deficits should be corroborated by other sources of data. Also, the test results should be viewed in relation to academic achievement and potential learning disabilities. This part should include explanations as to how and why WM weaknesses and deficits impair learning and performance (see Chapter 4). Finally, interpretation of assessment information should lead to recommendations for intervention. Chapter 9 illustrates how to integrate multiple sources of data and connect the data with achievement and interventions.

In addition to the analytical procedures detailed in the previous section, general interpretation steps are discussed here, followed by discussions of specific WM weaknesses and deficits.

1. If IQ or a cognitive composite was not used during the analysis procedures discussed in the previous section, it should now be considered. The examiner should informally compare this global cognitive score with the individual WM components. A difference of 12 to 15 or more standard score points should be considered significant. In cases where the examinee has a relatively high IQ, intra-individual weaknesses may not be identified as deficits because the WM scores are within the average range. In such cases, the extent of underachievement and frustration with learning should be taken into account because such individuals may certainly benefit from appropriate interventions. When no cognitive composite or IQ is available, overall ability should be estimated from available information.
2. A "clinical" WM composite should be computed and interpreted. If a within-WM-only analysis was conducted, the mean used in the analysis can be used. Otherwise, the WM component scores from the analysis worksheet should be averaged and used as an estimate of overall WM ability. When referring to this clinical composite, it should be stated that it

includes both visual-spatial and verbal WM functioning, as well as the STM aspect of WM. The purpose is to estimate the level of overall WM functioning. However, when there are significant differences among WM components, this estimate has less value. In such instances, it might be best to use the executive WM score as the best estimate of overall WM functioning.

3. Deficits and assets, as defined in the analysis procedures, should be emphasized more than weaknesses, and intra-individual weaknesses should be emphasized more than normative weaknesses.

4. If related cognitive processes (see Chapter 2) were not included in the analysis, they should now be considered, at least informally if scores are not available. These cognitive scores should be compared with overall cognitive ability, using an IQ or a cognitive composite if available. If none is available, the mean of the cognitive scores can be used (see Dehn, 2014b). A difference of 12 to 15 or more standard score points should be considered noteworthy. Second, related pairs of WM components and cognitive processes should be evaluated (see Rapid Reference 5.15 for suggested pairs), and the implications should be discussed (see Chapter 9 for some examples of this). For example, phonological STM and phonological processing should be compared. Although consistency is expected and partially corroborates related WM scores, divergent abilities are fairly common. When both a cognitive process and its related WM component are weak, the individual will encounter more cognitive and learning challenges.

5. When WM weaknesses or deficits have been identified, working memory's impact on LTM functioning needs further consideration if it has not already been assessed. At the very least, an informal investigation of the individual's LTM processes should be conducted. When testing, the emphasis should be on encoding (learning), retrieval fluency, and recognition subtests. Knowing the relative strength of LTM compared with WM has important implications for interventions, as an average or stronger LTM can be used to support WM.

6. Finally, the impact of WM weaknesses and deficits on learning and daily functioning needs to be considered and discussed.

Phonological Short-Term Memory

A weakness or deficit in phonological STM means that the examinee has difficulty with the brief retention of words and other speech-based and phonological information. Limited short-term storage capacity is probably the main cause of poor performance, but it may also be due to a lack of subvocal, automated rehearsal. To investigate this latter hypothesis, the examiner might ask the examinee to repeat a series of words several times in a row. Examinees who are unable to maintain the sequence during these repetitions may have poorly developed subvocal rehearsal. A slow speech rate may also decrease phonological STM span. When this WM component is weak, phonological processing should also be assessed and compared.

Deficiencies in phonological STM may have a detrimental impact on basic reading skills, math calculation skills, rote learning, spelling, vocabulary development, and language development. Children with this particular type of WM weakness may find the learning of a second language difficult. Fast processing speed, good executive skills, and a strong LTM may compensate somewhat for a weak phonological STM.

Caution is urged when interpreting results from a purported phonological STM task that introduces a distractor or interference. In experimental laboratory research, this type of activity is intended to prevent rehearsal and thereby obtain a "pure" measure of storage capacity. However, such approaches lack ecological validity because subvocal rehearsal is generally considered to be part of phonological STM. The result of interference will be a shorter span, giving a misleading impression as to the true storage capacity of the individual's STM. Moreover, introducing irrelevant interference will bring executive WM into play, making the task more of an executive WM measure than a phonological STM measure. When executive WM is poor, performance on the supposed phonological STM task will suffer even more.

Visual-Spatial Short-Term Memory

Individuals with a weakness in this WM component have difficulty with the brief storage of visual-spatial information, such as the identity of objects and their location. Whenever there are low scores for this component, the examiner should informally try to identify whether the weakness is primarily visual, primarily spatial, or both. Visual information is static, such as shape, color, and size. Spatial STM tracks and briefly retains location, motion, and direction. The spatial dimension seems to have more influence on learning and daily functioning. It is uncommon for visual-spatial STM performance to exceed visual-spatial processing ability. When visual-spatial processing without any memory demands is stronger than visual-spatial STM, then the STM storage aspect is the problem. In academics, this WM component has its most influence on the development of mathematics skills. Otherwise, the deficiency is most likely to be manifested in daily life, such as frequently forgetting where an object has just been placed. The best way to compensate for this particular weakness is to verbally recode both visual and spatial information, such as naming an object or stating where it is located.

Verbal Working Memory

A weakness or deficit in this WM component means that the examinee has difficulty holding and processing verbal information at the same time. Weaknesses in phonological STM, executive WM, verbal LTM, and LTM retrieval may contribute to a deficiency in this WM component. Poor verbal WM can have a detrimental impact on most aspects of language and literacy, including listening comprehension, oral expression, reading comprehension, and written expression. It may also lower the amount of new learning that is encoded and associated with related prior knowledge. In the cognitive domain, it has a close relationship with verbal fluid reasoning. Learning and memory strategies may support a deficiency in this WM component. Language development activities should also be included in the intervention.

Verbal WM performance should be compared with phonological STM. When phonological STM is lower, it is probably because of delayed phonological processing or poor speech fluency. Such individuals may do well with applied verbal skills, such as listening comprehension, but struggle with reading decoding. Conversely, when phonological STM is higher than verbal WM, it indicates shortcomings in the higher-level processes associated with verbal WM, while the storage and rehearsal functions of STM are intact. Such individuals may perform well at simple activities, such as spelling, but struggle with complex tasks, like written expression.

Visual-Spatial Working Memory

The interpretation, considerations, and implications of a deficiency in this WM component are the same as for visual-spatial STM, except mental imagery and movement, such as rotation, now come into play. Executive WM and visual-spatial LTM processes have strong influences on this visual-spatial WM. One implication for interventions is that visual mnemonics may not be beneficial when there is a weakness in visual-spatial WM.

Executive Working Memory

Poor performance on executive WM tasks means that the examinee has difficulty coordinating complex cognitive processing while simultaneously retaining and utilizing STM items and recently retrieved LTM information. There can be several underlying causes. The first is poor development of general executive functioning. The second is difficulty focusing, sustaining, and dividing attention, such as is observed in individuals with ADHD. The third cause may be difficulties with switching, inhibiting, or updating. Finally, poor development or limited use of strategies can influence executive WM performance. In general, any combination of these variables adds up to a poor ability to cope with high cognitive load. When executive WM is deficient, each of these potential causes should be pursued through appropriate forms of assessment.

A deficit in executive WM can have wide-ranging and serious impacts on many aspects of cognitive functioning, learning, LTM, and performance. Tasks that require integration of verbal and visual-spatial information will be especially challenging. With executive WM deficits, problems in related functions and skills will be more serious than when the WM deficits lie in nonexecutive components. For instance, individuals with SLD are most likely to have a deficit in executive WM rather than in any of the other WM components.

The domain-specific verbal and visual-spatial WM components will often be at a level of functioning similar to that of executive WM, unless the examinee has a relative strength in verbal or visual-spatial processing. A strength in verbal WM relative to executive WM indicates well-developed verbal abilities with a high capacity for storing and encoding verbal information. This outcome may also be due to strong support from activated LTM items. More fundamentally, it may mean that the individual does well at storing and processing verbal information, unless distractions and interference must be dealt with. When executive WM is better than verbal WM, it means that the individual has a stronger ability to inhibit irrelevant information in contrast with weak verbal abilities. Differences between executive WM and visual-spatial WM can be explained in a similar fashion. However, executive WM and visual-spatial WM are more likely to be similar because they are more closely related.

Automated STM functioning is somewhat immune from executive WM deficiencies. STM functioning can be normal while executive WM is below average. When this is the case, it means WM, in general, has more of a processing problem than a storage problem. When executive WM must support short-term storage by allowing time for rehearsal, STM retention tends to suffer.

Short-Term Memory Versus Working Memory Components

When STM components are higher than WM components, the examinee tends to do well with simple, rote tasks but struggles with more complex cognitive and learning activities. STM can function adequately without normal WM, but the converse is less likely because impairments in STM place more demands on WM as it tries to compensate for impaired short-term functions. As the load on WM increases, short-term spans tend to decline. When individuals do perform significantly better on more complex WM tasks than they do on simple-span tasks, it may be that they implement effective strategies when the task demands become more challenging. It may also be that the increased challenge motivates them to focus attention better.

SPECIFIC LEARNING DISABILITY DETERMINATION

The range and severity of specific WM deficits are related to the range and severity of specific learning disabilities. As documented by research (Swanson, Cochran, & Ewers, 1990), the more WM components that are below average and intra-individual weaknesses, the greater the likelihood of comorbid learning disabilities and the more severe the disabilities are likely to be. The probability of a specific learning disability (SLD) is also high when executive WM is deficient.

One contemporary approach to the identification of specific learning disabilities is the application of the processing pattern of strengths and weaknesses (PSW) model. Essentially, the model requires documentation of a PSW among cognitive processes that are highly related with academic learning (Dehn, 2014b). There are two ways of using WM assessment results in a PSW model. First, a WM "clinical" composite can be used to represent overall WM functioning. This composite is arrived at by averaging the WM components' scores. It can then be compared with an IQ or the mean of other cognitive processes to evaluate whether it is a weakness. The alternative is to use a significant intra-individual weakness or deficit from any one of the five specific WM components. However, this weakness or deficit should not only occur within WM but also emerge when the specific WM component is compared with other cognitive processes. That is, an intra-individual weakness in verbal WM that occurs only when it is compared with the mean of the WM components may be insufficient evidence in the PSW approach. It is stronger evidence when verbal WM is an intra-individual weakness relative to IQ or the mean of the cognitive processes and the memory components that have been tested. Furthermore, the specific WM weakness or deficit should be consistent with research-identified relations with specific academic skills. For instance, a phonological STM deficit is consistent with a basic reading skills deficiency but not with a mathematics problem-solving deficiency (see Rapid Reference 4.3).

MEMORY PROCESSES ANALYZER

The Memory Processes Analyzer (MPA; Dehn, 2014d) is a commercially available computer software program that conducts a statistical analysis of memory component and process scores. The primary purpose of the MPA is to identify statistically significant memory strengths and weaknesses within the individual. The analysis conducted by the MPA is very similar to that of the *Working Memory Analysis Worksheet*, discussed earlier in this chapter. The main difference between the two formats is that the MPA is automated and conducts statistical significance testing. Consequently, the results of the MPA are more acceptable than those of the worksheet.

The MPA examines up to 11 memory components and processes. Five of them are WM components and six are LTM processes (see Rapid Reference 5.19). The categorization of composites and subtests allowed in the MPA is consistent with the integrated model of working memory proposed in this book. Composites and subtests are drawn from 30 different scales (see the list in the online resources). The composites and subtests are classified by the primary memory process required to complete the subtest task, not necessarily according to the subtest name or the structure of the scale. The MPA can be used to conduct an analysis of WM components without any LTM entries being required. The predicted score

---

≡ *Rapid Reference 5.19*

Memory Processes Included in the MPA

- Phonological Short-Term Memory
- Visual-Spatial Short-Term Memory
- Verbal Working Memory
- Visual-Spatial Working Memory
- Executive Working Memory
- Long-Term Memory Verbal Recall
- Long-Term Memory Visual-Spatial Recall
- Long-Term Memory Encoding/Learning
- Long-Term Memory Consolidation
- Long-Term Memory Storage/Recognition
- Long-Term Memory Retrieval Fluency

can be a cognitive composite or the mean of the memory components. More details on the MPA can be found in the online resources.

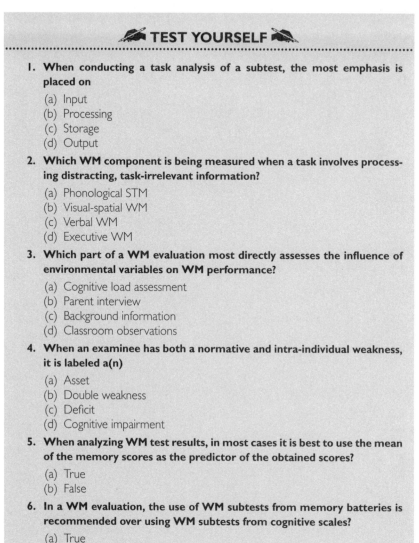

TEST YOURSELF

1. When conducting a task analysis of a subtest, the most emphasis is placed on
   (a) Input
   (b) Processing
   (c) Storage
   (d) Output

2. Which WM component is being measured when a task involves processing distracting, task-irrelevant information?
   (a) Phonological STM
   (b) Visual-spatial WM
   (c) Verbal WM
   (d) Executive WM

3. Which part of a WM evaluation most directly assesses the influence of environmental variables on WM performance?
   (a) Cognitive load assessment
   (b) Parent interview
   (c) Background information
   (d) Classroom observations

4. When an examinee has both a normative and intra-individual weakness, it is labeled a(n)
   (a) Asset
   (b) Double weakness
   (c) Deficit
   (d) Cognitive impairment

5. When analyzing WM test results, in most cases it is best to use the mean of the memory scores as the predictor of the obtained scores?
   (a) True
   (b) False

6. In a WM evaluation, the use of WM subtests from memory batteries is recommended over using WM subtests from cognitive scales?
   (a) True
   (b) False

7. Which relationship indicates that WM processing is the weakness and not storage?

(a) Executive WM > verbal WM
(b) Verbal WM < phonological STM
(c) Executive WM < phonological STM
(d) Processing speed < executive WM

Answers: 1. b; 2. d; 3. a; 4. c; 5. False; 6. False; 7. c

Six

PSYCHOLOGICAL SCALES THAT MEASURE WORKING MEMORY

The table in Appendix C classifies composites and subtests from 30 different psychological scales or batteries. The table specifies the WM component that is measured by each composite and subtest. Chapter 5 explained the guidelines and procedures used to determine these classifications. This chapter provides details on subtests and composites from 18 of the scales (see Rapid Reference 6.1) in Appendix C. The online resources include the same table as that found in Appendix C. The online version will be periodically updated as new psychological scales are released.

The subtest information in this chapter includes brief descriptions of the task, unique characteristics, cautions regarding usage, the rationale for classification, and some interpretative advice. Such information will help examiners select appropriate measures, understand their use, and facilitate interpretation of scores. For example, the details provided will help practitioners understand why the examinee's performance may vary across subtests that measure the same WM component.

Many of the scales reviewed contain some kind of "working memory" composite. Some of these composites are not named "working memory," even though all the subtests involved primarily measure one or more WM components. Each of these is different in its composition. One may be made up of a phonological STM subtest and a verbal WM subtest; another might consist only of executive WM tasks; and so on. None of these composites adequately sample all five aspects of WM as defined in the integrated model. Consequently, none of them should be used to represent overall WM functioning. Interpretation of these composites should specifically identify what is measured by the composite; for instance, the examiner might state, "This working memory composite measures verbal and executive working memory, but does not directly measure the short-term storage or visual-spatial aspects of working memory."

CAUTION

....

Working memory composites that measure multiple WM components should be avoided when analyzing test scores to determine WM strengths and weaknesses. Such composites also should not be used to represent overall WM functioning.

Furthermore, composites that include measures of more than one WM component should not be used when determining the examinee's specific WM strengths and weaknesses. That is, such composites should be avoided when using the *Working Memory Analysis Worksheet* or the *Memory Processes Analyzer*. This is why these "mixed" composites are not listed in Appendix C or included in the tables provided in Chapter 5. The composites that are classified and recommended are only those that are classified as measuring just one specific WM component.

≡ Rapid Reference 6.1 Psychological Scales Reviewed in This Chapter

....

Child and Adolescent Memory Profile (CHAMP)

Cognitive Assessment System, Second Edition (CAS-II)

Comprehensive Test of Phonological Processing, Second Edition (CTOPP-2)

Differential Ability Scales, Second Edition (DAS-II)

Kaufman Assessment Battery for Children, Second Edition (KABC-II)

NEPSY, Second Edition (NEPSY-II)

Stanford-Binet Intelligence Scales–Fifth Edition (SB5)

Test of Auditory Processing Skills, Third Edition (TAPS-3)

Test of Memory and Learning, Second Edition (TOMAL2)

Wechsler Adult Intelligence Scale-Fourth Edition (WAIS-IV)

Wechsler Intelligence Scale for Children-Fifth Edition (WISC-V)

Wechsler Intelligence Scale for Children Fourth Edition Integrated (WISC-IV Integrated)

Wechsler Memory Scale, Fourth Edition (WMS-IV)

Wechsler Preschool and Primary Scales of Intelligence, Fourth Edition (WPPSI-IV)

Wide Range Assessment of Memory and Learning, Second Edition (WRAML2)

Woodcock-Johnson IV Tests of Achievement (WJ IV ACH)

Woodcock-Johnson IV Tests of Cognitive Ability (WJ IV COG)

Woodcock-Johnson IV Tests of Oral Language (WJ IV ORAL)

CHILD AND ADOLESCENT MEMORY PROFILE (CHAMP)

The Child and Adolescent Memory Profile (CHAMP; Sherman & Brooks, 2015) is a recently developed, four-subtest scale that assesses both WM and LTM. With delayed recall and recognition versions of the four subtests, six different memory indexes can be derived. None of the CHAMP indexes are suitable composite scores for WM assessment. Specifically, the *Immediate Memory Index* should not be used to represent broad STM or WM because it includes a list learning subtest with repeated trials. Also, none of the CHAMP subtests tap executive WM (as defined in the integrated model in this text) in a challenging manner. Nonetheless, it has three subtests that measure specific WM components.

Visual-Spatial STM: Objects

The *Objects* subtest has stimuli that vary in shape, texture, detail, and three-dimensional characteristics. This subtest uses abstract stimuli designed to reduce naming. However, it is unique in that the abstract stimuli are colorful, realistic, contemporary, and visually interesting. After viewing a page of the same class of stimuli, the examinee selects from options on a response page.

Verbal WM: Instructions

The immediate recall version of the *Instructions* subtest has good ecological validity in regards to the ability to briefly retain a set of detailed instructions that might be spoken in a home or school environment. After the examiner reads the paragraph, the examinee is directed to recall as much as possible. Points are earned by recalling the concrete nouns embedded in the narrative.

Visual-Spatial WM: Places

The *Places* subtest is more complex and challenging than Objects because the examinee must discriminate between response choices that vary only slightly in spatial configuration and contextual details. The pictures used are of familiar, everyday scenes, such as a living room in a home.

COGNITIVE ASSESSMENT SYSTEM, SECOND EDITION (CAS-II)

The Cognitive Assessment System, Second Edition (CAS-II; Naglieri, Das, & Goldstein, 2014) is a Lurian-based test of cognitive abilities and processing that is highly predictive of academic learning and very useful in identifying psychological processing strengths and weaknesses. The four CAS-II composites (known as PASS) are *Planning*, *Attention*, *Simultaneous Processing*, and *Successive Processing*. The CAS II does not contain any measures of verbal ability, acquired knowledge, or crystallized intelligence.

Composites

Successive processing involves recognizing and maintaining the sequential arrangement of stimuli. At first glance, the CAS-II *Successive Processing* composite seems to represent overall WM ability because all of the subtests that contribute to it are considered WM measures. However, the *Successive Processing* score is not recommended during analysis of specific WM components because it includes both visual-spatial and phonological/verbal subtests. The *Successive Processing* score also should not be used to represent WM because it does not tap visual-spatial or executive WM.

The CAS-II has a supplemental *Working Memory* composite, but its use is not recommended because it includes the *Verbal-Spatial Relations* subtest, which also contributes to the CAS-II's *Simultaneous Processing* composite. *Verbal-Spatial Relations* certainly requires some challenging verbal-spatial processing and reasoning. However, it is not considered an appropriate measure of WM because the examinee is not required to retain any information. The visual stimuli and the printed question remain within the examinee's view until a response is given.

Subtests

Phonological STM: Word Series. Although classified as a measure of Successive Processing on the CAS-II, *Word Series* is a classic phonological STM measurement paradigm. Words are presented at the rate of one per second, and the examinee must repeat them in the same order. Although there is a different sequence and selection each time, the words for each item are selected from the names of nine common objects. At first glance, this appears to make the task easier; however, this is unlikely, as proactive interference probably builds throughout the subtest.

Visual-Spatial STM: Figure Memory. *Figure Memory* is classified as a Simultaneous processing task by the CAS-II authors. *Figure Memory* is herein considered a WM measure because it seems to be measuring visual-spatial STM as much as visual-spatial processing. After a 5-second exposure to a geometric figure, the examinee must draw the same figure within a more complex design. The subtest is unique in that a verbal response to a visual stimulus is not required.

Visual-Spatial STM: Visual Digit Span. A visual analog of the classic digit span forward task, *Visual Digit Span* is part of the CAS-II *Successive Processing* scale. The task requires an examinee to maintain a series of numbers in the same order shown on a stimulus page that is displayed from 1 to 5 seconds. Although an oral response to visual stimuli is required, the task remains primarily a visual-spatial task.

Verbal WM: Sentence Repetition. *Sentence Repetition*, another Successive processing task, is for ages 5 to 7. It consists of nonsensical sentences, with all the nouns, verbs, and modifiers being colors. For example, a sentence might read something like "A blue greened a brown purple." Although the examinee can depend somewhat on knowledge of sentence structure, chunking into phrases and visual imagery will be of little use. Normally, a sentence repetition task would be considered a phonological STM task. However, the novel aspect of this task will induce some processing and elevate the task to verbal WM.

Verbal WM: Sentence Questions. In lieu of the *Sentence Repetition* subtest, examinees 8 years and older complete *Sentence Questions*. This is a challenging verbal WM task because they must answer questions about nonsense sentences, such as "Who greened a brown purple?" With the questions requiring semantic processing, the task is surely tapping verbal WM. Moreover, because the items are nonsense sentences, WM will receive little assistance from LTM.

COMPREHENSIVE TEST OF PHONOLOGICAL PROCESSING, SECOND EDITION (CTOPP2)

The Comprehensive Test of Phonological Processing, Second Edition (CTOPP2; Wagner, Torgesen, Rashotte, & Pearson, 2013), measures the phonological processing abilities related to reading. For ages 4 through 24, it comprises 12 subtests that contribute to several composites, including *Phonological Awareness*, *Phonological Memory*, and *Rapid Symbolic Naming*. One advantage of the CTOPP2 is that performance on the closely related abilities of phonological processing and phonological STM can be directly compared within the same battery.

Phonological Memory Composite

What the CTOPP2 calls the *Phonological Memory* composite is the equivalent of phonological STM. The two subtests that produce this composite are both phonological STM measures. Consequently, the CTOPP2's *Phonological Memory* composite score should be directly used to represent phonological STM capacity, rather than the average of its two subtests.

Subtests

Phonological STM: Memory for Digits. This subtest is the classic phonological STM task of recalling digits without needing to manipulate them. The presentation of the digits (from an audio recording) is unique in that the rate is two digits per second. The intent of presenting the digits twice as fast as the usual rate of one per second is to prevent between-digit rehearsal by the examinee. However, for individuals who don't employ the rehearsal strategy, rapid presentation may be an advantage because it reduces the interval over which the digits need to be retained.

Phonological STM: Nonword Repetition. Nonwords are an ideal phonological STM measure because LTM semantic memory is unable to provide much support. This CTOPP2 subtest has 30 items, some of which are two syllables long. To facilitate standardized administration, the items are presented from an audio recording.

DIFFERENTIAL ABILITY SCALES–SECOND EDITION (DAS-II)

The Differential Ability Scales–Second Edition (DAS-II; C. Elliott, 2006), with norms for ages 2:6 to 18, offers a comprehensive assessment of the cognitive processes that are highly related with learning. The DAS-II is also known for child-friendly tasks and for subtests that have high specificity and reliability. Subtest specificity refers to the degree to which a subtest measures a specific ability or process, as opposed to multiple constructs. With its high subtest specificity, examiners can more confidently interpret subtest profiles of strengths and weaknesses. The DAS-II also minimizes the examinee's frustration and sense of failure by using an item-set approach instead of traditional basals and ceilings.

A validity study reported in the DAS-II technical manual found that students with learning disabilities performed poorly on STM and WM subtests. Subjects with a reading disability performed significantly lower than matched normal children on *Recall of Digits Forward, Rapid Naming, Recall of Sequential Order*, and *Recall of Objects*.

Working Memory Composite

The *Working Memory* composite from the DAS-II can be used to directly represent executive WM. The composite includes the *Recall of Digits Backward* and *Recall of Sequential Order* subtests. The latter task involves a component that places high demands on executive WM. Thus, this DAS-II composite should be used directly to represent executive WM capacity.

Subtests

Phonological STM: Recall of Digits Forward. For this traditional phonological STM measure, the examiner presents the digits at the rate of two per second, a speed twice as fast as most digit span tasks. The quicker delivery of the items is intended to prevent rehearsal; however, it appears that the forward and backward spans obtained on the DAS-II are very similar to those from digit span subtests that present digits at the traditional rate of one per second. Perhaps the shorter retention interval counterbalances the reduced opportunity to rehearse between digits.

Visual-Spatial STM: Recall of Designs. According to the DAS-II factor structure, this subtest is primarily aligned with visual-spatial processing. However, it can appropriately be considered a measure of visual-spatial STM because the task involves the short-term recall of visual and spatial relationships. After viewing an abstract line drawing for five seconds, the examinee is required to reproduce it with pencil and paper. Because of the abstract nature of the stimuli and short exposure time, verbal recoding of the stimuli is unlikely, making it a relatively strong measure of visual-spatial STM.

Visual-Spatial STM: Recognition of Pictures. During this subtest, the examinee is shown a picture of one or more familiar objects for 5 seconds, and then must select the previously viewed object(s) from a response page that includes distracters. Although examinees might subvocally name the objects during this activity, it seems to be primarily measuring visual-spatial STM.

Executive WM: Recall of Digits Backward. Like *Digits Forward*, the *Digits Backward* items are presented at the rate of two digits per second. Historically, digits backward tasks have been considered valid measures of executive WM, because manipulation of the digits is required in order to reverse the sequence. However, digits backward taxes executive WM only in a minimal manner, as no distractors are introduced and there is no multimodel processing. Consequently, under the integrated model of working memory, digits backward might be a better fit for verbal WM. Nonetheless, for the sake of consistency, it is allowed as an executive WM measure in the DAS-II and other scales that include it.

Executive WM: Recall of Sequential Order. In *Recall of Sequential Order*, the child hears a list of body parts and must order them from highest to lowest. For the easiest items, a picture of a child remains exposed as the examinee orders and recalls the body parts. At the next level, the examinee recalls body parts without a picture; and at the highest level, the examinee must sequentially recall body parts when other object names are mixed in with the list. Because this task includes distractors and requires the integration of verbal and visual information, it places high demands on executive WM, especially for older children who progress to the third task within the subtest.

KAUFMAN ASSESSMENT BATTERY FOR CHILDREN–SECOND EDITION (KABC-II)

The Kaufman Assessment Battery for Children–Second Edition (KABC-II; Kaufman & Kaufman, 2004) is a five-factor cognitive assessment instrument. The KABC-II's *Sequential Processing* composite is similar to the *Successive Processing* composite in the CAS-II. The KABC-II authors allow interpretation of the *Sequential Index* as a measure of STM under CHC theory. As defined by the integrated model of working memory, the KABC-II's *Sequential Index* comprises one phonological STM subtest and one executive WM subtest. Consequently, it could be considered a WM composite, but it does not adequately represent overall WM functioning.

Phonological STM: Number Recall

The *Number Recall* subtest, which does not include a digits backward condition, clearly measures phonological STM. Although the digits are presented at the typical rate of one per second, examiners should not drop their voice at the end of sequence, a practice that is typical with other batteries. Consistent with the research on the effect of articulation speed, the number "seven" is omitted from the subtest because it has two syllables.

Visual-Spatial STM: Face Recognition

The KABC-II places the *Face Recognition* subtest under the *Simultaneous Processing Index*, and the author allows alternative interpretation of the index as a measure of visual-spatial processing. Although recalling faces is a unique memory task, it can be classified as a visual-spatial STM measure. The task consists of showing the examinee one or two faces for 5 seconds and then having the examinee pick out the faces from a group of faces on the response page. Interestingly, the stimulus photos are tightly cropped so as to display only the face, whereas most of the body is shown on the response page.

Visual-Spatial STM: Hand Movements

According to the KABC-II manual, this measure of visuospatial STM is administered only when a *Nonverbal Index* is desired. This unique subtest consists of hand movements (there are three positions) presented at the rate of one per second. The examinee must repeat the movements in the correct sequence. Although psychomotor abilities come into play, this subtest primarily measures visuospatial

STM. If fine motor difficulties are suspected, performance on this task should be compared with the KABC-II's other visual-spatial STM subtests.

Executive WM: Word Order

Word Order is classified as an executive WM task because it requires both visual-spatial and verbal processing, and because the higher-level items include interference. For the lower-level items, the examinee is shown a card with five pictures (silhouettes of common objects), the pictures are covered, the examiner says the names of some of the pictures that were displayed, the pictures are uncovered, and then the examinee points to the pictures in the exact sequence. When the higher-level items are reached, the number of pictures is increased to seven and interference is introduced. The interference, which makes rehearsal difficult, consists of naming the colors of two rows of colored squares before pointing to the correct pictures.

THE NEPSY II

The NEPSY II (Korkman, Kirk, & Kemp, 2007) is a neuropsychological battery designed specifically for children ages 3 to 16:11. It consists of 34 subtests that are used to assess six domains: attention and executive functioning, language, sensorimotor functioning, visuospatial processing, social perception, and memory and learning. LTM encoding and delayed recall complement the WM subtests discussed ahead. The NEPSY-II offers a unique opportunity to conduct within-scale comparisons between WM and LTM, as well as between WM and attention and executive functioning.

Phonological STM: Repetition of Nonsense Words

The NEPSY-II authors have placed this measure of phonological STM under the language domain, but it is clearly a memory task because it requires repetition of nonsense words that have been presented aloud. When using the Working Memory Analysis Worksheet or the Memory Processes Analyzer (MPA) to analyze relative performance across WM components, the *Repetition of Nonsense Words Total Score* should be used.

Verbal WM: Narrative Memory

Narrative Memory is a story-retelling task that primarily measures verbal WM performance with some assistance from LTM. There is a twist to this commonly used memory task. After immediately retelling the story (the free recall part), the examinee is asked questions designed to elicit details not included in the immediate free recall. At this stage of the task, activated prior knowledge and information just encoded into LTM will come into play, making this subtest more complex than a typical verbal WM measure. Consequently, when analyzing the examinee's performance, only the *Narrative Memory Free Recall Total Score* should be used.

Verbal WM: Sentence Repetition

The administration of this verbal WM task is limited to children ages 3 to 6. As no interference or secondary processing is introduced, *Sentence Repetition* does not appear to draw on executive WM. The *Sentence Repetition Total Score* should be used when analyzing the scores for strengths and weaknesses.

Verbal WM: Word List Interference

For this task, the examinee is read two lists of words. The examinee must immediately repeat each list after it is read and then recall both lists. Thus, each list creates interference for the other list. The interference is limited to the verbal domain, and it is the type of interference that naturally occurs during verbal presentations. Therefore, the subtest is considered more a verbal WM task than an executive WM task. When analyzing scores, the *Repetition Total Score* is recommended.

Visual-Spatial STM: Memory for Faces

The examinee views a series of faces for 5 seconds each, stating the gender of each face during its exposure. After the faces have been presented, the examinee selects a previously displayed face from an array of three faces. The photos have been cropped to show only the faces. When analyzing scores, the *Memory for Faces Total Score* should be used.

Visual-Spatial STM: Memory for Designs

For this task, the examinee is shown a 4×4 grid with 4 to 10 designs that are difficult to name. After the stimulus page is removed, the examinee must then select the designs from a set of cards and place them in the grid in the same locations previously shown. This particular subtest places more demands on the spatial aspect than most visual-spatial subtests. When analyzing scores, the *Memory for Designs Total Score* should be used.

STANFORD-BINET INTELLIGENCE SCALES–FIFTH EDITION (SB5)

The Stanford-Binet Intelligence Scales, Fifth Edition (SB5; Roid, 2003) has one "verbal" WM subtest and one "nonverbal" WM subtest. Because the tasks change as difficulty level increases, neither of the two subtests can be assigned to a WM component. Accordingly, SB5 subtests are omitted from the classification tables in this text, and the WM subtest scores are not allowed in the MPA. Nonetheless, the tasks mixed within the subtests (for which no separate scores can be derived) are appropriate WM activities that are worthy of mention, and performance on them can provide valuable clinical information.

Visual-Spatial STM: Delayed Response

In the SB5 *Nonverbal Working Memory* subtest, young children and those with low cognitive functioning are administered a "testlet" (part of a subtest) referred to as *Delayed Response*. In this variation of the classic "shell game," a small toy is hidden under a plastic cup that either remains in position, is switched with another cup, or is hidden behind a screen. After a brief delay, the child must identify the cup that is covering the toy. Because it uses and manipulates actual objects, the task has validity in regards to everyday visual-spatial STM functioning. Delayed Response also provides an opportunity to informally assess the visual-spatial STM functioning of very young or delayed children who cannot yet manage images well.

Verbal WM: Memory for Sentences

This activity requires examinees to repeat brief phrases or sentences. At the lower level, there are brief phrases; at the higher level, the stimuli are complete sentences. Credit is given for less than perfect recall. Two points are awarded for perfect recall, and 1 point is awarded if the examinee makes a single mistake. As there is no transformation of the information or any secondary processing task, this activity seems to be a fairly pure measure of verbal WM.

Visual-Spatial STM and WM: Block Span

Block Span is the second WM testlet in the SB5 *Nonverbal Working Memory*. In this variation of the Corsi block span task, eight blocks are placed on a card that has two rows, one yellow and the other red. Using another block, the examiner taps a sequence of blocks at the rate of one per second. This part of the task measures visual-spatial STM. As the items progress, the task becomes more challenging as the examinee must sort the taps occurring on the blocks placed on the yellow strip from those placed on the red strip and then tap the yellow series before the red. With the addition of this processing requirement, the activity evolves into a visual-spatial WM task.

Executive WM: Last Word

Last Word is the final activity in the SB5 *Verbal Working Memory* subtest. The Last Word task is the classic listening span activity in which the examinee must retain the last word in a series of sentences while dealing with interference. The interference is introduced by requiring the examinee to answer two unrelated questions after each sentence is read aloud. With the interference, this task is considered a measure of executive WM, rather than verbal WM. This particular type of span has been found to have a very strong correlation with reading comprehension (Daneman & Carpenter, 1980).

TEST OF AUDITORY PROCESSING SKILLS, THIRD EDITION (TAPS-3)

The Test of Auditory Processing Skills, Third Edition (TAPS-3; Martin & Brownell, 2005), assesses the auditory, phonological, and memory skills necessary for the development, understanding, and production of language. The four subtests described ahead produce a Memory Index score. However, this index should not be used to represent overall WM functioning because it does not include any visual-spatial subtests.

Phonological STM: Number Memory Forward

The administration details for *Number Memory Forward* do not specify the rate at which the digits should be spoken. This subtest also has an unusual scoring procedure. Two points are awarded for no errors. One point is awarded when the response includes all of the correct digits but they are out of sequence. Allowing credit for out-of-sequence responses may produce scores that are inconsistent with most other phonological STM measures. Given that maintaining a sequence is considered an essential aspect of phonological STM, the number of 1-point responses on this subtest needs to be considered when the subtest score is reported. When the majority of responses are 1-point responses the resulting score may be an overestimate of the examinee's phonological STM capacity.

Phonological STM: Word Memory

Similar to Number Memory Forward, examinees can earn partial credit (1 point instead of 2) when the words are out of sequence. Thus, the use and interpretation of this subtest come with the same concerns as those expressed earlier.

Verbal WM: Sentence Memory

This subtest also has 1- and 2-point scoring, with 1 point being awarded when all the words are present but out of sequence. Sentence memory tasks in other scales usually do give 2 points for a perfect response and 1 point when there is only one error. However the TAPS-3 *Sentence Memory* gives no credit when a word is omitted, substituted, or inserted.

Executive WM: Number Memory Reversed

Number Memory Reversed also awards the examinee 1 point when the reversed sequence is not correct but all of the numbers are included. Given that random responses can earn partial credit and boost the overall subtest score, performance on this subtest may not represent executive WM functioning very well. The number of 1-point responses will need to be considered before the subtest score is interpreted.

TEST OF MEMORY AND LEARNING–SECOND EDITION (TOMAL-2)

The Test of Memory and Learning, Second Edition (TOMAL-2; Reynolds & Voress, 2007), provides in-depth sampling of WM, especially visual-spatial STM, with several subtests that are traditional WM measurement paradigms. Nonetheless, the TOMAL-2 does not offer a composite that represents overall WM functioning. Also, the TOMAL-2 does not provide any composites that differentiate between immediate and long-term memory. Rather, all of the immediate and delayed recall subtests are classified as "Verbal" or "Nonverbal" memory.

Phonological STM: Digits Forward and Letters Forward

In addition to the traditional *Digits Forward* task, the TOMAL-2's *Letters Forward* subtest provides an opportunity to measure phonological STM without digits. This option is useful when the examinee has significant delays in numeracy and arithmetic skills. Under the TOMAL-2 structure, these two subtests and similar subtests are placed under the Attention/Concentration Composite and/or the Sequential Recall Composite.

Visual-Spatial STM: Abstract Visual Memory

Abstract Visual Memory is considered a visual-spatial STM task because there is no interference and no manipulation of the stimuli is required. The stimuli are abstract figures whose recall is unlikely to be affected by verbal recoding or LTM.

Visual-Spatial STM: Facial Memory

Because memory for faces is a specific type of memory, performance on *Facial Memory* may be quite different than recalling inanimate objects and abstract stimuli. Nonetheless, memory for faces is considered a type of visual-spatial STM. No verbal response is required on this task.

Visual-Spatial STM: Manual Imitation

Manual Imitation uses four different hand movements to present a sequence of gestures that the examinee must repeat. Although psychomotor abilities come into play, this subtest primarily measures visual-spatial STM. If fine motor difficulties are suspected, performance on this task should be compared with the TOMAL-2's other visual-spatial STM subtests.

Visual-Spatial STM: Memory for Location

Memory for Location is a visuospatial STM task with an emphasis on the spatial dimension. After viewing dots on a grid, examinees recall the locations by placing chips on a blank grid. Performance on this task might be compared with scores on TOMAL-2 subtests that do not include a spatial aspect, such as *Abstract Visual Memory.*

Visual-Spatial STM: Visual Sequential Memory

Visual Sequential Memory requires the examinee to retain the sequence of geometric designs. Performance on this subtest might be contrasted with the TOMAL-2's other visual-spatial STM measures that do not require maintaining the sequence of the stimuli.

Verbal WM: Memory for Stories

One *Memory for Stories* credit is given for each element (words or phrases) of the story recalled correctly. Elements need not be verbatim or in order. Although associations with long-term semantic memory may cue recall, the immediate recall version primarily taps verbal WM. After 30 minutes has elapsed, there is the option of assessing delayed recall of the stories.

Executive WM: Digits Backward and Letters Backward

Digits Backward and *Letters Backward* are administered and scored in the same fashion. Some examinees may obtain a longer Digits Backward span because they can more easily chunk digits than letters. Although the TOMAL-2 places these subtests under its Attention/Concentration composite, from a WM perspective they both tap executive WM.

THE WECHSLER INTELLIGENCE SCALES

There are three Wechsler intelligence scales: the Wechsler Adult Intelligence Scale, Fourth Edition (WAIS-IV; Wechsler, 2008), the Wechsler Intelligence Scale for Children, Fifth Edition (WISC-V; Wechsler, 2014), and the Wechsler Preschool and Primary Scales of Intelligence, Fourth Edition (WPPSI-IV; Wechsler, 2012). The adult and children's versions share many of the same subtests and composites (see Rapid Reference 6.2), whereas the preschool version has two different, age-appropriate subtests. Of course, the adult and children's subtests differ in terms of difficulty levels.

Composites

The Wechsler *Working Memory* indexes do not represent overall WM well because none of them adequately sample all five WM components. However, the WPPSI-IV *Working Memory Index* can be used as a visual-spatial STM composite. The other working memory indexes differ in their composition. The WAIS-IV is made up of *Digit Span* and *Arithmetic*, with the supplemental *Letter-Number Sequencing* allowed as a substitution. The WISC-V *Working Memory Index* consists of *Digit Span* and *Picture Span*, with no substitutions allowed. The WISC-V also has an ancillary *Auditory Working Memory Index*, comprising *Digit Span* and *Letter-Number Sequencing*.

≣ Rapid Reference 6.2 Wechsler Measures of Working Memory

Wechsler Scale	WM Component	Composite or Subtest
WAIS-IV	Phonological STM	Digits Forward
	Executive WM	Arithmetic
		Digit Span Backward
		Digit Span Sequencing
		Letter-Number Sequencing
WISC-V	Phonological STM	Digits Forward
	Visual-spatial STM	Picture Span
	Executive WM	Digit Span Backward
		Digit Span Sequencing
		Letter-Number Sequencing
WPPSI-IV ·	Visual-Spatial STM	WORKING MEMORY
		Picture Memory
		Zoo Locations

Subtests

Phonological STM: Digit Span Forward. This classic forward digit span task is part of the *Digit Span* subtest. The Wechslers include all three digit span tasks in the *Digit Span* subtest score, but also offer separate scaled scores for each of the three digit span tasks. These separate scaled scores are the ones that should be used during an analysis of WM strengths and weaknesses.

Visual-Spatial STM: Picture Memory. For the WPPSI-IV *Picture Memory*, the child views pictures of one or more common objects on a stimulus page, and then must select the correct options from items on the response page. Children under age 7 are usually not verbally recoding the objects that they see. Thus, the subtest is a relatively specific measure of visual-spatial STM.

Visual-Spatial STM: Picture Span. *Picture Span* is the newest Wechsler WM measure. Its inclusion in the WISC-V *Working Memory Index* broadens what the Index represents. Picture Span requires examinees to recall pictures of objects in the sequence they were displayed. Because the stimuli are nameable, examinees with strong verbal recoding skills may score higher on this task than on subtests that utilize abstract stimuli.

Visual-Spatial STM: Zoo Locations. This is an age-appropriate, engaging WM task for children as young as 2.5 years of age. For the *Zoo Locations* subtest, the child views pictures of animals placed on a zoo layout for 3 to 5 seconds and then must place the proper animal in the correct location. This task includes a visual as well as a spatial dimension.

Executive WM: Arithmetic. For the *Arithmetic* subtest, the examinee listens to detailed arithmetic story problems and must solve them without pencil or paper within a specified time. Although mental arithmetic certainly involves WM, it may not be the primary process being assessed. Moreover, the Wechsler Arithmetic subtest is not based on any established WM measurement paradigm. Not surprisingly, Keith et al. (2006) concluded that the WISC-IV Arithmetic subtest was primarily measuring fluid reasoning. The WAIS-IV continued to include Arithmetic under its Working Memory Index, but the recently released WISC-V no longer places Arithmetic under its Working Memory Index. Despite the controversy and inconsistencies between the scales, the Arithmetic subtest can be considered a measure of executive WM, with significant influences from fluid reasoning and quantitative reasoning.

Executive WM: Digit Span Backward and Digit Span Sequencing. *Digit Span Sequencing* is the latest addition to the digit span activity. After hearing a series of random numbers that may include duplicates, the examinee must put them in numerical sequence. This reordering seems to be as challenging as arranging digits backward; thus, the sequencing task should also be considered a measure of executive WM. The special scaled process scores for the backward and sequencing tasks should be used when analyzing scores, rather than the *Digit Span* subtest score.

Executive WM: Letter-Number Sequencing. After listening to a randomly ordered series of letters and numbers spoken by the examiner, the examinee must first repeat the numbers in ascending order, then the letters in alphabetical order. Credit is also given when the examinee says the letters before the numbers, as long as both groups are arranged correctly. The rationale for allowing this exception is that the load on WM arises from arranging each series, not from remembering which group goes first. Because of the need to separate and reorder the two codes, the subtest is a challenging executive WM activity, despite its verbal content.

DON'T FORGET

The Wechsler *Digit Span* score should not be used when analyzing WM strengths and weaknesses. Rather, the scaled scores for *Digits Forward*, *Digits Backward*, and *Digits Sequencing* should be used.

WISC-IV INTEGRATED

Although not designed solely for WM assessment, the Wechsler Intelligence Scale for Children–Fourth Edition, Integrated (WISC-IV Integrated; Wechsler et al., 2004), offers an in-depth and efficient assessment of WM components. The WISC-IV Integrated is the combination of the standard WISC-IV battery (Wechsler, 2003) and 16 supplemental process subtests. The process subtests can be administered in a selective fashion without prior administration of the WISC-IV standard battery. Many of the process subtests are derivations of the standard WISC-IV subtests; only the scoring procedures or the presentation formats have changed. The WM process subtests consist of some derived and some new subtests. Because of its comprehensive WM sampling, the WISC-IV Integrated offers a unique opportunity for within-battery comparisons of specific WM components.

Phonological STM: Letter Span Rhyming and Nonrhyming

The *Letter Span* subtest consists of two item types, each with its own scaled score: *Letter Span Rhyming* and *Letter Span Nonrhyming*. The rhyming and nonrhyming items are interspersed, not divided into separate lists. Each item consists of four trials, two with nonrhyming letters and two with rhyming letters. The examinee is not informed that some of the trials consist entirely of rhyming letters. Consistent with research, most children obtain shorter Letter Span Rhyming than Letter Span Nonrhyming spans because rhyming letters interfere with each other more than nonrhyming letters.

Visual-Spatial STM: Spatial Span Forward

Spatial Span is a block-tapping activity that includes a forward and a backward condition, each with its own scaled score. This task is a visual-spatial analog to digits forward and backward. The examinee must tap a sequence of blocks in the same order they were touched by the examiner. In contrast to *Visual Digit Span*, *Spatial Span* depends more on spatial memory as opposed to visual memory. Also, performance may be mediated by motor planning and execution.

Visual-Spatial STM: Visual Digit Span

In Visual Digit Span, the examinee must repeat a sequence of digits that are visually presented for 1 to 5 seconds. Unlike the standard aural digit span, the entire string of digits is presented simultaneously, and there is no backward condition. Although Visual Digit Span is classified primarily as visual-spatial STM, many examinees will verbally recode or rehearse the digits, making this less a visual-spatial measure than subtests that utilize pictures of objects. Chunking is another strategy that could be employed during this subtest.

Visual-Spatial WM: Spatial Span Backward

Reversing the sequence elevates the block-tapping activity to the WM level. Because there is no interference and little opportunity to verbally encode the tapping sequence, this task is considered more visual-spatial WM than executive WM.

Executive WM: Letter-Number Sequencing Process Approach

The process version of this subtest is the same as the standard WISC-IV *Letter-Number Sequencing*, except that two of three trials in each item have letters that spell a word, and only the trials with embedded words are scored. The embedded word may function as a retrieval cue. Curiously, the examinee is never informed of the possibility of embedded words. Consequently, the examinee should be queried when the subtest is complete to determine whether he was aware of the cues and attempted to utilize them. Examinees who were aware of the embedded words are likely to retain longer sequences. The scaled score on this process subtest should be compared with the standard version of the subtest to assess whether cuing and strategy use improved performance for the individual.

> **DON'T FORGET**
>
> Select subtests from the processing part of the WISC-IV Integrated may be administered without administering any of the standard WISC-IV subtests.

WECHSLER MEMORY SCALE, FOURTH EDITION (WMS-IV)

The Wechsler Memory Scale, Fourth Edition (WMS-IV; Wechsler, 2009), is an adult memory battery for individuals ages 16 to 90, with a shorter form for older adults ages 65 to 90. Four core subtests are used to assess immediate and delayed recall, and two additional subtests are designed for visual WM testing. The *Auditory Memory* and *Visual Memory* indexes include both immediate and delayed recall subtests. Similarly, the *Immediate Memory* and *Delayed Memory* indexes combine both verbal and visual-spatial memory scores.

Composite

The *Visual Working Memory* index includes the *Spatial Addition* and *Symbol Span* subtests. For WM assessment purposes, this index can be used to represent visual-spatial WM. Even though Symbol Span is not complex enough to require more than visual-spatial STM, Spatial Addition is an exceptionally challenging visual-spatial WM task. Thus, the index is weighted toward the WM level and can be used appropriately to represent visual-spatial WM. This composite is not available in the Older Adult version of the battery. The WMS-IV Immediate Memory index is a mixed composite that includes performance on a multiple-trial learning task. Therefore, it should not be used to represent overall WM.

Subtests

Visual-Spatial STM: Designs I. The official structure of the WMS-IV does not consider *Designs I* to be a WM measure, but does include it under its Immediate Memory index. The task involves recalling the grid location of four to eight designs. Designs I presents a unique opportunity to contrast visual and spatial memory. Responses can be separately scored for visual (design) and spatial (location) accuracy. The two scaled scores can then be statistically compared, using a WMS-IV contrast score.

Visual-Spatial STM: Symbol Span. This task uses abstract stimuli that are difficult to verbally recode. After viewing some symbols on a page, the examinee must select symbols on the response page in the same order they were first presented. Although the WMS-IV labels *Symbol Span* as a visual-spatial WM measure, it is more appropriately classified as visual-spatial STM.

Visual-Spatial STM: Visual-Reproduction I. *Visual-Reproduction I* also contributes to the WMS-IV *Immediate Memory* index but not the *Visual Working Memory* index. After an exposure of 10 seconds each, the examinee is directed to draw five figural designs from memory. Scoring is complex, as up to 13 points can be earned per item. This subtest is a fairly direct measure of visual-spatial STM, but performance may be mediated by fine motor planning and skills.

Verbal WM: Logical Memory I. *Logical Memory I* consists of two short stories that are read aloud (older adults receive only one story). Points are awarded for each element (words or phrases) the examinee recalls. Some elements need to be verbatim and others can be paraphrased. The items need not be recalled in sequence. This task is a measure of verbal WM, as no interference or additional processing is introduced.

Visual-Spatial WM: Spatial Addition. *Spatial Addition* is a unique and challenging visual-spatial WM activity that probably requires some support from executive WM. The examinee is sequentially shown two grids with blue or red circles on them. The red circles are distractors and are to be ignored. The locations of the blue circles need to be retained, and the examinee must discriminate between locations covered by a blue circle on only one grid versus locations covered in both displays. When responding, the examinee must put a blue circle where a blue circle appeared only once and white circle where a blue circle appeared twice.

WIDE RANGE ASSESSMENT OF MEMORY AND LEARNING–SECOND EDITION (WRAML2)

The Wide Range Assessment of Memory and Learning, Second Edition (WRAML2; Adams & Sheslow, 2003), consists of six subtests, two for each of the three main factors: Verbal Memory, Visual Memory, and Attention/ Concentration.

Composites

The *Attention/Concentration* composite should not be used to represent overall WM ability, but it does adequately sample the STM level with both a phonological and visual-spatial task. The WRAML2 does have an official *Working Memory* index comprising two subtests that make significant demands of executive WM. Although it should not be used to represent overall WM, the *Working Memory* composite can be used for executive WM.

Subtests

Phonological STM: Number Letter. This variation of a simple STM span task combines digits and letters. The examinee needs only to repeat the mixed sequence as presented. There is no requirement to sort the numbers and letters. The WRAML2 includes the *Number Letter* subtest under its Attention/ Concentration index, but the more appropriate classification is phonological STM.

Visual-Spatial STM: Design Memory. This procedure consists of exposing geometric designs for 5 seconds and then having the examinee reproduce them from memory. Scoring criteria must be used to award points for separate aspects of the drawings. Up to 12 points can be earned for each of the four drawings. The fairly lenient scoring criteria diminish the influence of fine motor ability, while maintaining the emphasis on short-term visual-spatial recall.

Visual-Spatial STM: Finger Windows. For this subtest, the examiner sequentially touches holes in a card at the rate one per second and the examinee repeats the sequence. The WRAML2 classifies *Finger Windows* as a measure of attention/concentration. However, because the activity is analogous to the Corsi block task, it seems more appropriate to consider it as a measure of visual-spatial STM.

Verbal WM: Sentence Memory. As the name implies, this subtest requires the examinee to repeat sentences dictated by the examiner. Two points are awarded for an entirely correct response and 1 point when one error occurs. As no interference or multiple trials are involved, it seems to be a relatively direct measure of verbal WM.

Verbal WM: Story Memory. This traditional memory measure is classified as a verbal WM subtest, although there is some influence from LTM. Some of the details must be recalled verbatim to earn credit, but others can be paraphrased. The information need not be recalled in sequence. There is an option of contrasting verbatim with gist scaled scores.

Visual-Spatial WM: Picture Memory. For this subtest, the examinee is shown four common but visually complex scenes for 10 seconds, then shown a similar but altered scene, and next asked to identify the elements that have moved, changed, or been added by marking each part of the picture that is different. Because of the transformations and distractors involved, this task is more challenging than a basic visual-spatial activity. Therefore, it is considered a visual-spatial WM measure.

Executive WM: Symbolic Working Memory. Only examinees 9 years of age and older are administered this subtest, which is part of the WRAML2's *Working Memory* index. For Level A of *Symbolic Working Memory,* the examiner first orally presents a series of random numbers, and then shows the examinee a card that has numbers arranged in sequence, such as all the numbers from 1 through 8. The examinee must then point to the numbers that were spoken and select them in correct numerical sequence. At Level B, the examinee hears a list of numbers and letters, followed by the presentation of a card with numbers and letters in order. The examinee must first point to all the stimulus numbers in the correct sequence, followed by pointing to the letters in the correct sequence. This task includes both auditory and visual stimuli, and it requires transformation of information while inhibiting distractors (the extra numbers and letters). Consequently, it is a fairly strong measure of executive WM.

Executive WM: Verbal Working Memory. Only examinees 9 years of age and older are administered this subtest, which is part of the WRAML2's *Working Memory* index. Despite the subtest's name, overall it places high demands on executive WM. Level A, which is primarily a verbal WM task, requires the examinee to separate animal and nonanimal words. Level B requires the examinee to incorporate visual imagery as he must now sequence the animals by size from smallest to largest before saying the nonanimal words. At Level C, the examinee must rearrange both the animals and nonanimals by size. Thus, at levels B and C the examinee is transforming the information in two different ways.

WOODCOCK-JOHNSON IV TESTS OF ACHIEVEMENT (WJ IV ACH)

The Woodcock-Johnson IV Tests of Achievement (WJ IV ACH; Schrank, Mather, & McGrew, 2014a) is not a cognitive or memory battery, but it does have a reading comprehension subtest that is structured and scored in such a way that it can appropriately be used as a verbal WM measure. The subtest is called *Reading Recall* and is officially used to measure reading comprehension. The examinee is directed to silently read a short passage once, the passage is covered, and then the examinee recalls as much information as possible. There are no actual comprehension questions. To earn points, some words or information need to be verbatim and other information can be paraphrased. Essentially, the task is scored in the same fashion as the recall of oral passages in memory scales. For students with adequate reading fluency, *Reading Recall* seems to be a rather direct measure of verbal WM.

WOODCOCK-JOHNSON IV TESTS OF COGNITIVE ABILITIES (WJ IV COG)

The Woodcock-Johnson IV Tests of Cognitive Abilities (WJ IV COG; Schrank, McGrew, & Mather, 2014) is a comprehensive cognitive abilities scale. The main advantage to using the WJ IV COG to assess WM is that its WM scores can be directly compared with scores of related cognitive processes. The "Intra-Cognitive Variations" table from the online WJ IV scoring report may be used to determine how WJ IV working memory test performance compares with the other WJ IV cognitive abilities. The table's "Discrepancy SD" column should be used to determine relative strengths and weaknesses. For example, a discrepancy SD of −1.51

for the *Short-Term Working Memory* cluster indicates that WM is a significant intra-individual weakness relative to the mean of the scores from the other cognitive clusters or subtests. Alternatively, the examiner may enter the WJ IV COG scores into the Working Memory Analysis Worksheet and conduct a specific WM component analysis, with the option of including related cognitive processes.

Composites

The WJ IV COG has an executive WM composite known as the *Short-Term Working Memory* cluster. The standard version of this cluster consists of *Verbal Attention* and *Numbers Reversed*, while the extended cluster includes the additional *Object-Number Sequencing* subtest. Given their composition, both of these clusters seem to be strong measures of executive WM. When used in conjunction with the WJ IV Tests of Oral Language (WJ IV OL; Schrank, Mather, & McGrew, 2014b), the *Sentence Repetition* subtest can be paired with *Memory for Words* to produce what's called the *Auditory Memory Span* cluster. This is a nonexecutive WM composite that is informative but should be interpreted cautiously because it includes both a phonological STM test (Memory for Words) and a verbal WM test (Sentence Repetition).

Subtests

Phonological STM: Memory for Words. *Memory for Words* is a classic test of phonological STM in which the examinee is directed to repeat lists of unrelated words in the correct sequence. The items include both monosyllable and two syllable words. To maintain standardized administration, it is best to play the items from the CD that accompanies the test battery.

Visual-Spatial STM: Picture Recognition. *Picture Recognition* is officially part of the WJ IV's *Visual Processing* cluster. However, the format of the task is identical to common visual-spatial STM activities. One or more pictures of common objects are presented for 5 seconds, and then the examinee selects the previously presented items from a page that includes distracters. Justifiably, *Picture Recognition* can be used as a visual-spatial STM measure. *Picture Recognition* makes verbal recoding of the stimuli difficult, as each item contains varieties of the same category, such as a stimulus page that contains several houses.

Verbal WM: Story Recall. *Story Recall* is a typical immediate memory activity that can be considered a measure of verbal WM, even though LTM becomes involved, especially as the stories become longer than a sentence or two. Legitimately, the WJ IV places this subtest under its *Long-Term Retrieval* cluster, but the task also taps verbal WM in a significant manner. The examinee listens to a sentence or brief story and then retells as much as can be remembered. Points are awarded for elements (single words or phrases) that are recalled; some elements must be stated verbatim, whereas others can be paraphrased.

Executive WM: Numbers Reversed. *Numbers Reversed* is the classic backward digit span paradigm, with the examinee required to repeat a series of numbers in reverse sequential order. The WJ IV COG does not include a forward digit span task.

Executive WM: Object-Number Sequencing. The examiner orally presents a series of intermixed numbers and object words. Then the examinee must first recall the objects and then the numbers in the order they were presented. Both groups of items must be completely correct in order to receive credit for the item. Due to the complexity of the required processing, it is considered more an executive than a verbal WM task.

Executive WM: Verbal Attention. *Verbal Attention* is another WJ IV COG subtest with verbal content only that can be considered more of an executive than verbal WM activity because of the challenges it involves. The orally presented items consist of intermixed numbers and animal names. After the sequence is presented, the examinee is directed to state only specific animals or numbers, such as, "Tell me the second animal and then the first number." The position and types of words requested vary with each item. Thus, the examinee never knows what information is going to be requested and must maintain the sequence until the directive is given. Consequently, this task is extremely demanding of various WM components and executive skills, such as inhibiting the words and numbers that are not requested. Also, the task is unique and very appropriate for executive WM because span is not being measured. Examinees who utilize an appropriate strategy during this task, such as conscious rehearsal, are more likely to succeed.

WOODCOCK-JOHNSON IV TESTS OF ORAL LANGUAGE (WJ IV OL)

The Woodcock-Johnson IV Tests of Oral Language (WJ IV OL; Schrank et al., 2014b) assess oral language development, as well as cognitive processes that contribute to oral language development and production. Among these are long-term retrieval and WM.

Verbal WM: Sentence Repetition

In the WJ IV OL, *Sentence Repetition* is part of the *Oral Expression* cluster. Nonetheless, the format and scoring procedures of the subtest are identical to sentence recall subtests in memory batteries. Consequently, it is herein classified and recommended for use as a measure of verbal WM. No partial credit for one error is given; the response must be perfect in order to award 1 point.

Executive WM: Understanding Directions

Understanding Directions is another WJ IV OL subtest that is recommended as an unofficial measure of WM. The WJ IV OL battery uses this subtest for assessing listening comprehension. Although it certainly requires listening comprehension and probably has high ecological validity in regards to listening comprehension, it also places high demands on executive WM. Without adequate WM functioning, the examinee will not be very successful at this task. After comprehending what is said (which also requires WM), the examinee must maintain the information while pointing to specific stimuli. While viewing a natural scene with many items in it, the examinee must point to select items in a certain sequence after the oral directions are completed. Another reason this task is primarily executive WM is that the examinee must integrate verbal and visual-spatial information. The WJ IV OL also has a Spanish version of this subtest, which provides a unique opportunity to assess executive WM in individuals with Spanish language proficiency.

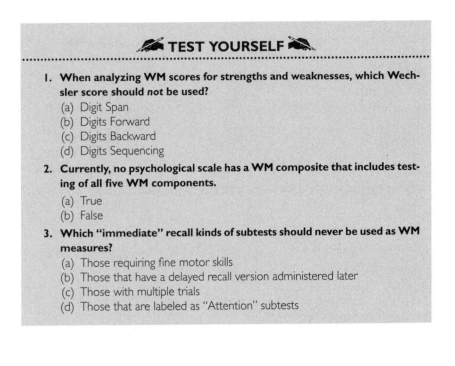

🐟 TEST YOURSELF 🐟

1. **When analyzing WM scores for strengths and weaknesses, which Wechsler score should *not* be used?**
   (a) Digit Span
   (b) Digits Forward
   (c) Digits Backward
   (d) Digits Sequencing

2. **Currently, no psychological scale has a WM composite that includes testing of all five WM components.**
   (a) True
   (b) False

3. **Which "immediate" recall kinds of subtests should never be used as WM measures?**
   (a) Those requiring fine motor skills
   (b) Those that have a delayed recall version administered later
   (c) Those with multiple trials
   (d) Those that are labeled as "Attention" subtests

4. **The theoretical basis and structure of the psychological scale should determine how its WM measures are interpreted.**
   (a) True
   (b) False

5. **WM subtests from memory batteries are preferable and more valid than WM subtests from cognitive scales.**
   (a) True
   (b) False

6. **Some psychological scales use traditional WM measurement tasks to measure other cognitive abilities without altering the format or scoring procedures.**
   (a) True
   (b) False

Answers: 1. a; 2. True; 3. c; 4. False; 5. False; 6. True

Seven

WORKING MEMORY INTERVENTIONS THAT CHANGE THE BRAIN

W M functioning can be improved through evidence-based interventions. Despite some controversy, there is a well-established research base supporting the efficacy of WM training, strategies, and other forms of intervening. Although computer-based training has received the most attention, there are other options when intervening. These include the teaching of strategies, hands-on WM exercises, modifications to instruction and the classroom environment, metamemory training, accommodations, strengthening LTM, reducing cognitive load, and strengthening related cognitive functions. This chapter will focus on brain-based training, hands-on exercises, and strengthening related cognitive functions. Chapter 8 presents information on the remaining approaches. The other difference between this chapter and Chapter 8 is that this chapter is intended primarily for individual and small group interventions, whereas Chapter 8 is intended for classroom-wide and academically related methods. However, the two chapters overlap in that the methods in Chapter 8 can also be applied to individuals.

DON'T FORGET

Individuals with normative WM weaknesses may benefit as much from interventions as learners with intra-individual WM weaknesses.

WM interventions are appropriate for individuals with either normative or intra-individual weaknesses, but essential for those with deficits. For those with a normative weakness but no intra-individual weakness, WM interventions are still appropriate, but low functioning in related cognitive processes may limit improvement. Although the interventions advocated in this and the next chapter would also benefit most adults with WM impairments, these intervention methods are primarily intended for children and adolescents.

TYPES OF WORKING MEMORY INTERVENTIONS

WM and related cognitive processing interventions can be categorized as remedial or compensatory. Remedial interventions have the expressed goal of correcting a brain-based deficit by directly addressing the weakness. From a neurological perspective, the purpose of remedial interventions is to strengthen the affected brain structures. In the past 20 years there has been ample research supporting the belief that WM brain functions can be strengthened. The primary method of remediating or strengthening WM is computer-based training.

Efforts to directly strengthen WM may be necessary because there is no clear evidence that the human brain is able to compensate for WM deficits or dysfunctions. Research on human brain plasticity has demonstrated that the brain is capable of compensating for functional loss by using other brain regions to perform cognitive functions not normally associated with those regions (Berninger & Richards, 2002; Shaywitz, 2003). However, this finding may not apply to WM because there is little or no evidence that other brain structures are able to perform the functions of the prefrontal cortex. Nonetheless, stronger cognitive processes that are highly interrelated with WM may support or help to compensate for a deficient WM. Such processes include fluid reasoning, processing speed, phonological processing, and long-term memory, as well as attentional control and general executive processes. Consequently, compensatory approaches that include attempts to strengthen related cognitive processes should be incorporated into a WM intervention.

A common compensatory intervention for WM impairments is the teaching and application of strategies. The intent of WM strategies is to make the most effective use of existing WM capabilities. They are not designed for the purpose of directly strengthening WM brain functions. However, the observed outcome may be the same as that resulting from WM training. Both methods improve WM performance, such as a longer memory span. Strategy training can be conducted one-on-one, with small groups, or classroom wide. Students with low WM spans typically benefit the most from strategy training, even though they may be slower to learn the strategies than trainees with high WM spans (Turley-Ames & Whitfield, 2003). Details about WM strategies that can be taught are provided in Chapter 8.

SELECTING WORKING MEMORY EXERCISES AND STRATEGIES

Interventions for WM problems should be closely tailored to the cognitive processing and WM profile of the student, thereby increasing the likelihood of positive outcomes. The methods selected should address the specific WM weaknesses. (Rapid Reference 7.1 lists some recommended exercises and strategies by WM component.) For instance, an intervention for a deficit in phonological STM should be somewhat different from an intervention for a deficit in executive WM. Nonetheless, given the interactive nature of WM components and processes, an intervention should never be limited to one specific component. Although there is little or no evidence of general brain plasticity in regards to WM overall, there is evidence of plasticity across WM components. For example, training that primarily contains visual-spatial exercises has been shown to also strengthen verbal WM (Klingberg, 2010). The hierarchical structure of WM also needs to be considered. Executive WM is a higher-level process that "supervises" the STM storage components. Consequently, strengthening executive WM is a "top-down" approach that is likely to also improve the performance of STM components (Dehn, 2014e).

≡ *Rapid Reference 7.1*

Recommended Exercises and Strategies* for Specific Working Memory Deficits**

Phonological STM
- Online exercises that require sequential recall of verbally presented items
- Verbal Span Practice
- Rehearsal
- Chunking

Visual-Spatial STM
- Online exercises that require recall of visual-spatial stimuli
- Visual-Spatial Recall
- Visualization

Verbal WM
- Online exercises that require sequential recall of verbally presented items
- Rehearsal
- Last Word
- Arithmetic Flash Cards

Visual-Spatial WM
- Online exercises that have visual-spatial stimuli that move or rotate
- Visual-Spatial Recall
- Dual Encoding

Executive WM
- Online exercises that require the integration of verbal and visual-spatial information

- N-back
- Counting Span
- Arithmetic Flash Cards
- Following Directions
- Switching and Updating

*See Chapter 8 for details on strategies.
**This list is also in the online resources.

Given the list of exercises and strategies from which to draw, the challenge is to select options that best meet the learner's needs, without overly relying on trial and error. A single exercise or strategy will seldom be sufficient (Dehn, 2014c). For successful WM training, several exercises are recommended, with each of them being practiced for several minutes during each training session. However, it is not necessary to practice or learn every available exercise or strategy. The trainer and trainee should focus on exercises and strategies that seem to be working for the trainee.

In addition to the trainee's WM weaknesses and deficits, other factors should be considered when selecting WM exercises and strategies. These include:

- *The trainee's other needs and impairments.* For example, with a child who has an oral language delay, it may be more appropriate to prioritize language development and include only WM intervention methods that directly support language development, such as strengthening phonological STM.
- *Related cognitive processing weaknesses.* For instance, with a trainee who has slow processing speed, exercises that require quick responding may only add to the trainee's frustration.
- *The number and severity of the WM deficits.* Individuals with broad-ranging WM deficits or those with severe deficits will require a longer intervention. In such cases, the exercises and strategies should change over the course of the intervention. That is, simple exercises and strategies may be practiced and learned first before challenging exercises and complex strategies are introduced. Also, such individuals will require some of the accommodations, such as memory aids, that are recommended in Chapter 8.
- *How well the methods generalize and how long the gains are maintained.* Exercises, training programs, and strategies that have the best documentation of generalization and maintenance should be preferred.
- *The extent of practice required to obtain fluency with the strategy.* Time constraints and the motivation of the learner need to be considered.

- *The learner's age, cognitive ability, and extent of metamemory awareness.* The methods selected need to be appropriate for the trainee's developmental level.

Phonological STM Methods

Individuals with a specific weakness or deficit in phonological STM will benefit from learning effective rehearsal (oral or subvocal repetition; see Chapter 8 for details) methods and from practicing rehearsal as an exercise. Low test scores on measures such as digits forward or memory for words are evidence of a phonological weakness or deficit. However, informal assessment is also necessary. For instance, examinees should be asked about their use of rehearsal and asked to demonstrate how they do it. The children most in need of rehearsal training and practice are those who do not rehearse, those who use rehearsal infrequently, those who rehearse incorrectly, and those who are unable to maintain a verbal sequence during rehearsal.

With school-aged children, it is never too early to start rehearsal strategy training (see Chapter 8). There is empirical evidence that even 5-year-old children can be trained to use verbal rehearsal and that this improves their recall (Henry & Millar, 1993). Chunking is another strategy (see Chapter 8 for details) that has been demonstrated to increase phonological STM span (Parente & Herrmann, 1996).

Repetitive verbal span practice may also improve phonological STM capacity and performance. Currently, this type of exercise is not available with computer-based training because the programs do not use voice recognition programs. Although the computer-based programs may present verbal spans orally, the trainee must respond by clicking on items displayed on a computer screen. An oral response from the trainee is important because it eliminates support from the visual-spatial domain and because oral responding may stimulate verbal rehearsal. Nearly any type of content may be used for verbal span practice: phonemes, letters, digits, words, pseudowords, and sentences.

> **DON'T FORGET**
> ....
> One disadvantage of computer-based WM training programs is that they do not require oral responses.

Verbal Working Memory Methods

Verbal WM practice and strategies are more involved and complex than those utilized for phonological STM training. Even the rehearsal involved is more complex. For example, trainees might be required to group items semantically before rehearsing them (see Chapter 8 for details), or they might be directed to associate the verbal information with related prior knowledge before rehearsing it (Banikowski & Mehring, 1999). Verbal WM exercises also introduce a processing element not contained in phonological STM exercises. For example, trainees may be required to read sentences while remembering the sequence of the last words in each sentence, or they might complete arithmetic calculations while remembering all the answers in sequence.

For individuals with severe limitations in verbal WM, such as those with language and literacy disabilities, training them to compensate by more effectively utilizing their visual-spatial WM memory may prove extremely beneficial (Gathercole & Baddeley, 1993). A basic approach is to visualize verbal information by picturing it in one's mind. Practicing this strategy might involve visualizing words consisting of objects and actions. Such recoding is seldom employed by those with verbal WM deficits until they are explicitly taught to do so. An advanced application of this approach is to encourage individuals to do more consciously directed visualizing as they read.

Visual-Spatial STM Methods

Individuals with a specific weakness or deficit in visual-spatial STM will benefit from repetitive visual-spatial exercises that are the mainstay of most WM online training programs. In addition to low scores on standardized measures of visual-spatial STM and visual-spatial processing, such individuals may also display inattentive behaviors (Bedard, Martinussen, Ickowicz, & Tannock, 2004). Recalling sequences is not as important for visual-spatial STM as it is for phonological STM. Therefore, online or hands-on exercises need not require sequential recall; identification of the stimuli in any order is sufficient. Also, these training exercises should include a spatial component (recalling the location of the stimuli) to ensure that they adequately challenge visual-spatial STM.

In general, visual-spatial STM exercises are quite simple. Typically, stimuli are briefly presented, and then the trainee must click on, identify, or position the stimuli. Ideally, the stimuli should be abstract or within the same class of objects to make it more difficult for the trainee to name them. Naming brings in phonological STM and LTM to support visual-spatial STM. However, in instances of severe deficits in visual-spatial STM, a naming strategy should be taught as a compensatory method. That is, the trainee should name each object as it appears and keep rehearsing the sequence until the response is complete. For example, if pictures of a ball, bat, and glove are presented, the child should say, "Ball, bat, and glove" and keep repeating this until the visual-spatial response is complete.

Visual-Spatial Working Memory Methods

What sets visual-spatial WM training apart from visual-spatial STM training is that the WM component training includes a significant processing requirement. The processing is often verbal, such as counting objects on different cards or completing mathematical calculations. Ideally, the processing aspect should be visual-spatial in nature. Rotation of the background after presentation of the stimuli is the best example of visual-spatial processing. Naming the stimuli and rehearsing the sequence are an effective verbal strategy that can be incorporated into this kind of training. To juggle processing and rehearsal simultaneously, the trainee may need to be taught how to continually switch back and forth between rehearsing and processing.

Executive Working Memory Methods

Any exercise or strategy that requires the integration of verbal and visual-spatial information will involve executive WM. Because of their complexity, such online or hands-on exercises can be very challenging for individuals with executive WM weaknesses or deficits. Consequently, there may be higher levels of frustration and observable progress may be slow. Yet, these kinds of exercises have strong evidence supporting them (e.g., Tageuchi et al., 2010). Executive WM exercises include a significant processing dimension and usually require trainees to constantly update, switch, and inhibit. At the very least, trainees must continually switch between rehearsing and processing. Because of this demand, trainees should be taught the strategy of switching between rehearsing and processing, especially when they reach the point where improvement on the exercise becomes minimal. The best example of a challenging and evidence-based executive WM exercise is n-back. With n-back (see details later in this chapter), trainees must remember items that were exposed a certain number of items before. Numerous variations of n-back are offered on brain training websites, such as Lumosity, but the exercise is easily conducted face-to-face. Executive WM training exercises also improve attentional processes and ADHD symptoms (Klingberg et al., 2005). This is probably because executive WM training exercises require focusing attention while inhibiting irrelevant information.

MEASURING PROGRESS

Before any training begins, pretesting should sample the trainee's span (the number of items the trainee can recall in the correct sequence) in each of the five WM components. It is better not to use a standardized measure for this purpose because most WM training programs will not last long enough to avoid the practice effects that occur when a standardized measure is readministered within a year. Another problem with standardized tests is that there is seldom a significant change in standardized scores even when there has been meaningful improvement. Informally constructed verbal span word lists can be used instead. The items should consist of nonrhyming and monosyllabic words. For visual-spatial assessment, items should be difficult to name or be in the same class of objects. When conducting post-testing, different but equivalent items should be used. It is also important that the tasks used to measure progress from pre- to post-testing are different from the training tasks themselves. (See Chapter 5 for more details on WM assessment.)

> **DON'T FORGET**
> ....
> When assessing the effectiveness of WM training with pre- and post-tests, it is important to use nontrained tasks.

In addition to pre- and post-testing, performance during each training session should be recorded, regardless of whether the practice is with strategies or exercises. The primary variable to measure during each practice round is the length of the trainee's span. With simple exercises, increases in span may occur rapidly, at least during the initial practice sessions. However, with complex exercises such as n-back, span increases may be very slow. With such complex exercises, it is better to note the number of successful responses the trainee produces at his current span level.

Improved performance on the hands-on or computer-based exercises is to be expected. As humans practice a particular task, they usually become better at it. Improvement on a practice task must occur before there can be near or far transfer. Thus, the tracking conducted by computer-based programs and span performance during hands-on exercises is important. However, transfer of the new or enhanced skill is better evidence that there has been improvement in WM (see Rapid Reference 7.2). That's why nontrained tasks should be used to measure progress. When there are notable gains on measures of near transfer, then there's a good chance that brain-based WM functioning has improved.

Far transfer (also known as generalization) is the long-term goal of WM exercises and strategy training (Zinke et al., 2014). With students, improved academic learning and performance are usually the long-term objective. Typically,

≋ *Rapid Reference 7.2 Methods for Measuring Progress During a Working Memory Intervention*

- Standardized pre- and post-tests
- Informal verbal span word lists
- Length of span during practice exercises
- Curriculum-based measures
- Scores on classroom tests
- Academic grades
- Parent and teacher rating scales
- Recall when using a new strategy

deficient academic skills are assessed for changes. Again, the use of standardized measures may not be the most appropriate form of assessment. Curriculum-based measures that document small improvements would be better documentation. Tracking general academic progress with grades and scores on classroom tests may be the best method of assessing far transfer. Standardized teacher and parent rating scales can also provide objective data that is not subject to practice effects. In addition to a WM rating scale, the most appropriate rating scales are those that assess executive functions, psychological processes, and attention. (See Chapter 5 for a review of appropriate rating scales.) As discovered in some WM training studies, far transfer to academics may not be immediate (Holmes, Gathercole, & Dunning, 2009). Academic progress should be monitored for at least a few months following termination of a WM training program.

When strategy training is involved, there is another important method of evaluating the effectiveness of the intervention. First, recall should be measured after no strategy or an existing ineffective strategy is used by the trainee. Following this, the new strategy should be introduced and then recall measured after it is used the very first time. Recall scores should then be compared. When performance is notably better with the new strategy, this provides valuable evidence. For example, the trainee might be asked to review a list of words in his typical manner and then his recall is recorded. Next, a rehearsal, chunking, or visualization strategy might be introduced and recall after using the new strategy is recorded. Note that recall after using a strategy need not be sequential. Also, measuring recall after using or practicing new strategies should continue during subsequent sessions.

METAMEMORY TRAINING

Metamemory instruction is discussed in depth in Chapter 8, but it is mentioned here because it is also a crucial component of individual and small group training. Metamemory training is especially important when strategies are taught because it is crucial that trainees understand how and why a new strategy works for them. In particular, they need to realize the personal efficacy of the strategy. Ways of imparting this knowledge are to continually show and discuss improvement data. Metamemory is also important when training primarily consists of online or hands-on WM exercises that do not include explicit strategy instruction. In such instances, trainees should, at the very least, learn about how WM works, their WM weaknesses, and how the exercises are designed to strengthen WM.

THE EFFICACY OF WORKING MEMORY TRAINING

Any given intervention method is not going to work with every individual. This is true of even the most robust methods. For example, in education, not every student benefits from direct instruction; in psychological treatment, not every client benefits from cognitive-behavioral therapy. This reality emerges even in the best designed scientific research. When investigators conclude that a researched method is effective, their conclusion is based on the mean performance of the sample. Thus, interventions that are judged to be effective may work with the majority of individuals, but not everyone. Another reality of empirical investigations is that there is never 100% consistency across studies. No matter what type of intervention is under consideration, results will vary across studies. Inconsistencies are due to the fact that the variables are always different in each study. For example, there may be differences in the populations sampled, in the specific intervention methods and how they were delivered, in the assessments used to measure the constructs, and in how the data were analyzed.

Given that scientific research, especially in the fields of psychology and education, has inherent weaknesses, the evidence for emerging WM interventions should not be held to higher standards than other types of interventions. As long as an intervention can do no harm, using what works for

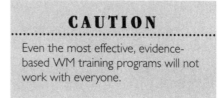

CAUTION

Even the most effective, evidence-based WM training programs will not work with everyone.

a majority of individuals is appropriate professional practice. The key is to monitor the individual's response to each intervention method and change to another approach when objective measures of improvement indicate a lack of progress.

In the field of WM interventions and research, computer-based WM training is a recent development (most of it has emerged since the year 2000). Dozens of studies on the efficacy of such training have been conducted. These studies have the same inherent weaknesses and inconsistencies found in other fields of research, opening the door to questions and criticisms. The result is that brain-based WM training has become controversial. Consequently, a review of the research is provided here so that practitioners can make informed decisions about WM training.

Concerns About the Efficacy of Working Memory Training

As defined in this text, WM training refers to hands-on exercises, computerized exercises, and training programs that are available on the Internet. This type of training has been referred to as "implicit" training, as opposed to "explicit" training (Klingberg, 2010). Implicit training is based only on repetition, practice, and immediate feedback. In contrast, explicit training involves conscious strategies for handling the material. WM training is usually considered implicit primarily because there is no instruction about how to use strategies to improve performance. Klingberg (2009) believes that the introduction of strategies may reduce the effectiveness of the training. Klingberg was the founder of Cogmed, one of the first brain-based training programs dedicated to WM improvement. The efficacy of Cogmed has been the focus of dozens of studies (Jaeggi, Buschkuehl, Jonides, & Shah, 2012).

Some critics (Melby-Lervag & Hulme, 2013; Shipstead, Hicks, & Engle, 2012) have questioned nearly all of the findings reported by studies of WM training. Their charge is that most studies do not meet standards for experimental design. As summarized by Dunning, Holmes, and Gathercole (2013), poorly designed studies may lack one or more of the following: random assignment of subjects, adequate sample sizes, a control group, enough training time, multiple measures, and measures with high construct validity. These concerns are valid, but the field of WM research is not the only type of psychological and educational research with such weaknesses. One reason is that with applied research (as opposed to research conducted in a laboratory) it is difficult to control all of the main variables involved. On the other hand, the ecological (real-world) validity of results obtained from well-designed laboratory research is often questioned.

In response to criticism regarding research methodology, Dunning et al. (2013) conducted a randomized, controlled trial investigation. They found that adaptive, computerized training led to improvements on multiple untrained tests of visual-spatial STM, verbal WM, and visual-spatial WM. Gains in verbal WM were sustained 1 year after training. However, after 20 to 25 training sessions with Cogmed, there were no significant gains on academic achievement tests and no improvement in WM-related classroom tasks, such as following instructions.

Even when experimental design shortcomings are ignored and all of the findings of WM training studies are accepted, critics (e.g., Melby-Lervåg & Hulme, 2013) point out that the evidence for effectiveness is weak. It's not that the majority of WM investigations do not find significant improvements in some aspects of WM performance. Nearly all of them do report significant changes on nontrained measures of WM. Rather, the primary concerns are that the changes are not sustained and generalization (also referred to as far transfer) does not occur, at least not in any consistent fashion. The presumption behind this charge is that genuine improvements in WM capacity should transfer to highly related functions. For example, fluid reasoning should increase because it is highly correlated with WM (Perrig, Hollenstein, & Oelhafen, 2009), and academic skills and performance should improve because they depend heavily on WM capability.

Melby-Lervåg and Hulme (2013) conducted a meta-analytic review of 23 studies that met stringent experimental design criteria. For instance, studies that did not have an untreated control group were excluded. The average duration of training was 12 hours. The meta-analysis found that nearly all of the studies produced short-term improvements in practiced skills. However, the authors concluded that there was no convincing or consistent evidence for far transfer to related functions and skills.

Cognitive and Academic Gains Produced by Working Memory Training

Psychologists agree that repeated performance of a task always leads to improved performance on that particular task. The important question is the extent to which the training-induced gains transfer to nontrained tasks. With WM training, near transfer almost always occurs. Near transfer is documented by significant pre- to post-test gains on untrained measures of WM. Evidence for far transfer occurs when there are significant improvements in other cognitive constructs, everyday behavior, and academic learning and performance.

Near Transfer. Many studies have found adaptive, computerized WM training to increase WM capacity and bring about changes in associated brain activity in all types of subjects (Klingberg et al., 2002, 2005; Olesen, Westerberg, & Klingberg, 2004). For instance, in a meta-analysis of 25 training studies conducted with ADHD children, Rapport, Orban, Kofler, and Friedman (2013) reported that WM training had a moderate effect size of .63 on STM performance. Another meta-analysis of 23 studies conducted with nondisabled subjects led Melby-Lervag and Hulme (2012) to conclude that WM training programs produce reliable short-term improvements in WM skills. Van der Molen, Van Luit, Van der Molen, Klugkist, and Jongmans (2010) examined the performance of subjects with mild to borderline intellectual disabilities and discovered a significant increase in verbal WM. In children with initially poor WM, Holmes et al. (2009) found substantial gains in all types of STM and WM. Also, some studies have reported sustained gains. Holmes et al. reported that WM increases were still present after 6 months. Maintenance of the gains also has been documented over intervals up to 18 months (E. Dahlin, Nyberg, Backman, & Neely, 2008).

Near transfer is typically measured with untrained standardized and informal WM tasks. For instance, Westerberg et al. (2007) measured the performance of treated subjects with a digit span test. As a result of training, the digit span of the treated subjects improved from a mean of 5.8 to 7.3, an effect size of 1.58.

Online WM training primarily consists of visual-spatial exercises. Yet, there usually is significant near transfer to verbal WM (Klingberg, 2010; Van der Molen et al., 2010). However, the trained tasks improve more than performance on untrained tasks. Trained tasks typically improve 30% to 40%, whereas untrained WM tasks often improve about 15% (Klingberg, 2010). These fairly consistent findings have led Klingberg (2010) to conclude that intrinsic (no strategy) visual-spatial training tasks lead to improvement in general WM capacity.

Far Transfer. Results regarding far transfer are more mixed, and typically only one instance of far transfer is found per study. One type of far transfer is improvement in related cognitive processes. For instance, after online WM training, Alloway and Alloway (2009) discovered a significant increase in crystallized intelligence among their sample of LD students.

Fluid reasoning is another cognitive ability that is highly related with WM. Jaeggi, Buschkuehl, Jonides, and Perrig (2008) reported that WM training improved fluid reasoning. Participants with initially lower fluid reasoning showed the largest gains in fluid reasoning. The study used a dual *n*-back task (see the *n*-back section later in this chapter); one task was auditory and the other visual. The gains in fluid reasoning are not surprising given that *n*-back is an extremely challenging task.

Subjects with ADHD often display changes in behavior following computerized WM training. The Klingberg et al. (2005) study was one of the first to report this observation. As reported by parents, the ADHD subjects in this early study had reduced behavioral symptoms of inattention following WM training. Using a structured observational system, C. T. Green et al. (2012) discovered significant reductions in off-task behavior. In another study, ADHD and LD college students had fewer ADHD symptoms and fewer cognitive difficulties after a 5-week intensive WM training program (Gropper, Gotlieb, Kronitz, & Tannock, 2014). The changes were still present when reassessed after 2 months. In a study with comorbid ADHD/LD adolescents, Gray et al. (2012) found that those who improved the most on WM training tasks demonstrated the greatest reduction in ADHD symptoms. For example, parent ratings of home behaviors indicated that these subjects had become less inattentive and hyperactive. More recently, a meta-analysis of the Cogmed training program found that it significantly improved inattention in daily life (Spencer-Smith & Klingberg, 2015).

Regarding improvements in academic skills and functioning, the results are also mixed and typically limited to one aspect of academics. In a study by Loosli, Buschkuehl, Perrig, and Jaeggi (2012), WM training resulted in significantly enhanced reading performance in typically developing children aged 9 to 11. Similarly, improvements in reading comprehension were reported by K. Dahlin (2011). Improvements in mathematics reasoning, mathematics skills, and performance have been reported in some studies. Swanson, Jerman, and Zheng (2008) documented how growth in WM is related to growth in word problem solving accuracy for children with mathematics LD. Holmes et al. (2009) discovered significantly improved mathematics ability as a result of WM training. Although Alloway and Alloway (2009) reported improvement in following classroom instructions, positive changes in academic performance have been documented less frequently.

Perhaps those searching for evidence of far transfer are not allowing enough time for it to occur. Some studies have found evidence for transfer effects as much as 6 months later. For instance, Holmes et al. (2009) reported delayed improvement in arithmetic skills. A neurological explanation for this phenomenon is that improvement in WM functioning may take some time to have an impact on related functions.

HOW WORKING MEMORY TRAINING CHANGES THE BRAIN

True WM performance deficits are due to underlying weaknesses or impairments in the neurological structures and functions that are responsible for WM functions. Thus, the primary goal of WM training is to create positive changes in these neurological structures and functions. When measurable change in WM performance occurs, the presumption is that there have been changes in brain-based WM capacity. The extensive evidence for brain plasticity supports this presumption. There is no reason to suspect that WM is any different than other parts of the brain. The synaptic connections determining WM capacity are governed by the same laws of plasticity that characterize other parts of the brain (Klingberg,

2010; Rabipour & Raz, 2012). Therefore, training directed at improving WM has the potential to change the WM parts of the brain.

Although psychologists and neuroscientists do not fully understand the mechanisms involved when WM functioning improves (Buschkuehl, Jaeggi, & Jonides, 2012), findings from several studies are consistent with the current understanding of the neuropsychology of WM. In these studies, the neural correlates of the improved performance have been measured (Morrison & Chein, 2011).

The first line of evidence is increased connectivity among brain structures involved in STM and WM functioning. In a groundbreaking neuroimaging study, Tageuchi et al. (2010) discovered measureable growth in the brain's white matter (connective tissue) that was correlated with the extent of training and the amount of improved performance. The majority of the white matter growth was within the parietal cortex and adjacent to an area of the corpus callosum closely linked with the prefrontal cortex. There was also increased connectivity between the parietal region and the dorsolateral prefrontal cortex. The new white matter in the corpus callosum seemed to be connecting the bilateral dorsolateral prefrontal cortices, which are the key structures involved in WM. Thus, there was increased hemispheric information transfer between the prefrontal cortices. According to Klingberg (2010), stronger frontoparietal connectivity is one potential mechanism behind higher WM capacity. Tageuchi et al. also found indications that myelination had increased. Tageuchi et al. used intensive adaptive training, 25 minutes per day for 2 months. The training consisted of three tasks: a visual-spatial WM task, an *n*-back task, and a dual *n*-back task that required recalling both the identity of items and location of items *n*-stimuli ago.

The second kind of reoccurring evidence involves changes in brain activity levels. Early on, Olesen et al. (2004) discovered that WM training resulted in increased activity in the prefrontal and parietal cortices. Klingberg (2010) also reports that WM training is associated with changes in activity in the frontal and parietal cortices and the basal ganglia. Paradoxically, decreases in brain activity are also a sign of improvement. This is because neural responses become more efficient as a function of training. Thus, activation decreases are attributed to increased neural efficiency. Functional MRI has found decreased brain activation in the prefrontal cortex as a function of WM training, especially *n*-back training (Buschkuehl et al., 2012).

The third influence that WM training may have on the brain is to increase dopamine levels and/or dopamine utilization. It is well known that dopamine plays an important role in WM function and in improving WM capacity. For example, medications that act on the dopamine system, such as methylphenidate, improve WM performance. Backman and Nyberg (2013) believe that WM training, especially training that requires updating, is associated with increased release of dopamine. Klingberg (2010) believes that WM training creates changes in dopamine receptor density.

For WM training to have a positive impact on the brain, it needs to meet certain characteristics. First, the program must be adaptive (difficulty levels change to match the trainee's performance). Research has clearly established that nonadaptive programs fail to show improvement

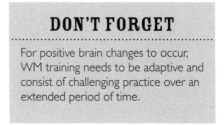

DON'T FORGET
······································
For positive brain changes to occur, WM training needs to be adaptive and consist of challenging practice over an extended period of time.

(Klingberg et al., 2005). Second, it must consist of challenging practice over an extended period of time (Westerberg et al., 2007).

Regarding transfer effects, the training must share at least some neural components with the neural components involved with the outcome tasks; that is, the training and transfer tasks must engage similar processes and brain regions. For example, WM and fluid reasoning share overlapping neural networks in the prefrontal cortex. Far transfer may also occur because of improved control over attention, improved executive control, increased ability to inhibit distraction, and developing and using more effective strategies (Jaeggi et al., 2012; Rabipour & Raz, 2012). Moreover, WM training programs may also promote metamemory and the development of compensatory strategies.

CONCLUSIONS REGARDING THE EFFICACY OF WORKING MEMORY TRAINING

Given the strong relations between WM and academic learning, it is surprising that only a few WM training studies have produced improvements in academic learning. Closer examination of the training tasks employed in many programs sheds some light on potential explanations for these discouraging outcomes. The disconnect between successful near transfer and limited far transfer may begin with a faulty theoretical framework and a failure to conduct a detailed task analysis of the exercises involved. It seems that the underlying assumption of many training programs is that simple exercises that repeatedly load high on a limited cognitive resource will lead to an increase in capacity. Although such tasks may in fact boost capacity, the improvements may be limited to STM (Melby-Lervag & Hulme, 2012).

Unfortunately, what is often the most in need of improvement are the higher levels of WM, especially executive WM. Task analysis of WM training programs that have failed to reach expectations reveals that many of their exercises are simple span (STM) tasks when complex span (WM) tasks are called for. For example, observing a sequence of flashing objects and then clicking on that sequence amounts to a simple span task. After a review of the training tasks involved in 25 studies, Rapport et al. (2013) concluded that most tasks in programs marketed as WM training could be more accurately classified as STM training. Thus, the lack of far transfer effects to improved cognitive and academic functioning may be due to the incongruence between the deficits and the WM areas in need of training. Also, the trainee's ability to more quickly respond to stimuli may not mean that the underlying ability has actually increased (Melby-Lervag & Hulme, 2012).

DON'T FORGET

....

Some computerized WM training programs may fail to produce far transfer because they consist primarily of STM tasks rather than complex tasks that challenge higher levels of WM.

The other main reason for the failure of online WM training to live up to its promise may be because it is limited to implicit training. Perhaps, some explicit training should be combined with implicit training. Explicit training would include teaching the trainees to use effective strategies to increase their WM span. Holmes et al. (2009) asked subjects what they thought led to their WM improvement. Of the responses, 37% reported concentrating harder by closing their eyes or focusing on the presented information, and 27% reported using a variety of other strategies, such as rehearsal or tracing the pattern on the screen with their eyes. Also, Holmes et al. hypothesized that the amount of effort put into WM training had the largest impact on treatment outcomes.

INTERNET-BASED WORKING MEMORY TRAINING

A few of the commercial "brain-training" programs available on the Internet are reviewed in this section. Most of them consist of multiple exercises and claim to train several cognitive abilities, including attention, speed, problem solving, and memory. Only a couple of them are dedicated solely to WM training. All of them have a game-like format, although children may not consider some of the more challenging tasks to be fun games.

There are several advantages to web-based WM exercises. These include: the ability to train alone, flexible training times and locations, consistent application of the procedures, the speed of presentation, recording of response time, immediate corrective feedback, an automated adaptive feature, and automated record-keeping.

There are also some serious disadvantages, including an overreliance on visual-spatial stimuli, an inability to accept oral responses, lack of strategy training, a significant guessing factor, and too many simple span exercises that do not require enough processing to challenge the higher-level WM components. Also, when trainees complete exercises alone there is no one to monitor and encourage their effort and motivation. Furthermore, there is no provision of metacognitive information that might ensure generalization and maintenance.

When selecting games/exercises from any of these brain-training websites, the user should keep in mind that WM tasks are not always labeled or categorized as such. For example, appropriate WM exercises might be placed under such categories of attention, intelligence, or even people skills. Guidelines for selecting WM tasks are at the end of this section.

Cogmed

Cogmed (www.cogmed.com) is a comprehensive, evidence-based WM training program that was developed by psychologists in Sweden (Klingberg et al., 2005; Olesen et al., 2004). Marketing and distribution to U.S. psychologists began in 2001. Pearson Education purchased Cogmed in 2010 and now promotes its use in schools. It is available in three different packages: JM for ages 4 to 6, RM for ages 7 to 18, and QM for adults. All versions have the same visual-spatial tasks and algorithms. Some tasks involve a combination of verbal and visual-spatial information, but oral responses are not accepted. The typical response consists of clicking on target objects in the correct sequence (Roche & Johnson, 2014).

The software is intended to improve the WM span and attention span of children who have WM deficits, especially those who are diagnosed with ADHD. Research summarized by Pearson Education indicates that approximately 80% of children who complete the training show measurable improvement in WM and attention. Of those who benefit from training, 79% still demonstrate benefits a year later, according to parent reports.

Cogmed recommends daily sessions of approximately 25 to 45 minutes, 5 days a week, for 5 weeks. Each training session consists of eight (out of 12 available) short visuospatial and verbal activities, or some combination thereof. Children can complete the sessions independently at school or at home. The computer program is adaptive, automatically adjusting difficulty level up or down.

The program tracks several aspects of the trainee's responses, including time of day and speed of responding. The trainee's compliance and performance are monitored through the Internet by a "coach" who has been trained to understand the data and to give appropriate guidance and feedback.

Given the computerized medium, the training is more visuospatially loaded than verbally loaded, including visual items that rotate after the sequence is provided. This emphasis seems to be a particularly good match for children with ADHD, who are typically more deficient in visual-spatial WM than verbal WM. The training essentially entails the practice of memory span activities, some of which can be classified as complex-span tasks, thereby involving executive WM to some extent.

Jungle Memory

Jungle Memory (www.junglememory.com) is another evidence-based, adaptive program dedicated to WM improvement. Jungle Memory consists of three exercises intended for children ages 7 to 16. One of the games involves mental arithmetic, and in another game the user must remember the location of letters and words. Research with Jungle Memory has found evidence of near and far transfer, including improvement in IQ and language and math test scores (Melby-Lervag & Hulme, 2012). The improvements were sustained for at least 8 months.

Lumosity

Lumosity (www.lumosity.com) is a popular cognitive training website that has a variety of games, only some of which are WM exercises. The WM training tasks are derived from tasks reported in WM research. For instance, several of the WM games are n-back tasks. The stimuli used in the challenging n-back tasks include faces, a frog jumping on lily pads, letters, symbols, and rhyming words. Lumosity requires that users be at least 13 years of age.

Brain HQ

Brain HQ (www.brainhq.com) is another example of a brain training website that has WM games derived from WM research. Brain HQ offers the typical n-back exercises but also has some interesting games that apply WM to everyday living. For example, one task requires the trainee to remember conversation details, and in another the user must match a face with details about an individual. Many of the Brain HQ exercises challenge WM because they require the integration of verbal and visual-spatial information.

Guidelines for Internet-Based Working Memory Training

The Internet offers numerous websites, exercises, games, and apps that all claim to improve WM. Unfortunately, some of them are just games that fail to meet the design requirements of evidence-based WM exercises. Consequently, the "buyer beware" adage applies to the selection of online WM training, especially when selecting "apps."

For WM training programs, exercises, games, or apps to be considered effective, they should meet *all* of the following criteria:

- The procedures used should have documented efficacy, such as *n*-back, be derived from procedures that have an evidence base, or clearly meet criteria for tasks that challenge WM. An alternative is that the overall training program has several studies documenting its effectiveness.
- The program or game must be adaptive, immediately adapting difficulty level as the user succeeds and fails. For example, when the user responds correctly several times in a row, the required span might be increased by one.
- The program or game keeps track of the user's level from one session to the next. For example, when the user returns to a game a day later, the level presented to the user is the same as when the session ended a day earlier.
- The training regimens consistently demand high cognitive workloads at the level the user is working at.
- The exercise, game, or app requires simultaneous processing and storage. That is, the trainee must "do" some cognitive task in addition to retaining a sequence of items. For example, simply repeating a series of words does not include sufficient processing to qualify as a WM exercise. However, remembering the sequence of answers to math calculation problems does require processing while retaining information.
- At least some of the exercises should require the integration of visual and verbal information.
- Regardless of age, training sessions should consist of at least a few different exercises and last for a minimum of 25 minutes.
- The exercises should be available on a daily basis over an extended period of time. At a minimum, 20 to 25 lessons should be available over of period of 4 to 6 weeks.

The only exceptions to these guidelines would be cases where an individual's deficit is clearly in STM storage components and not in higher-level WM processes. In such instances, the individual has a strong ability to strategically process information and manage a high cognitive load, but lacks STM storage capacity.

For instance, such an individual might score very poorly on a digits forward task but very well on digits backward. In such instances, simple span exercises that require minimal processing would be appropriate.

HANDS-ON WORKING MEMORY EXERCISES

For some individuals, face-to-face, hands-on WM exercises are more appropriate and likely to be more effective than computerized training. Individuals who might especially benefit from hands-on exercises are younger children, those with severe WM impairments, those who are not motivated to do exercises independently, those who are unable to maintain a sequence of items during rehearsal, and those who are delayed in metamemory and strategy development. Moreover, because of the limitations of computerized training, face-to-face exercises are particularly needed with individuals whose WM impairments are primarily phonological, auditory, or verbal in nature.

In addition to meeting the foregoing needs, one-on-one training allows the opportunity to incorporate strategy training. Although computerized training exercises generally do not prevent trainees from using strategies, many trainees do not apply or develop strategies during computerized training. Consequently, an opportunity to learn effective strategies and further improve WM performance may be lost. For example, learning a systematic method of maintaining information while updating and switching could be an extremely valuable lesson. Nonetheless, trainers should not teach task-specific strategies until the trainee's level of performance on a task has plateaued.

Many of the recommended hands-on exercises are adaptations of computerized exercises, some are derived from procedures reported in research studies, and some have been designed by this author. Those without a specific research base meet the requirements of effective WM exercise design, such as those specified in the preceding section. All of them can easily be applied in a home or school setting. The most important factor is that the trainers apply these procedures with integrity. Step-by-step instructions for each can be found in the online resources. Additional details are available in Dehn (2011).

Most of the exercises recommended ahead are complex span tasks because they require processing of information while maintaining information in short-term storage. Most of them are also exercises that challenge executive WM (see Rapid Reference 7.1). Because they are all span tasks (remembering the stimuli in the correct sequence) the difficulty level can be adjusted by simply increasing or decreasing the length of the span. For example, once the trainee has been successful a few times with a span of three, then the span should be increased to four. Also, in the exercises described ahead, specific techniques for making each task more difficult are suggested.

The following WM exercises are recommended for use with children, adolescents, and adults who have significant WM deficits.

N-Back

N-back requires the individual to remember an item that was presented a certain number of items previously. For example, with *2*-back, the trainer might display and remove a series of letters one at a time. If the letters are *b-q-f-j-r*, then the student would say "*b*" when the *f* is displayed, "*q*" when the *j* is displayed, and "*f*" when the *r* is displayed. Almost any type of stimuli can be used for this exercise. A convenient set of materials is a deck of regular playing cards. The general procedures for *n*-back are: (a) Display each item for 1 to 2 seconds; (b) have the trainee name the appropriate *n*-back item when it is time to do so; (c) start the process over whenever the trainee makes an error; (d) increase the *n*-back by 1 when the trainee successfully completes a sequence of 10 items three times in a row. More step-by-step details are provided in the online resources.

The effectiveness of *n*-back has been well documented. All of the studies using the approach have produced significant gains in WM. In fact, the study that found increased connectivity in the brain was one that used *n*-back as the training method (Tageuchi et al., 2010). *N*-back is very effective because it challenges executive WM by requiring continual updating, switching, and inhibiting. The only concern with *n*-back is that it is too challenging for younger children, especially those less than 8 years of age. For adults and those who handle *n*-back well, the task can be made more challenging by creating a dual *n*-back, such as having to remember both auditory and visual information about an item presented *n*-items before.

For *n*-back, trainees should be taught a rehearsal strategy that involves conscious updating, switching, and inhibiting. For example, given a *2*-back task with the letters *b-q-f-j-r*, the examinee should keep rehearsing "*b-q*" until the *f* is shown, then say "*b*," then forget the *b* (this is inhibiting), begin repeating "*q-f*" (this is updating) until the next letter is shown, and so on. The switching occurs when the trainee switches from rehearsing to providing a response and looking at the new item and then back to rehearsing. Even without the application of this strategy, *n*-back should be considered an executive WM exercise.

Counting Span

In this activity the trainee counts aloud the number of randomly arranged items on a series of cards displayed and removed one at a time, and then must recall the count for each card in the correct sequence. For materials, cards with dots or stars on them would be appropriate. If the first card has seven items, the second has four items, and the third has nine items, the student would say "seven, four, nine" after the last card has been counted and removed. Each time the student successfully completes three series, another card should be added to the sequence. This exercise is appropriate for younger children who can count but still find counting a process that demands their attention. The task can be made more challenging by including distractor stimuli, such as items of a different color that are to be ignored. Because there is minimal processing and little integration of verbal and visual-spatial information, this task is mostly visual-spatial WM, rather than executive WM.

Arithmetic Flash Cards

For this exercise, only arithmetic facts that the individual has mastered or nearly mastered should be used. For example, multiplication flash cards could be used with a student who knows multiplication tables. The procedure is similar to that for counting span. The student computes and says the answer for each card as it is displayed, and then must recall the answers in the correct sequence after all the cards have been presented. Incorrect calculations should be accepted, provided the trainee says the same number when recalling the sequence. When the math facts are known, errors are an indication that the trainee is focusing on maintaining the sequence of answers at the expense of making processing errors. To make the task more challenging, different arithmetic procedures can be mixed together, such as addition and subtraction problems in the same series. This task should be considered an executive WM exercise.

Visual-Spatial Recall

The materials for this activity are a sheet or board with a grid, such as an "8 × 12," and tokens, such as chips. For each trial, the trainer should display a set number of tokens on random squares for 5 seconds, then remove the chips, and then have the trainee place them in the correct locations. In addition to increasing the number of chips, difficulty can be increased by increasing the number of squares or by using chips of two different colors and requiring that the correct color be placed in each location. Because there is very little processing involved and locations can be recalled without a strategy, this task primarily involves visual-spatial STM.

To make it a visual-spatial WM task, rotation should be added. After the chips have been removed from the board, rotate it 90 degrees and then require the trainee to place the tokens on the squares where they were located before the board was rotated.

Following Directions

For this exercise, complex scenes containing several items should be used. For example, a picture of a school playground with children would be appropriate. The trainer states a series of items that the trainee must point to in the correct sequence after the directions are complete. For example, the trainer might say, "Point to the swing, then the teacher, and then the bush next to the building." This task involves integrating verbal and visual-spatial information and is therefore classified as an executive WM exercise.

Verbal Span Practice

Younger children may benefit from simply being required to recall verbal spans. For example, the trainer says a few common words at the rate of approximately one per second and then the trainee is required to repeat them. With young children, a typical starting point would a list of three words. As the trainee masters each span, another word should be added to the list. In addition to words, trainers can also present letters, nonwords, and digits. Nonwords are especially challenging because the trainee cannot rely on much support from LTM. It is best if all of the items used are monosyllabic.

Last Word

Last word is a task that challenges verbal WM. The trainer will first need to create a list of basic questions to which the trainee must respond with a "yes" or "no." For example, the first question might be, "Do cats bark at people?," to which the trainee should answer "No." Additional questions might be, "Do cows drive cars?" and "Do houses have rooms?" Then after the series of questions, the trainee must say, "People, cars, rooms."

Rehearsal as an Exercise

Rehearsal is subvocal repetition of information. It is usually considered a strategy, and recommendations for teaching it as a strategy are in Chapter 8. However, for some young children, practicing rehearsal can function as an exercise that will strengthen their phonological STM and verbal WM. Children who are most in need of this training exercise are those who are not yet using rehearsal, those who are using rehearsal incorrectly, and those who are unable to maintain a sequence of items during rehearsal.

Practicing rehearsal is fairly straightforward (detailed steps are provided in the online resources). Trainers say a series of words, and the trainee is required to repeat them at least five times in order. A cumulative version in which the trainee must keep adding new words to the list being rehearsed should also be practiced. After students have mastered the approach, they are directed to whisper during rehearsal, and then finally to subvocalize. To accurately assess whether there is growth in span, it is important that all of the words are monosyllabic or contain the same number of syllables. Once a trainee understands how to correctly apply rehearsal, require the trainee to use rehearsal (in a whispering mode) during all hands-on WM exercises. When presenting items be sure to pause long enough for rehearsal to occur.

INTERVENTIONS THAT IMPROVE RELATED COGNITIVE PROCESSES

There are several cognitive processes and skills that are highly interrelated with WM, especially attention, executive functions, phonological processing, and processing speed. (Details on their relations are provided in Chapter 2.) For example, speech fluency is associated with phonological STM span; the faster an individual can speak, the longer the span. Because of this brain-based interaction, interventions that focus solely on strengthening WM may not be the most effective. Rather, including related processes in a WM intervention may improve the chances of changing the brain and lead to transfer to WM. As one or more related cognitive processes improve, WM performance may also improve.

Attention

Processes that control attention are intricately interwoven with WM. In fact, stimulant medication for ADHD, such as methylphenidate, improves performance in visual-spatial, verbal, and executive WM tasks as much as 10% in children with ADHD (Bedard et al., 2004; Minear & Shah, 2006). Medication is thought to enhance WM performance by suppressing distracting, irrelevant information and by increasing the efficiency of WM. Computer-based exercises designed to train sustained, selective, alternating, and divided attention are another alternative

(Tamm et al., 2010). Finally, cognitively focused interventions for attention, such as self-monitoring training, may also benefit WM functions and performance (Reid, Schartz, & Trout, 2005).

Self-monitoring is an evidence-based procedure (K. Harris, Friedlander, Saddler, Frizzelle, & Graham, 2005) that involves a multistage process of observing, evaluating, and recording one's behavior, such as whether one is "paying attention." Self-monitoring makes the individual more aware of his regulatory processes and serves as a cue to maintain the target behavior and cognition. As metacognitive self-awareness increases, attentional control improves.

Self-monitoring training is typically used with young students who have difficulty maintaining their focus during academic tasks. A high degree of accuracy is not necessary for the effects of self-monitoring to occur. Reinforcers may be incorporated to reward trainees, but external reinforcers frequently are unnecessary.

Self-monitoring training might be conducted in a classroom during regular learning activities or while the student is completing homework in another setting. One approach is to have the student wear a device that vibrates at random intervals, ranging from 10 to 90 seconds. Immediately upon feeling the vibration, the student is taught to self-assess by asking, "Was I paying attention?" The student then self-records whether he was on task when the vibration occurred. As the training proceeds, intervals may be lengthened. Another option is to have the student appraise whether he was paying attention during the entire interval since the last self-evaluation. Teachers may provide an external check on the accuracy of the student's assessment by recording their evaluation of the interval alongside the student's (Reid et al., 2005). Bonus points may be earned when teachers agree with the student's assessment. Worksheets for self-monitoring training are provided in the online resources.

Executive Functions

More than 30 specific executive functions, one of which is WM, have been identified (McCloskey & Perkins, 2013). Of these, interventions for planning are selected because of the important role planning plays in academic production. Recommendations for other executive functions interventions can be found in McCloskey, Perkins, and Van Divner (2009).

Several studies have documented the efficacy of educational interventions designed to facilitate planning (R. Conway & Ashman, 1989; Kar, Dash, Das, & Carlson, 1993). Following the training, students have performed better on planning tasks and on mathematics, a skill that depends heavily on planning and WM (Naglieri & Gottling, 1997; Naglieri & Johnson, 2000).

Planning instruction should be explicit and include: teaching students about plans and strategy use; requiring students to verbalize their planning process, and encouraging students to develop, use, and evaluate their own planning strategies. When mathematics is included in an intervention for a planning weakness, students are taught how to be self-reflective, how planning is important, how to formulate plans, how to verbalize their plans, and how to select efficient problem-solving strategies. More details on planning interventions can be found in Naglieri and Pickering (2010).

Phonological Processing

Phonological processing deficits frequently underlie weak phonological STM. Consequently, phonological processing and phonemic awareness training are highly recommended when phonological STM deficits are present. With an overall effect size as high as .86 (National Reading Panel, 2000), phonological processing training has an excellent track record. Transfer to reading and other literacy skills is also well documented (Bus & Van IJzendoorn, 1999).

There are evidence-based, commercial training programs available. However, it is easy to conduct phonological processing training without software or a curriculum. Basically, all phonological processing training involves manipulation of phonemes. These are the essential activities to include:

- Rhyming with familiar words increases awareness of the different sounds in words.
- Alliteration, generating words that begin with the same sound, is another way of increasing awareness of sounds in words.
- Isolating and identifying phonemes, such as having children identify the three phonemes in "cat" are crucial first steps in phoneme manipulation.
- Blending begins with blending syllables and then progresses to phonemes. The trainer says words a syllable or phoneme at a time, and the trainee puts all the word parts together into a smoothly pronounced word.
- After blending is mastered, children are ready for segmentation. Again, students should practice dividing words into syllables before saying them phoneme by phoneme. Because the ability to segment words into phonemic units is the hallmark of phonological awareness, it should be the focus of any phonemic awareness training.
- As trainees progress, segmenting and blending should be conducted during the same exercise.
- The most advanced stage of training is replacing phonemes to form different words or deleting phonemes at the beginning, middle, or end of a word.

Processing Speed

A few published studies have reported faster processing speed following computerized training designed for this purpose. A training study by Mackey, Hill, Stone, and Bunge (2011) with children 7 to 10 years of age reported that processing speed can be increased through training. Their intervention emphasized rapid visual detection and rapid motor responses during performance on a variety of commercially available games with simple rules. The method taxed processing speed by requiring the subject to maintain focus and concentration.

Another study found that playing action video games can increase processing speed (Dye, Green, & Bavelier, 2009). For example, when novices played the same video game for a total of 50 hours, their reaction time decreased 13% on untrained tasks. Playing action video games requires rapid processing of information and rapid decision making and responding.

In a review of seven studies C. S. Green and Bavelier (2008) report that rapid processing required by video games does transfer. It appears that playing video games that require speed may have benefits for any task, such as visual-spatial WM, for which speeded visual processing influences performance. Also, the faster reaction times reported in these studies have been reported to correlate with performance on higher-level cognitive tasks, such as WM (A. Conway et al., 2002).

Processing speed training is not something that can be accomplished with hands-on exercises. A computerized program is necessary. However, trainees are no longer limited to using video games for this purpose. Brain-training websites, such as Lumosity, have several games designed specifically for increasing speed.

🏹 TEST YOURSELF 🏹

1. **What is the main purpose of WM strategies?**
   (a) To increase WM capacity
   (b) To compensate for weak executive functions
   (c) To improve academic learning
   (d) To make effective use of existing WM capabilities
2. **Which WM intervention method can be considered both an exercise and a strategy?**
   (a) N-back
   (b) Rehearsal
   (c) Metamemory
   (d) Chunking

3. **One hallmark of executive WM exercises is that they:**
   (a) Involve the use of verbal strategies
   (b) Are unrelated to other types of WM exercises
   (c) Involve the integration of verbal and visual-spatial information
   (d) Are available only through online training programs

4. **Which WM exercise requires the most updating, switching, and inhibiting?**
   (a) N-back
   (b) Visualization
   (c) Following directions
   (d) Counting span

5. **What is the primary concern regarding the effectiveness of WM training programs?**
   (a) They are not challenging enough.
   (b) They lack near transfer.
   (c) There is no transfer between WM components.
   (d) They lack far transfer.

6. **All of the following have been reported to improve as a result of WM training except:**
   (a) Fluid reasoning
   (b) Processing speed
   (c) Attention
   (d) Crystallized intelligence

7. **Which brain change has been observed as a result of WM training?**
   (a) Increased connectivity
   (b) Decreased dopamine levels
   (c) An enlarged prefrontal cortex
   (d) Increased brain activity

8. **Computerized WM exercises are most likely to fail when:**
   (a) They are too lengthy.
   (b) They are visual-spatial only.
   (c) They are nonadaptive.
   (d) They require simultaneous processing.

9. **Interventions with related cognitive processes are recommended for all of the following except:**
   (a) Visual-spatial processing
   (b) Processing speed
   (c) Executive functions
   (d) Phonological processing

Answers: 1. d; 2. b; 3. c; 4. a; 5. d; 6. b; 7. a; 8. c; 9. a

Eight

SUPPORTING WORKING MEMORY IN THE CLASSROOM

The working memory elephant in the classroom should not be ignored. At least 10% of students in the typical classroom have WM deficits that impair their academic learning and performance (Alloway & Gathercole, 2006). Although their academic deficiencies are frequently targeted for intervention, almost never is the underlying WM impairment directly addressed. Given that WM may be the most important cognitive and metacognitive ability necessary for successful learning and performance, ignoring it seems almost unconscionable. Knowing the crucial roles WM plays throughout a learner's day (see Chapter 4) is not enough. Action is warranted. Many educators and related professionals who understand WM and its relations with learning may not act because they believe that there are no evidence-based interventions for WM deficits. However, this is a misconception; there are evidence-based interventions for WM (see Chapter 7 for more interventions).

At the very least, the learning environment can be modified to accommodate the needs of students with below average WM capacity. Most of these accommodations and modifications reduce cognitive load, thereby allowing the student to acquire more skills and knowledge. Some of the practices that reduce cognitive load involve changing how instruction is delivered. Other modifications allow the student to cope with otherwise high cognitive load material and activities. Students might even be taught how to better manage cognitive load internally.

An alternative is to teach WM-impaired students evidence-based strategies that will enhance their WM functioning and learning. This approach is distinct from the WM exercises designed to increase WM capacity that are discussed in Chapter 7. The premise underlying strategy instruction is that strategies can allow an individual to more effectively utilize existing capability. Delivering strategy instruction to an entire class is probably the most efficient approach. Even students with normal WM ability are likely to benefit from the training (Mastropieri, Sweda, & Scruggs, 2000).

When a psychologist or other related professional works one-on-one with an individual who has a WM impairment, it is helpful to know that individual's WM profile. For example, knowing that the trainee has a deficit in verbal WM and normal visual-spatial WM will allow the design of an individualized intervention that best meets the trainee's needs. However, classroom teachers can be effective without knowing the WM profiles of their WM-deficient students. The first reason for this is that most of the practices recommended in this chapter will improve WM performance, regardless of the specific weaknesses. For example, reducing cognitive load will support any type of WM weakness. The second reason is that teachers are being asked to adopt classroom-wide methods that will benefit nearly all learners. Finally, when teachers do need to differentiate their instruction, they can respond appropriately to academic deficiencies and the student challenges they observe without needing to know the WM profile. For instance, the assistance provided to students who struggle to put words on paper is basically the same regardless of each student's WM profile.

THE MNEMONIC-BASED CLASSROOM

Classroom-based WM interventions begin with teachers considering the roles WM plays in the learning process and making a commitment to providing more support for memory. This approach to supporting and emphasizing memory is referred to as "the mnemonic-based classroom." First, teachers need to learn more about brain-based memory functions. To accomplish this goal, support staff, such as school psychologists and special education teachers, might provide teachers with consultation, training, and resources. Next, teachers should adopt the philosophy that WM is so essential it must be considered and supported throughout the school day. In a mnemonic-based classroom, teachers adopt procedures and offer accommodations that reduce cognitive load. They also teach students some basic memory strategies. Throughout the school day, mnemonic-oriented teachers provide learners with prompts and reminders to utilize strategies and study practices that support WM limitations and enhance WM performance.

CAUTION

"Mnemonic-based classroom" refers to a classroom that emphasizes memory-based instruction. As used here, the term *mnemonic* is not limited to structured memorization techniques known by that name.

Mnemonic-focused classroom practices are not solely for students with identified WM weaknesses. A classroom-wide approach is recommended. All learners are likely to benefit, although students with below average WM capacity usually benefit the most (Mastropieri et al., 2000). A mnemonic-based classroom may also incorporate methods that support and enhance LTM.

Teachers who conduct a mnemonic-based classroom will be rewarded for their efforts. In a meta-analysis of 34 studies involving the teaching of memory strategies to students with learning disabilities, Scruggs and Mastropieri (1990) reported a large effect size of 1.62 across a variety of content areas and instructional settings. This large effect size translates into a rather significant increase in students' retention and recall of information. For example, Carney, Levin, and Levin (1993) found that mnemonic-based instruction doubled students' recall of information.

In the mnemonic-based classroom, teachers focus on WM limitations and apply methods that support WM and enhance learning. Effective, mnemonic-focused teachers do the following:

- Engage in instructional practices and offer accommodations and modifications that reduce cognitive load (see later section on cognitive load).
- Provide metamemory instruction (see later section on metamemory).
- Beginning in first grade, teach students how to rehearse correctly (see later section on rehearsal).
- At all grade levels, continually remind students to use memory strategies during learning activities.
- Model the use of memory strategies, through thinking aloud and explaining their processing. For example, a teacher might model the chunking strategy (see later section on chunking).
- In developmentally appropriate terms, teach about WM, how it works, and how students can improve their WM performance.
- Regularly emphasize the efficacy of WM strategies to the students, using student data as evidence.
- Reinforce students for applying strategies and for self-managing cognitive load.
- Incorporate memory-enhancing instructional practices into all of their instruction.
- Structure content in a manner that facilitates strategy use. For example, providing highly structured materials encourages children to group them categorically.
- Allow time for students to practice WM exercises (see Chapter 7).

Incorporating all of the foregoing practices into an already crowded curriculum may be challenging. Teachers are already very busy. However, adopting just a few of these recommendations could have a significant impact on student learning. For instance, first graders taught by "mnemonic-focused" teachers spend significantly more time independently using memory strategies than first graders in nonmnemonic-based classrooms (Ornstein, Grammer, & Coffman, 2010). Several studies (e.g., Carney et al., 1993) have confirmed that mnemonic-based instruction is more effective than traditional instructional methods.

METAMEMORY INSTRUCTION

Metamemory instruction should be an integral component of the mnemonic classroom. The major components of metamemory instruction are: teaching students about human memory functions; increasing students' self-awareness of their individual memory strengths and weaknesses; helping students understand why specific practices and strategies work; and demonstrating the efficacy of memory practices, exercises, and strategies (Dehn, 2010, 2011). Without metamemory instruction, students are less likely to maintain and generalize the memory-enhancing practices and strategies they are taught. Students who receive metamemory instruction continue to independently use effective memory strategies and are more successful academically (Ornstein et al., 2010). Also, metamemory instruction promotes further metamemory development in students. Students with more advanced metamemory development are more strategic in their learning and study habits.

> **DON'T FORGET**
>
> Metamemory refers to knowledge about human memory functions, an individual's self-awareness of memory strengths and weaknesses, conscious control of memory, and knowledge and regulation of memory strategies.

Metamemory instruction begins with teaching how memory works in everyone. Key principles to impart to students are:

- Forgetting is normal. Having memory problems does not mean the learner is stupid. Even smart children and adults forget.
- People have two main kinds of memory: verbal memory and visual-spatial memory.
- Some information is easier to remember than other information, especially information about something the learner knows well.
- There are three memory systems—short-term, working, and long-term. They all involve taking in information, storing it for a period of time, and then recalling it.

- Information is stored in short-term and WM for only a few seconds. After this short interval, any information recalled is probably being retrieved from long-term memory.
- The WM storage interval can be extended by repeating information over and over.
- Everyone has a limited WM.
- WM is used whenever a person must think and remember at the same time, such as when a person is reading, writing, doing math, or completing an assignment.
- When WM is weak, an individual is likely to forget what he was doing and will have to start over, which explains why such individuals take longer to complete multistep tasks.
- People are more likely to forget things when their WM gets overloaded.
- Individuals can do things that will make their memory stronger.

Metamemory instruction continues with helping children understand their own memory strengths and weaknesses, such as recognizing that their visual-spatial WM is much stronger than their verbal. Without individual assessment results on students, a classroom teacher may be limited to having students reflect on their within-child differences. For example, a teacher might ask, "Which do you remember better—things you see or information you hear?"

As students learn memory strategies, the final component of metamemory instruction is necessary. Students should be taught when, where, why, and how to use a strategy. This type of knowledge, referred to as "conditional knowledge," is a form of metamemory. Conditional knowledge includes knowing how to use a strategy in different situations, knowing why a strategy works from a memory perspective, and knowing the personal efficacy of a strategy. The greater the conditional metamemory knowledge, the more likely a learner will maintain and generalize a strategy (O'Sullivan & Pressley, 1984). When children and adolescents understand the conditional factors and the usefulness of a memory strategy, their motivation to continue using the strategy will be increased. Consequently, conditional knowledge instruction should be embedded in strategy training and reiterated regularly.

INSTRUCTION THAT REDUCES COGNITIVE LOAD

Cognitive processing utilizes WM resources. When cognitive processing occurs, the amount of information that can be retained in the short-term storage component of WM is reduced. The cognitive processing portion of WM is referred to as "cognitive load" (see Chapter 4 for more details). The greater the

DON'T FORGET
....
When a learner experiences high cognitive load, tasks become more difficult to complete and less information is encoded into LTM, resulting in reduced learning.

cognitive load, the less information can be maintained in WM, resulting in less information being encoded into LTM. Thus, academic learning decreases as the load on WM increases (Paas, Renkl, & Sweller, 2004). Also, completing assignments efficiently becomes more challenging as cognitive load increases.

The structure, materials, and instructional practices in the typical classroom easily create high cognitive load and overwhelm most students' WM capacity many times each day. For learners with WM deficiencies, the continual loss of information before it can be processed or stored permanently must be very frustrating. Cognitive load is created by the nature of the material, the manner in which the material is presented, and the learner's own internal processes. For example, excessive cognitive load occurs when material is complex, when the instruction is disorganized, and when the learner is distracted by irrelevant thoughts.

Instructors can help students with WM difficulties by reducing cognitive load in the classroom (T. de Jong, 2010). Minimizing processing demands in the learning environment will help impaired students overcome the WM deficits that are impacting their learning and performance (J. Elliott, Gathercole, Alloway, Holmes, & Kirkwood, 2010).

Here are methods for minimizing the load arising from the nature of the content and materials:

- Material should be divided up into small units and presented one unit at a time. Smaller units of information require less integration and relational processing, and there also is less information to maintain while processing. Additional units of information should be added gradually so that there is time to process each piece of information before going on to the next.
- Complex material needs to be simplified so that it is at the learner's level.
- Material should be sequenced from simple to complex.
- When the subject matter is new, background knowledge needs to be provided first, or the method of elaboration needs to be applied (see later section on elaboration).
- Materials should be well organized. Requiring the learner to integrate disorganized materials will add significantly to cognitive load. For example, presenting the information on multiple sheets of paper increases processing

demands because the learner must combine several sources of information (Jang et al., 2011).

- The information to be processed and the information to be recalled at a later time should be the same. An example of inconsistency would be requiring a learner to locate each capital on a map during the lesson, but then later requiring the learner to match the names of states and capitals.
- Worked examples or partially completed examples should be provided. Having examples available reduces the need to hold several elements in temporary storage.
- All the required information should be presented in an integrated manner. If multiple sources of information must be used during a self-study task, they should be arranged in a side-by-side fashion (Jang et al., 2011).
- Arithmetic problems should be presented vertically, rather than horizontally (Alloway, 2011).
- Materials should allow the student to focus on processing without the need to maintain task-relevant information. Keeping lists of information or procedural steps in view reduces load. Written reminders of problem-solving steps reduce problem-solving search and evaluation strategies that impose a heavy cognitive load. Other examples include number lines and a list of frequently misspelled words (Barrouillet, Portrat, & Camos, 2011).
- Students should be taught to ask for help when it is too difficult to process and retain information simultaneously.

The following teacher behaviors and instructional variables also reduce cognitive load:

- Oral instruction should be simple and concise with consistent wording. This allows the learner to focus on the required processing.
- Lessons should be brief. Lengthy lessons create more proactive and retroactive interference as more and more information is added. The need to inhibit interference from too much information being presented adds to cognitive load.
- Enough time should be allowed for both processing and maintenance of information. The need to switch between processing and rehearsal adds to the time it takes to complete a task.
- Only one processing task should be required at a time. For example, listening and copying notes at the same time involve two processes. WM-impaired students should never be required to multitask.
- A quiet learning environment is important for memory (Gathercole & Baddeley, 1993). The need to inhibit interference from noise and distractions increases processing load.

- The use of direct instruction procedures may be necessary. Direct instruction has built-in repetition so that the learner can focus more on processing and less on maintenance (see later section on direct instruction).
- Nonessential, irrelevant, or confusing information should not be mentioned. All information and required processing should be germane to the task or the material to be learned.
- Procedural steps should not be presented until they are actually needed.
- Material should be presented both verbally and visually. This may reduce processing challenges in students with a relative weakness in one modality (T. de Jong, 2010).
- Students should be guided through schema construction and modification. Such guidance might include helping the student to classify, interpret, exemplify, differentiate, and infer (T. de Jong, 2010).

The cognitive load caused by the learner's cognitive abilities and internal processing may be difficult for instructors to influence. However, teachers should be aware of these variables so that they can talk with students about how to cope with and control them. Intrinsic variables that influence the extent of cognitive load include:

- The ability to inhibit internally generated irrelevant thoughts.
- The learner's levels of mastery, expertise, and prior knowledge. The less developed these are, the greater the amount of processing required.
- Other cognitive factors related to WM performance, such as the learner's processing speed and fluid reasoning ability. Slow processing speed will increase cognitive load and decrease retention because rehearsal cannot occur frequently enough.
- The use and automaticity of memory strategies, such as chunking. Strategies that are mastered and automated can function effectively without creating additional cognitive load.
- The level of metamemory development (Dehn, 2010). Older learners with advanced understanding of memory functions, cognitive load, and their personal memory weaknesses can make informed decisions and selections to regulate the type and amount of processing they engage in during learning and WM tasks.

DON'T FORGET

Learners can add to their own cognitive load, especially when their general executive functioning is delayed. For example, poor inhibition of distracting thoughts adds to cognitive load.

Isolated application of any of the procedures just recommended should be helpful, but the more that are applied, the greater the reduction in cognitive load. In general, learners will have difficulty maintaining information in the short-term and encoding it into long-term memory whenever the learning task requires them to engage in very attention-demanding processing activity. Students with impaired WM can learn effectively if they have ample exposure to material while demands on WM are minimal.

Some students with WM deficits may require more than methods that minimize cognitive load. They may need additional, individualized interventions and accommodations that support WM and allow them to learn and perform better. These include: frequent repetition, reteaching, and review; scaffolding during the initial stages of learning when cognitive load is higher; and help with monitoring the quality of their work. Additional helpful classroom practices include advance organizers, helping students complete challenging activities, teaching WM strategies, and structuring information in a manner that encourages and supports the use of memory strategies.

ACCOMMODATIONS AND MODIFICATIONS FOR SPECIFIC ACADEMIC SUBJECTS

Individuals with deficiencies in WM will be more sensitive to elevated cognitive load than individuals with normal WM. What might be a manageable cognitive load for most students may significantly impair learning and performance in a student with a WM impairment. Consequently, students with WM deficits may need more accommodations and modifications than those recommended in the previous section. Regardless of whether such students have mastered basic skills, they may still need the subject-specific procedures recommended in this section.

Modifications for Written Expression

Transforming ideas into written expression always creates significant cognitive load, even after basic writing skills have been mastered. The high cognitive load results from the several steps involved in written expression. These steps include brainstorming ideas, organizing thoughts, planning how to communicate ideas, constructing sentences, recalling grammar rules, and monitoring the writing. At the same time, there is a lot of information to maintain in short-term storage, especially the words and sentences that the writer wants to put on paper. In general, written expression places high demands on the executive WM processes of updating, inhibiting, and switching.

Signs of too much cognitive load during the act of writing include omitting words, repeating words, not being able to start writing, not detecting errors, and forgetting what was going to be said. In extreme cases, the student may be unable to independently transfer ideas to words on paper or onto the word processing screen. Specific recommendations for written expression assistance include:

- Shorten the writing assignment.
- Allow shorter sentences.
- Disregard basic skills errors during the initial stages of writing.
- Allow revisions after feedback is provided.
- Allow abbreviations and symbols in the first draft.
- Separate the planning from the writing by having the student do an outline or graphic organizer before beginning to write.

In extreme cases, a teacher, parent, aide, or peer may have to serve as either the writer's scribe or the writer's short-term storage. When a scribe does the writing for the student, the steps are:

1. Have the writer express the idea orally.
2. Help the writer convert the idea into an oral sentence.
3. Direct the writer to keep repeating the oral sentence.
4. The scribe writes the sentence the learner is expressing orally.
5. The scribe reads the written sentence back to the learner.

The alternative is for the assistant to serve as short-term storage as the learner writes. These steps are:

1. The learner expresses the sentence orally.
2. The assistant maintains the sentence by subvocally rehearsing it.
3. The assistant states the sentence a word or phrase at a time as the learner writes.

If neither of the foregoing methods works well, then a closure approach might be helpful. In such instances, the assistant writes the sentence the learner has expressed orally, but omits some words that the learner must complete.

In order to achieve independence at converting oral expression to written expression, the writer should be taught to use the strategy of switching between rehearsal and the process of writing. Here are the steps:

1. The student repeats the sentence orally a few times before beginning to write.
2. The student writes a word or phrase that does not take more than a few seconds.
3. The student pauses to repeat the sentence a couple more times, this time omitting the part that has been written.
4. Steps 2 and 3 are repeated as necessary until the written sentence is complete.

Revising is another aspect of the writing process that can be challenging for students who cannot tolerate a high cognitive load. The main approach to supporting such students is to break the revising process into small, discrete steps. The result is that the student checks the written product several times, each time checking for only one of these:

- Capitalization
- Punctuation
- Spacing between letters and words
- Upper and lower case lettering
- Omitted words
- Repeated words
- Spelling
- Grammar
- Whether the sentence makes sense
- Whether the sentence conveys the intended message

Modifications for Taking Notes

Listening to instruction while copying or taking notes presents challenges very similar to written expression. Students with limited WM capacity find note taking to be very difficult. Appropriate accommodations include:

- Providing a note-taker.
- Providing a copy of the notes.
- Providing a template or partially completed notes.
- Teaching the student to use abbreviations.
- Teaching the student to use codes or symbols for frequently repeated words.
- Teaching the student to use some basic shorthand.
- Allowing the student to record the lesson and listen to it later.

Modifications for Mathematics

Mathematics calculation and problem solving can also place high demands on WM, especially when arithmetic facts have not been mastered. Signs of too much cognitive load during mathematics performance include finger counting, losing one's place while counting, computation errors when facts are known, ignoring the signs, inability to do mental arithmetic, omitting calculation steps, and not recognizing the procedures required for a story problem.

Methods for reducing cognitive load include allowing calculators, allowing facts tables, providing a list of step-by-step procedures, allowing extended time on math tests, teaching the student to use a number line, and helping the learner identify story problem words that signify the type of procedure involved.

Modifications for Basic Reading Skills

Until reading fluency and decoding automaticity are attained, WM-deficient readers will benefit from support with processing and storage. Support is especially needed for sounding out phonemes and during blending. When the student does not recognize the word and does not attempt the word, saying the first phoneme of the word may serve as a prompt. When students forget some of the sounded-out phonemes when reaching the blending stage, the assistant should slowly say the phonemes or syllables, and then require the reader to blend them together. When the blended word is not said fluently or smoothly, the reader should be directed to say the word smoothly.

Modifications for Reading Comprehension

Reading comprehension is another task that places high demands on WM processes and storage. Suggestions for WM support for reading comprehension include:

- Prior to reading, requiring the student to preview the selection so that related prior knowledge is activated.
- During oral reading, allowing the reader to substitute words that are consistent with the meaning.
- Requiring the reader to reread sentences that were not read fluently.
- Reading the selection to the student so that the student can focus on comprehending.
- Having the student pause after each sentence or paragraph and reflect on its meaning.

GENERAL ACCOMMODATIONS

In addition to the subject-specific modifications recommended in the previous sections, there are general accommodations for WM deficits. These include:

- Extended testing time on all types of tests.
- Presenting information visually, as well as verbally.
- Repeating information verbatim.
- Providing cues and prompts.
- Repeating information in a simplified manner.

- Providing written checklists to guide task completion.
- Providing lists of step-by-step procedures or directions.
- Requiring the student to complete only one task at a time.
- Slowing down instruction so the student has time to process and rehearse the information.
- Providing preferential seating to reduce distraction.

INSTRUCTIONAL PRACTICES THAT SUPPORT WORKING MEMORY

In addition to the specific instructional practices and modifications discussed earlier, there are some effective teaching practices that can support and enhance WM. These are familiar practices that are commonly applied in classrooms. Their consistent application supports the normal WM limitations of most learners, not just those with WM deficits.

Visually Oriented Instruction

The old adage that "one picture is worth a thousand words" applies well to students with verbal WM weaknesses. The implication is that a picture or visual image may contain much more information than a few pieces of verbal information. When such a picture or image can be maintained in short-term storage, it may allow the learner to process and encode into LTM more information than would be possible with verbal information only.

When classroom instruction and presentations are primarily verbal, the visual-spatial dimension of WM may not be fully engaged, thereby limiting the effectiveness of WM functioning. When visual input is limited, the full storage and processing capabilities of WM are being underutilized. Although processing and short-term storage compete for WM resources, phonological and visual-spatial storage apparently do not. That is, the amount of content being stored in one component should not reduce the amount that can be held in the other (Baddeley, 1986). From a cognitive load perspective, fully utilizing both types of storage may increase the total amount of information that can be maintained during processing (Barrouillet et al., 2011).

Furthermore, most students with learning problems have stronger visual-spatial abilities than verbal abilities, and this strength usually carries over to WM and LTM. When classroom instruction and presentations are primarily verbal, these students are not able to fully utilize their WM strength. Consequently, instructors should make an effort to present material in a visual format along with verbalization (Cook, 1989).

The long-term memory benefits of presenting information in both a visual and verbal mode have been known for decades, if not longer. For instance, Pavio and Csapo (1969) demonstrated that concepts presented once in verbal form and once in visual form were remembered better than concepts presented twice in one mode or the other.

Mnemonic-oriented teachers do not need to actually display pictures of everything being presented verbally. When learners create images of verbal information in their minds, it may be just as beneficial, if not more so, than viewing a visual provided by a teacher. This type of visualization is not something that all students automatically do. Thus, students may need to be taught a visualization strategy (see section later in this chapter). Once students are familiar with this strategy, teachers need only to prompt and encourage them to visualize the verbal information they are receiving, as well as allow them time to create the internal visual images.

Direct Instruction

Direct instruction refers to a structured curriculum that incorporates effective teaching techniques in a scripted fashion. Direct instruction procedures include: well-sequenced and focused lessons; modeling and shaping of correct responses; reinforcement of appropriate responses; corrective feedback; continuous assessment of performance; lots of repetition; frequent review of material; and an emphasis on mastery at each step in the learning process (Gersten, 1985; Swanson, 1999). Direct instruction methods have been embedded in many effective curricula, and the general principles of direct instruction can be applied to the teaching of nearly every academic skill and subject.

The primary reason for direct instruction's documented success is that it successfully addresses the cognitive load limitations of challenged learners (Rosenshine & Stevens, 1986). Direct instruction characteristics that reduce cognitive load include frequent repetition of new material and practice until a high level of mastery is reached.

DON'T FORGET

Most teaching practices identified as *effective* or as *direct instruction* support the storage and capacity limitations of WM by minimizing the demands and cognitive load placed on WM.

Direct instruction has proven to be an extremely effective teaching approach, especially with children who need it most: younger children, slow learners, at-risk children, and those with learning disabilities (Gersten & Keating, 1987). In a meta-analysis of 25 studies comparing different instruction methods (White, 1988), direct instruction, with a very significant effect size of .84, emerged as the most effective instructional method for students in special education. Consequently, teachers who wish to support and enhance WM performance should adopt direct instruction approaches and try to incorporate them into their instruction, especially basic skills instruction.

Repetition and Review

A very natural, common, and immediate way of supporting WM is to simply repeat information and keep repeating it until the recipient of the information has completed processing it. Although teachers are constantly repeating information for the benefit of all students, the amount of repetition required by some WM-impaired students may be more than teachers can deliver individually. Some solutions to this instructional challenge are to provide these students with written directions, have peers repeat information for them, and teach these students to use basic strategies such as rehearsal (see section later in this chapter).

In addition to immediate and frequent repetition during the course of a lesson, periodic review will give students another opportunity to encode new information. It is a well-established fact that periodic review increases long-term retention of new learning (Bahrick, 2000). Reviews that occur with longer and longer intervals between them are the most effective (Karpicke & Roediger, 2007). For students with WM and LTM deficits an ideal review schedule might be: (a) at the end of the lesson; (b) the next day; (c) after a delay of 2 or 3 days; (d) after another delay of a week; and (e) after 2 weeks have passed since the last review.

Mastery and Automaticity

The acquisition of mastery and automaticity enhances WM performance, primarily because automaticity reduces cognitive load. A task or procedure is said to be "automated" when it is overlearned or mastered to the point where it can be performed with little, if any, conscious, cognitive effort. A prime example is the acquisition of reading fluency. A fluent reader has automated word decoding processes that "free up" WM capacity for processing and for retaining more information, leading to better reading comprehension (Garcia-Madruga, 2013).

Any curriculum, instruction, or intervention that improves student mastery of basic skills increases automaticity, and automaticity reduces load on WM, thereby allowing WM to operate more efficiently (D. Brown & Hulme, 1996). Automaticity speeds up processing, reduces cognitive load, and increases retention of information because the processing involved requires little attention. Also, automaticity increases the speed of task completion. More information can be processed and retained when it is processed quickly. With automaticity, those with WM deficits can focus on critical, higher-level processing. Consequently, a mnemonic-oriented teacher is one who strives to develop basic skills mastery and automaticity in WM-deficient students.

Elaboration

Elaboration is another instructional method that enhances the learning of students with WM and LTM deficits. From a memory perspective, elaboration is the conscious, explicit linking of new information with related prior knowledge (Gagne, Yekovich, & Yekovich 1993). Elaboration occurs when a learner brings associated or related knowledge from long-term memory into WM and constructs a verbal or visual memory link between the prior knowledge and the information to be learned (Ritchie & Karge, 1996). The LTM outcome of this process is that more associations are made between new information and related knowledge. The WM outcome of teacher-provided elaboration is a reduction in the cognitive load that the elaboration process would create in the learner.

> **DON'T FORGET**
> ....
> Teacher-provided elaboration benefits WM-impaired learners because self-elaboration can create a heavy cognitive load.

Teachers can elaborate for learners or learners can elaborate on their own. With WM-impaired students, teacher-provided elaboration is recommended because self-elaboration can impose a heavy cognitive load that will interfere with short-term retention and LTM encoding. Self-elaboration occurs whenever a person thinks about how a specific piece of information is connected with information already stored in long-term memory (Ritchie & Karge, 1996). Thinking about why a penguin is a bird even though it doesn't fly is an example of self-elaboration.

Teachers can begin the elaboration process for students by helping them activate relevant schema. A structured manner of doing this is to use advance organizers. Advance organizers activate relevant knowledge prior to presentation of the new material; they also provide a structure for adding new information. Advance organizers include such things as metaphors, analogies, diagrams, models, and idea maps. Their effectiveness as a teaching strategy is well documented in educational research.

Once relevant information has been activated through advance organizers, elaboration procedures include identifying and emphasizing main ideas, providing examples that illustrate connections between ideas, directly relating the new material to prior knowledge, and drawing parallels to the students' own lives. Paraphrasing, summarizing, drawing inferences, semantic mapping, and generating questions are also elaborative processes (Ritchie & Karge, 1996). In general, teachers elaborate whenever they directly talk about the connections between two pieces of information. When doing so, elaborations should be as precise as possible (Pressley, Johnson, & Symons, 1987); vague or general elaborations are less effective. An example of a precise elaboration is stating that a penguin is a bird because it lays eggs, has feathers, and has wings. Finally, explaining "why" new information makes sense is an effective form of elaboration (Scruggs, Mastropieri, & Sullivan, 1994). For example, a teacher might say that it makes sense that a penguin is a bird because it has wings.

TEACHING WORKING MEMORY STRATEGIES

Another way to enhance WM performance in the classroom is to teach students WM strategies. The purpose of teaching strategies for STM and WM is not to reduce cognitive load or to increase WM capacity but rather to improve WM performance through effective utilization of existing WM abilities. Many children begin using

> **DON'T FORGET**
> ....
> The purpose of WM strategies is not to decrease cognitive load or increase WM capacity. Rather, the purpose is to make effective use of existing WM abilities.

simple memory strategies around 5 years of age or when they begin school. However, some children do not acquire strategies independently, and those who do often fail to use strategies consistently or in an effective manner. Consequently, explicit teaching of WM strategies to individuals or groups will produce a significant improvement in WM performance (St. Clair-Thompson, Stevens, Hunt, & Bolder, 2010). Students with low WM spans will benefit the most from training in WM strategies, even though they are slower to learn the strategies than trainees with high WM spans (Turley-Ames & Whitfield, 2003).

Strategy Training Guidelines

WM strategy training will be most effective when strategy training procedures are followed with integrity. The outcomes will be further enhanced when these general strategy guidelines are applied:

- Training sessions should be brief (less than 60 minutes) and focused on no more than three strategies.

- Training and practice sessions should be conducted at least twice weekly over a period of at least six weeks.
- Metamemory information (see section on metamemory) should be included in the lessons. For example, the students should be informed about the purpose and rationale for the strategy, including when, where, why, and how to use the strategy. Without this knowledge, the student will have difficulty selecting the most appropriate strategy for the task at hand.
- When introducing a strategy, all steps and components of the strategy should be modeled while thinking aloud. It is best to play a peer or coping model who sometimes struggles or makes errors, rather than an expert model.
- Each step in the strategy procedures should be explained and demonstrated in detail, with special attention paid to aspects of strategy use that are the most challenging.
- There should be plenty of relevant practice, beginning with overt, orally expressed practice and ending with practice that encourages internalization.
- Practice should continue until the strategy is overlearned and automatized.
- Immediate corrective feedback should be provided whenever the strategy is not conducted correctly.
- When strategies have multiple steps, it is helpful to give students nonverbal cuing.
- Students should receive positive reinforcement for using a new strategy.
- Improved performance should be attributed to strategy use. Students should also be provided with data that illustrates the personal efficacy of strategy use.
- Generalization should be encouraged by discussing applications of the strategy and practicing the strategy with different materials and under different situations.
- Practice should continue until the strategy is automatic or semi-automatic.

CAUTION

Learning and using a new strategy will put increased demands on WM, resulting in even less capacity left over for storage. This is a particular concern for individuals who have impaired WM capacity. In such instances, simple strategies should be taught first, and complex strategies should be taught and practiced step-by-step.

Rehearsal

Self-repetition of information is known as rehearsal (Gathercole, 1999). Although it can be subvocal and automatic, it is primarily vocal and effortful

(Cowan, 2005). For most individuals, it is the first memory strategy they acquire and the one they will use the most throughout life. The main purpose of rehearsal is to maintain information in STM and WM storage long enough to complete a process or obtain a goal that depends on that information, such as maintaining a phone number long enough to complete entering the digits on a keypad.

Rehearsal also maintains information long enough for it to be encoded into LTM, and rehearsal provides multiple opportunities for the information to be encoded. Thus, rehearsal is both a WM and an LTM strategy. For WM, rehearsal is extremely effective (Turley-Ames & Whitfield, 2003). For LTM, it is fundamental, but less effective than more elaborate strategies.

Baddeley (1986) views rehearsal as an integral component of short-term storage. From a cognitive load perspective, rehearsal that is conscious and requires some effort to maintain the sequential repetition does add to cognitive load. However, older children and adults can rehearse semiautomatically without the need to focus attention on the process, resulting in only minimal cognitive load (Cowan, 2005). Thus, having young children use and practice rehearsal until it becomes fairly automated will enhance its effectiveness. However, because of the simplicity of rehearsal, it will create less cognitive load than more complex strategies, even when the rehearsal lacks automaticity.

Most children begin using simple rehearsal strategies around age 5, but consistent application of verbal rehearsal strategies may not occur until age 10 (Gill, Klecan-Aker, Roberts, & Fredenburg, 2003). Students with learning disabilities often fail to develop rehearsal strategies or utilize them effectively. The development of subvocal rehearsal strategies is thought to be at least partially responsible for increased verbal WM span as children develop (Minear & Shah, 2006). Increased use of rehearsal corresponds with increases in recall from both WM and LTM, resulting in greater learning (Turley-Ames & Whitfield, 2003). Research on the effectiveness of classroom-wide rehearsal training has reported significant gains when the strategy is taught to first graders. Therefore, the ideal training opportunity for rehearsal may be when students are in first grade.

Review of Research on Rehearsal Training. Numerous studies have found explicit rehearsal training to significantly improve STM span, as well as the WM performance of children, with and without disabilities (Comblain, 1994; Conners, Rosenquist, & Taylor, 2001; Klingberg, Forssberg, & Westerberg, 2002; Minear & Shah, 2006). Research on the effectiveness of classroom rehearsal training has also discovered that rehearsal training leads to improved academic achievement (Comblain, 1994; Loomes, Rasmussen, & Pei, 2008).

Teaching rehearsal strategies may be particularly beneficial for students with learning or intellectual disabilities. Hulme and Mackenzie (1992) reviewed research that improved STM recall in subjects with moderate learning difficulties to the same level as that of age-matched normal control subjects. Other inquiries have reported that rehearsal training can improve WM in individuals with Down syndrome (Conners et al., 2001).

Normally developing students may also benefit from rehearsal training. For instance, Ornstein, Naus, and Stone (1977) found that second graders, who were already rehearsing one or two items together, were able to learn to rehearse more items together, and when they did, their recall became similar to that of sixth graders. Adults with low WM spans have also shown improvement after training in simple rote rehearsal strategies (McNamara & Scott, 2001; Turley-Ames & Whitfield, 2003). Many other investigations (reviewed in Ornstein et al., 1977) have demonstrated that children and adults can improve short-term verbal memory span by learning more active and effective rehearsal strategies. Moreover, there is evidence of improvement in untrained memory activities (Olesen, Westerberg, & Klingberg, 2004) and evidence for the maintenance and durability of rehearsal training, especially when extensive practice and overlearning are provided during the initial training phase (Broadley, MacDonald, & Buckley, 1994).

Serial Rehearsal Training Procedures. Basic rehearsal training is easily accomplished classroom-wide, in small groups or one-on-one. The key is to teach students to repeat sequences of words aloud. For practice, monosyllabic words should be used. Different words should be used with each practice round so that the words do not become memorized. Words that rhyme should not be presented within the same lists. Letters and digits may be used in lieu of words. For advanced training, nonwords should be used. The advantage to nonwords is that they place higher demands on short-term maintenance because the words don't exist in the learner's LTM.

Students may benefit from rehearsal training sessions of only 10 minutes per day over a period of 10 days, but daily training over a period of several weeks may produce better long-term change. As training progresses, the difficulty level can be adjusted by increasing the number of words (the span). With young children, training should begin with a span of two words. When the majority of the group or the child is easily handling two words, the span should be increased to three, and so on. Practice should continue until the child, or the majority of the group, appears capable of rehearsing semiautomatically. That is, the child appears to be rehearsing without needing to concentrate on the process. The training details ahead are also in the online resources.

The training steps for basic, serial rehearsal are as follows:

1. Model the procedure by repeating a short list of words (equal to the length of the student's memory span) five times in a row.

2. When presenting the items to students, say them at the rate of one per second.
3. Have the student(s) repeat the items aloud five times in sequence.
4. Keep practicing Steps 2 and 3 for at least 5 minutes, using different words in each span presented.
5. After the students can rehearse fluently and maintain the items in sequence, they should be directed to whisper the repetitions.
6. After the whispering stage, they should be directed to say the span items silently to themselves.
7. Periodically, check on their rehearsal by requiring aloud and whispered repetition.
8. Reinforce students for their effort and following the procedure correctly. Let them know that forgetting items during rehearsal or mixing up the sequence is normal when the spans become challenging.

Some students, usually those with limited WM spans, will have difficulty maintaining the sequence of items during rehearsal. These students should be trained individually or in small groups. Follow the same procedures as mentioned, but shorten the spans and have the student practice repeating the span faster and faster. Do not use nonwords with these students. To encourage these students, give them partial credit for recalling all of the items, even when the items are out of sequence.

Cumulative Rehearsal Training Procedures. Cumulative rehearsal is more challenging than simple serial rehearsal, but it is an important skill to develop because it involves updating. Cumulative rehearsal involves adding new items to the rehearsed span as the additional items become available. The general procedures are the same as serial rehearsal training, with these unique steps:

1. Begin with one item.
2. After the students say the item three times, say the second item on the list but not the original item.
3. The students should then add the new item to the span and say both items in sequence three times.
4. Then say the next item, and require the students to add the item to the previous two and rehearse all three items in sequence.
5. Continue Steps 3 and 4 until the students' span limit is reached.
6. When the students successfully demonstrate the strategy, vary the number of repetitions between presentations of additional items by directing the students to keep repeating the current list until they hear the next item presented.

An important training option is to teach students to use cumulative rehearsal in reverse. This strategy is especially applicable to completing multistep directions. For instance, when students must complete a simple art activity that involves the sequence of drawing, folding, cutting, and pasting, they should begin by rehearsing all the steps: "draw, fold, cut, paste." They should then keep repeating the sequence periodically as they work. After the first step is completed, they should update the sequence by dropping "draw" and continuing to rehearse, "fold, cut, paste." After each step is completed, the rehearsal list should be shortened to the remaining items.

Semantic Rehearsal. When the purpose of rehearsal is to support encoding into LTM (learning), then a more complex form of rehearsal is advised. The degree of learning and subsequent recall from LTM depends on the manner in which the information is processed in WM (Baddeley, 2006). According to the levels-of-processing theory advocated by Craig and Lockhart (1972), deeper processing of the information leads to better long-term retention than superficial processing, such as rote repetition. Variations of rehearsal that lend themselves to deeper processing have been shown to be very effective. One of these variations is semantic rehearsal. The steps involved are as follows:

1. Provide students with a list of words that can be grouped into semantic categories. With children ages 8-14, a list of about 12 words that can be clustered into three or four categories is recommended. For older students, a list of 16-20 words that can be clustered in four or five categories is appropriate.
2. Have the students group the words by categories. Provide assistance as needed.
3. Have the students rehearse each group of items separately, using the name of the category as the first item in the list.
4. After all the groups of items have been rehearsed, have the students recall the items, one group at time.
5. After an appropriate long-term recall interval, such as 30 minutes, have the students recall as many items as they can. Attribute their recall to the use of the strategy.

Chunking

Chunking refers to the pairing, clustering, or grouping of discrete items into larger units that are processed and remembered as a whole. Chunking increases the amount of information that can be held and processed in WM because WM is processing and retaining chunks, instead of discrete, smaller units. For example, for a beginning reader, each phoneme is a WM unit or chunk. As automatic blending, word recognition, and fluency increase, words become the chunks the young reader maintains in WM.

Like subvocal rehearsal, most children acquire basic chunking strategies without any specific training. The development of chunking may be a prerequisite for the formation of complex representations and schemas in LTM. During WM processing, preexisting chunks, which usually consist of associations (Cowan, 2005), are retrieved from LTM. Once in WM, chunks may be rapidly amended or enlarged as new information is considered. In addition to leading to more efficient encoding and retrieval, the development of chunking is crucial for efficient WM functioning.

Teaching young children to use a basic chunking strategy has been found to improve WM performance (Parente & Herrmann, 1996). Chunking is taught by requiring students to group items into larger units. Training often has students pair digits. For example, the digits "4," "6," "3," and "8" could be paired and recalled as "46" and "38." Memorizing the spelling of words by using syllables as chunks provides another opportunity to apply this type of training.

To train students to use a basic chunking strategy, follow these steps:

1. Begin with digits. Require the students to pair digits in a series, such as chunking "5, 1, 6, 9" into "51 (fifty-one), 69 (sixty-nine)."
2. After Step 1 is mastered, practice chunking three digits into a single number—for example, 2, 7, 6 becomes 276 (two hundred seventy-six).
3. Apply chunking to spelling. For example, the letters in "forget" could be chunked as "f, o, r" and "g, e, t."
4. Continuing training with words. For example, the words "cat, horse, dog, cow" could be paired as "cat-horse" and "dog-cow."
5. Once chunking is mastered, require the students to combine chunking and rehearsal. That is, they should first chunk the information. Then they should rehearse it in chunks.

Teaching the Strategies of Switching and Updating

Switching and updating are critical executive WM functions that allow individuals to hold and process more information. Thus, students should be taught switching and updating in conjunction with rehearsal. Switching involves going back and forth between rehearsing and processing. For example, an individual may repeatedly pause to rehearse the words he is trying to put into writing. Updating involves constantly changing the set of information being retained and processed. For example, people are constantly updating to keep up with the flow of a conversation.

The working memory exercise known as "*n*-back" is an excellent exercise for simultaneously practicing switching and updating (see Chapter 7 for details on this exercise). However, individuals may have difficulty generalizing unless the practice is applied directly to relevant tasks. For instance, imagine a young student who must complete a multistep art project that involves several sequential steps, such as "draw, fold, cut, staple, paste." While completing these steps the student should be required to pause every few seconds to repeat the sequence "draw, fold, cut, staple, paste." Updating practice can also be applied to this task by having the student drop each step from the rehearsal list as that step is completed.

> # DON'T FORGET
> ....
> Switching back and forth between processing and rehearsing is an effective strategy for maintaining information in short-term storage.

Students who are 7 years of age and older can be taught the strategy of switching when they need to maintain information and process at the same time. Switching includes rehearsal, especially cumulative rehearsal (see the previous section on rehearsal training). Thus, rehearsal training should be completed before teaching students to switch. Some of the WM exercises in Chapter 7 can be used to practice switching. For example, a classroom teacher might teach the whole class to switch by using the arithmetic flash cards exercise. Specifically, students must rehearse the answers from multiple flash cards in between doing the calculation for each card.

Students learn best under low cognitive load conditions, but when cognitive load cannot be reduced, switching is a strategy that can help a learner cope with a high cognitive load while retaining important information. To apply switching in any situation, an individual would switch back and forth between the processing task and rehearsing the information that needs to be retained. For example, when converting an oral sentence into a written one, the writer might first state the sentence, then write a few words of it, then repeat the sentence again, then write a few more words, then repeat the sentence again, and so on until the written sentence is complete. Without switching, information that needs to be maintained in short-term storage is usually lost before the processing task is completed. Successful switching can be challenging for young children (Liefooghe et al., 2008) and individuals with WM impairments. Consequently, modifications that reduce cognitive load are very important.

Teaching Visualization Strategies

Visual imagery involves transforming verbal content into visual information. The method is rather simple and straightforward. Essentially, individuals picture or imagine verbal information. For example, when trying to retain a list of words the individual should picture each word. Another example would be consciously making an effort to picture material that is being read. This type of visualization is distinct from visual mnemonics, which involve following structured techniques that pair or associate information, sometimes in ways that have no logical connection. Visual mnemonics primarily benefit LTM (Dehn, 2010). In fact, the cognitive load they create may actually reduce the amount of content that can be maintained in WM.

As discussed earlier in this chapter, visualizing, or recoding verbal information into visual information, more fully utilizes WM capacity. Visualization is especially beneficial with students who have language disorders or deficits in verbal WM (Clark & Klecan-Aker, 1992). Such students tend to possess strong visuospatial WM that can capitalize on imagery. Visual imagery may be particularly valuable in mathematics (McLean & Hitch, 1999).

When teaching students this strategy, it is important to first demonstrate the power of imagery. First, have students recall a list of words after they use rehearsal to learn them. Then give students a comparable list of words and direct them to form a visual image of each object or action instead of rehearsing it. When the recall of the two methods is compared, the vast majority of students will recall significantly more words with the visualization method.

When training visualization, begin with concrete images, as they are easier to recall than abstract images. For example, use a list of concrete words and have the learners close their eyes and form a mental image of what the item looks like. Remind students to use this approach whenever the opportunity presents itself, such as when they are reading for comprehension and recall. When a student is directed to visualize while reading, stop the student frequently and have the student describe the images he has created.

Dual Encoding

Visualization can be used without any verbal rehearsal. However, simultaneously rehearsing and visualizing can be more effective than either strategy alone. This combination is known as dual encoding. Once learners spontaneously use the verbal rehearsal strategy, they can be taught to visualize as an additional way of keeping information active in WM. To combine the strategies, a learner should be taught to verbally rehearse material while simultaneously visualizing it. For example, while rehearsing a series of steps an individual might visualize himself completing the steps.

This type of strategy may be particularly helpful for individuals with low verbal WM or with those who have a language impairment. The approach has been found to be more effective and enduring with language-disordered children than using verbal rehearsal alone. The concurrent use of visual imagery may tap the strength of a child with a language disability. Gill et al. (2003) discovered that language impaired children quickly learned to use and maintain the visualization strategy. Gill et al. concluded that adding a visualization component to a verbal rehearsal strategy was very effective.

Dual encoding also benefits individuals who possess strong verbal WM but weak visual-spatial WM. Like those with verbal WM weaknesses, such individuals seldom independently discover dual encoding and its benefits. Consequently, direct instruction of this strategy is necessary. Training is straightforward; just direct learners to verbalize what they see by describing it in detail. A practice exercise is available in the online resources.

BYPASSING WORKING MEMORY BY USING LTM STRATEGIES

For individuals with WM deficits, teaching LTM strategies as part of the intervention is also recommended. There are several reasons for incorporating LTM strategies. First, WM capacity is strongly influenced by genetics. Even the most effective brain-based training exercises may not increase WM capacity all that much (see Chapter 7). WM strategies also have their limitations; essentially they make more effective use of existing capacity without necessarily increasing it. Second, applying a WM strategy, such as chunking, may actually add to cognitive load, causing some information to be forgotten while other information is being chunked. Third, WM functioning is usually intertwined with and dependent on the knowledge and skills stored in LTM. For example, possessing vocabulary knowledge reduces the cognitive load required to understand the meaning of a sentence. Thus, long-term memory strategies that increase knowledge and skills indirectly enhance WM functioning.

If increasing learning efficiency is the main purpose of a WM intervention, then introducing LTM strategies is even more appropriate. Learning is accomplished when new information and procedures are effectively encoded into LTM. As explained earlier (see Chapter 4) WM plays a critical role during encoding by maintaining new pieces of information that need to be associated with prior knowledge. In instances where WM is severely impaired, it may be effective to "bypass" WM and focus directly on LTM strategies and structured mnemonics that make encoding more effective.

LTM encoding strategies and mnemonics that are appropriate for this purpose include semantic clustering, making associations, periodic review, self-testing, reducing interference, loci, and keyword. Instructions for teaching some of these strategies are found in the online resources. Additional practice with these and other LTM encoding strategies can be found in Dehn (2011). Such strategies and mnemonics will need to be introduced and practiced step-by-step so as not to overburden WM. Practice with a strategy should continue until the strategy is automatized. Once it is automatized, it should not add appreciably to cognitive load.

🐟 TEST YOURSELF 🐟

1. **In a mnemonic-based classroom focused on supporting WM, all of the following should be taught** *except*

   (a) Metamemory
   (b) Rehearsal strategies
   (c) Retrieval strategies
   (d) Encoding strategies

2. **What is a main concern when teaching a multistep strategy to someone with significant WM limitations?**

   (a) It will require too much practice.
   (b) It will create too much cognitive load.
   (c) It will be difficult to generalize.
   (d) It will require adequate LTM.

3. **When is probably the best time to teach rehearsal strategies?**

   (a) Preschool
   (b) First grade
   (c) Sixth grade
   (d) High school

4. **What is likely to happen if metamemory instruction is *not* part of the intervention?**

   (a) Trainees won't be able to remember the methods.
   (b) The methods will be more understandable to the trainees.
   (c) LTM methods will interfere with WM methods.
   (d) Trainees will not continue to use the methods they learned.

5. **Dual encoding includes which two strategies?**

   (a) Rehearsal and visualization
   (b) Rehearsal and chunking
   (c) Switching and updating
   (d) WM and LTM strategies

6. In the classroom, which is *not* one of the main variables that directly contribute to cognitive load?

(a) The learner's internal processes
(b) The teacher's instructional practices
(c) The learner's level of metamemory
(d) The complexity of the material

7. What method is recommended for someone who is supporting the writing process of a WM-impaired individual?

(a) Function as the individual's short-term storage
(b) Require practice until the individual masters the writing process
(c) Function as the individual's long-term storage
(d) Continually remind the writer of each step in the writing process

Answers: 1. c; 2. b; 3. b; 4. d; 5. a; 6. c; 7. a

Nine

CASE STUDY

T his chapter includes a case study of an elementary age child. The case study includes background, assessment, and intervention information, along with the outcomes of the interventions. The purpose of this chapter is to integrate and apply much of what has been presented in this book. Thus, the assessment results will be explained in more detail than would be included in a psychological report, with an emphasis on how the individual's background, difficulties, and profile are consistent with WM models and research. Also, the rationale for including certain methods in the interventions will be explained, and hypotheses that account for the outcomes will complete the picture.

WORKING MEMORY INTERPRETATION SECTION

In this chapter, only the interpretation section of an assessment report is illustrated. The other sections of a typical report, such as observations, interviews, background information, and recommendations, are omitted. For the type of information that should be included in such sections, see Chapters 5, 7, and 8. In the interpretative report section, only the information pertaining to WM is included.

A template for the WM interpretation section of an assessment report is available in the online resources. The structure of the template assumes that the results of the *Working Memory Analysis Worksheet* or the *Memory Processes Analyzer* will be displayed in a table. The narrative template begins

DON'T FORGET

The assessment report should include a paragraph that explains how the test scores were analyzed and how the scores of the working memory components were determined.

with an introductory paragraph that explains how the data was analyzed using the Working Memory Analysis Worksheet. Then, each WM component is defined and explained. This is followed by details on the examinee's performance on the WM component measures and statements regarding strengths and weaknesses. The template concludes with a summary paragraph.

The report template applies an integrated approach to report writing, rather than a test-by-test or method-by-method approach. That is, all of the assessment data pertaining to a specific WM component is presented in the section on that component, regardless of the source or method. Structuring the report in this fashion makes it easier for consumers of the report to understand the functioning of each component, without having to search through different report sections for relevant information. A method-by-method or test-by-test reporting style may be used in conjunction with the template. If so, this type of interpretation should be presented first. The memory interpretation section should still integrate information pertaining to each WM component, even if this is somewhat redundant.

Users of the template provided in the online resources should add any additional information to the narrative sections as needed or desired. For each WM component, the information that is prompted in the template includes:

- Identifying the specific scales, composites, and subtests that were used to test the component.
- Reporting the component standard score that was derived from the mean of select subtests or taken directly from a WM composite.
- Providing related information about the component standard score, such as the confidence interval, percentile, and range (e.g., average) within which it falls. (For percentiles, use Appendix A.)
- Explaining why WM subtest scores might be discrepant when they are nonunitary.
- Reporting when the component score is a normative strength or weakness.
- Reporting when the component score is an intra-individual strength or weakness.
- Reporting when the component score is a deficit or asset.
- Integrating observations from the testing session that relate to the component score.
- Integrating observations from the classroom that relate to the component score.
- Integrating any history that relates to the component score.
- Integrating any information from interviews that relates to the component score.

- Integrating any concurrent achievement test scores that are influenced by or related with the component.
- Integrating related scores or conclusions from testing conducted by others.
- Concluding with any hypotheses that might account for the scores.

> **DON'T FORGET**
>
> A report that presents all of the data pertaining to each memory component in an integrated fashion makes the assessment results easier to understand than a test-by-test report.

CASE STUDY ASSESSMENT

The case study is of a student who will be called "Jon." Jon was first evaluated by the author of this book when he was 8.4 years old and in mid-second grade. Jon's parents brought him in for an evaluation and for tutoring in reading because they were concerned about his slow progress in reading. This had been a concern since kindergarten, when Jon had difficulty recognizing and recalling shapes and letters. Jon was also struggling with written language skills, especially spelling. His performance in mathematics was generally average, although he did have difficulty memorizing arithmetic facts. There were no behavioral, social, emotional, or health concerns. Also, there were no indications that Jon had any problems with attentional control or executive functions.

Jon was born at 32 weeks of gestation, with a weight of 3 pounds, 4 ounces. Such extremely early births are a risk factor for memory problems, including WM problems. Research indicates that the cause might be poor or delayed myelination in the brain. Myelination, the coating of brain fibers, is important for fast and accurate transmission of information in the brain. Jon went home after a month's stay in the hospital that was due to feeding problems, not respiratory problems. Since then, Jon had been healthy, and his early childhood development was normal.

Jon began receiving Title I reading services in kindergarten, but his school had not yet evaluated him for a reading disability. Near the end of first grade, an optometrist recommended vision therapy. At the time of this initial evaluation, Jon had completed 24 weeks of vision therapy. At home, Jon's parents read to him and worked on his reading skills.

Jon had recently been evaluated by another private practice psychologist whose initial impression was that Jon had dysphonetic dyslexia. The clinician administered part of the Wechsler Individual Achievement Test, Third Edition (WIAT-III), and reported that Jon's sight word reading was a standard score of 83, his spelling was a standard score of 83, and his reading comprehension was a standard score of 79. On the Wechsler Abbreviated Scale of Intelligence, Second Edition, Jon obtained a Full Scale IQ of 92.

Given the referral concerns, educational history, and Jon's risk factor for memory problems, it was decided to conduct a broad assessment of cognitive abilities, with an emphasis on investigating WM components and LTM processes that are related to these types of concerns and history. No additional achievement testing was conducted because Jon had current scores and because his school had just initiated an SLD evaluation. The purpose of the evaluation was primarily to investigate underlying processing and memory problems that could account for his specific learning problems.

Results From the Initial Assessment

Jon was tested with the Woodcock-Johnson III Tests of Cognitive Abilities (WJ III COG), select subtests from the WISC-IV Integrated, and the Wide Range Assessment of Memory and Learning, Second Edition (WRAML2). His WJ III COG extended General Intellectual Ability (GIA) score was 98. The seven main cognitive abilities tested by the WJ III COG are grouped into three broad clusters. Of these, Jon had an above average score of 112 on Verbal Ability, a mid-average score of 98 on Thinking Ability, and a below average score of 89 on Cognitive Efficiency. Jon's high Verbal Ability score, based on measures of vocabulary and general knowledge, was corroborated through observations and reports from Jon's parents. It was reported that Jon was outgoing, inquisitive, and talkative, with strong oral language abilities. Jon's Thinking Ability score was consistent with his Fluid Reasoning score of 98, indicating that he had adequate reasoning ability for reading comprehension. His below average Cognitive Efficiency score was primarily due to a low score on the Memory for Words subtest. The other contributor to the Cognitive Efficiency cluster was a processing speed subtest, on which Jon had a mid-average score of 105.

Even before a multibattery WM component analysis was conducted with reclassified subtests, the WJ III results indicated some memory problems. All of Jon's WJ III COG cluster scores were within the average range, except Long-Term Retrieval, with a score of 84, and Short-Term Memory, with a score of 82. In contrast, his Working Memory cluster score was 94, mainly buoyed up by an Auditory Working Memory subtest score of 103, whereas Numbers Reversed had been a 90. The WJ III Intra-Cognitive Variations table revealed that Jon had significant intra-individual strengths in Comprehension Knowledge and Auditory Processing, while demonstrating significant weaknesses in Long-Term Retrieval and Short-Term Memory.

The official WJ COG STM and WM clusters address only phonological and verbal aspects of WM. Consequently, the WISC-IV Integrated was used to assess visual-spatial dimensions, as well as pursue phonological STM in more depth. The results indicated that Jon's visual-spatial STM and WM were mid-average to above average. Also, his performance on Phonological STM tasks was slightly stronger than his Memory for Words score on the WJ III COG (see Rapid Reference 9.1).

The WRAML2 Verbal Learning subtest was used to further investigate Jon's LTM encoding ability (see details under the LTM Encoding subsection that follows). Regarding other cognitive processes closely related with basic reading skills, Jon had cluster scores of 117 in Auditory Processing and 102 in Phonemic Awareness ability (see details under the Phonological Processing subsection that follows).

Analysis of Working Memory Results

A WM component analysis that included some LTM and other related cognitive processes was conducted with the Working Memory Analysis Worksheet (see Chapter 5 and the online resources). Using the classification of WM composites and subtests from Appendix C, all of Jon's relevant multibattery scores were placed under appropriate WM components and other LTM and psychological processes (see Rapid Reference 9.1). Chapter 5 presents detailed instructions for this type of analysis, but here are the general steps and guidelines:

1. All composite and subtest scores were converted to standard scores with a mean of 100 and a standard deviation of 15.
2. When more than one subtest was used to measure a component or process, the mean of the scores involved was computed and used to represent the level of functioning for that component or process.
3. In Jon's case, his GIA of 98 was used as the predicted score.
4. Discrepancies were determined by subtracting the predicted score from each component or process score.
5. Significant discrepancies were labeled as intra-individual strengths or weaknesses.
6. Normative weaknesses were identified when component or process scores were below 90, and normative strengths were identified when scores were above 109.
7. Intra-individual weaknesses were identified when discrepancies were −12 or greater, and intra-individual strengths were identified when discrepancies were +12 or higher.

8. Components and processes that had both a normative weakness and an intra-individual weakness were labeled deficits, and those that had both normative strengths and intra-individual strengths were labeled assets.

9. In Jon's case, analysis of related pairs of scores was not conducted because a cursory review indicated that none of the paired subtests would be significantly discrepant.

The subsections that follow discuss the results of each WM component, some LTM processes, and some related cognitive processes. The purpose of this discussion section is to explain how to interpret the results of the analysis (see Rapid Reference 9.1), to generate hypotheses that account for them, and to discuss implications. Basically, the section attempts to illustrate how an examiner might think through the results. Thus, this is not how the actual report should be written. An illustration of how the WM interpretation should be written in a formal assessment report follows later in this chapter.

Phonological STM. The Memory for Words subtest on the WJ III COG is a classic phonological STM measurement procedure. Because Jon performed poorly on it, further assessment was conducted with the two Letter Span tasks from the WISC-IV Integrated. Retaining the sequence of letters rather than words should more directly tap the phonological coding and storage processes in this WM component. Jon performed similarly on Memory for Words and Letter Span Nonrhyming but did slightly better on Letter Span Rhyming. For children with normal phonological processing ability, oral stimuli that rhyme can interfere with each other, reducing span. This type of interference is less likely in children who don't recognize phonemes well. If rhyming interference is having less of an effect on Jon, it may be that he is dysphonetic, as hypothesized by the first psychologist to test him.

Based on the results of the WM analysis, Jon's phonological STM is a deficit for him relative to his overall level of cognitive functioning. It is also his lowest WM component, the only one that is clearly in the low average range. The implication is that he has difficulty with the short-term storage of phonological information. Exactly what this may be due to is difficult to determine. One possibility is that Jon has not acquired or is not systematically conducting automated, subvocal rehearsal, an essential dimension of phonological STM. Nor is there any indication that he is consciously applying such a strategy; for instance, he displayed no signs of rehearsing during testing. How this WM deficit relates to his other WM components and related cognitive processes is discussed in subsequent subsections.

Rapid Reference 9.1   Working Memory Analysis Worksheet

Student's Name: _____ "Jon" _____ Date of Birth: _____ Gender: *Male* _____ Age: *8.4* _____ Grade: *2.5*

Date of Testing: _____

Memory Component or Process	Name of Scale	Names of Composites and Subtests	Obtained Standard Scores	Process or Component Score	95% Confidence Interval	Cognitive Composite WJ III COG	Discrepancy	Normative S or W	Intra-Individual S or W	Deficit or Asset
Phonological STM	WISC-IV Integrated	Letter Span Rhyming	(8) 90	85	75–95	98	–13	W	W	D
		Letter Span Nonrhyming	(7) 85							
	WJ-III COG	Memory for Words	80							
Visual-spatial STM	WISC-IV Integrated	Spatial Span Forward	(10) 100	98	88–108	98	0	—	—	—
	WJ III COG	Picture Recognition	95							
Verbal WM	WJ III ACH	Story Recall	89	89	79–99	98	–9	W	—	—
Visual-spatial WM	WISC-IV Integrated	Spatial Span Backward	(12) 110	110	100–120	98	+12	S	S	A
Executive WM	WJ III COG	WORKING MEMORY	94	94	84–104	98	–4			

(continued)

(continued)

Memory Component or Process	Name of Scale	Names of Composites and Subtests	Obtained Standard Scores	Process or Component Score	95% Confidence Interval	Cognitive Composite WJ III COG	Discrepancy	Normative S or W	Intra-Individual S or W	Deficit or Asset
LTM encoding	WRAML2	Verbal Learning	(9) 95	86	76–96	98	–12	W	W	D
	WJ III COG	Visual-Auditory Learning	76							
LTM retrieval fluency	WJ III COG	Retrieval Fluency	111	108	98–118	98	+10	—	—	—
		Rapid Picture Naming	105							
Processing speed	WJ III COG	PROCESSING SPEED	102	102	92–112	98	+4	—	—	—
Phonological processing	WJ III COG	PHONEMIC AWARENESS	102	102	92–112	98	+4	—	—	—

Visual-Spatial STM. Jon performed well on both visual-spatial STM activities he completed. The two tasks are quite different in nature. Spatial Span Forward requires retention of spatial and sequential information. In contrast, Picture Recognition is strictly visual and does not require any sequencing. Thus, there appears to be no difference between Jon's visual and spatial brief retention abilities. These memory abilities are consistent with his mid-average visual-spatial processing abilities and with his average to high average visual-spatial WM.

Verbal Working Memory. Jon's verbal WM component score is more of an estimate than his other component scores because it is based on only one subtest. Story Recall requires the examinee to immediately recall short passages presented orally. As the passages became longer, Jon recalled only the beginning of the passage. It seemed his recall was primarily for details, rather than gist, which is typical of 8-year-olds. Story Recall also involves LTM encoding. It may be that this element of the task was more challenging for Jon than the WM dimension, and pulled down his score. Thus, it is possible that Jon's verbal WM functioning is higher than indicated by his score of 89. This hypothesis is supported by Jon's mid-average oral expression ability. Oral expression depends on adequate verbal WM.

Visual-Spatial Working Memory. It appears that Jon has an asset in visual-spatial WM, although more testing to confirm this would have been ideal. His performance on Spatial Span Backward, primarily a spatial task, was better than even his visual-spatial STM performance. Jon's strengths in visual-spatial WM are consistent with his average skills in mathematics.

Executive Working Memory. The Working Memory cluster score of 94 from the WJ III COG provided the score for Jon's executive WM. Jon performed better on Auditory Working Memory (score of 104) than he did on Numbers Reversed (score of 91). There are other indications that Jon has average executive WM functioning, including good executive functioning skills, no problems with attentional control, and mid-average fluid reasoning. More telling is that Jon's average executive WM ability is consistent with his verbal WM and his higher ability in visual-spatial STM and WM.

Jon's profile of WM scores is that of an individual whose weaknesses within WM lie more with the storage aspects rather than with processing. Jon performed better on complex tasks that required processing in addition to storage. This is evident from his higher scores in verbal WM versus phonological STM and in visual-spatial WM versus visual-spatial STM.

This is an important insight into Jon's overall WM functioning and the memory difficulties he is experiencing. First, it indicates that Jon may be able to cope normally with increases in cognitive load. Second, from a neurological perspective, the development of Jon's dorsolateral prefrontal cortex (the WM control center) is most likely normal, but something is lacking in the more fundamental temporary storage areas of the brain, especially storage for phonological information. Given his risk factor for poor myelination, it may be that there are deficiencies in the connectivity and communication between the dorsolateral prefrontal cortex and the phonological storage area. An alternative hypothesis is that Jon's normally developed executive WM enables him to be consciously strategic when needed, leading to improved performance. In contrast, the more automated and unconscious functions of his phonological STM are deficient, and will reduce retention of information unless directed by a conscious executive WM. If these hypotheses are true, then Jon should benefit from learning and applying more strategies. Consequently, his intervention should include memory strategy training.

LTM Encoding. On the WRAML2's Verbal Learning subtest, Jon earned a standard score of 95, in contrast with his 76 on Visual-Auditory Learning on the WJ III COG. His higher performance on the WRAML2 encoding task might have been due to the fact that it is less complex than the WJ IV COG learning task, which requires the examinee to integrate verbal and visual-spatial information while new rebuses are added in a cumulative fashion.

For Verbal Learning, the examinee must recall the words from a list that is presented four times. Although Jon's overall score on this task was average, he was slow to initially learn the words. He recalled only 3 of 13 on the first two trials, whereas average 8-year-olds recall 4.9 and 6.3 words respectively. However, in the remaining two trials he recalled seven and nine words, an average retention for someone his age. Jon's slow start at learning the words is probably due to his weak phonological STM storage. As the task progressed, he either received enough repetitions to compensate for this weakness or applied a strategy that helped retain the words. Jon also demonstrated serial learning effects. Except for one word on the final trial, all of the words he learned were at the beginning or end of the list. Strong serial learning effects indicate that the examinee is quite susceptible to interference.

One hypothesis that accounts for the lower score on Visual-Auditory Learning is that it requires more support from executive WM processes. For example, updating is necessary as new rebuses are added in a cumulative fashion. Inhibition is required because some rebuses and the words associated with them are very similar, creating interference. Also, the ability to quickly switch back and forth between different aspects of the task is important. Although Jon performed adequately on executive WM subtests, the demands those subtests imposed on updating, inhibition, and switching are limited. Thus, Jon's development of these three fundamental executive WM processes is unknown. If they are relatively weak, they could have added to his LTM encoding challenges.

Another brain-based hypothesis that might explain why Visual-Auditory Learning was more difficult for Jon is that integrating verbal and visual-spatial information requires more interconnectivity and communication among different parts of the brain than the simpler Verbal Learning task required. Greater myelination facilitates transference of information within the brain. Given the likelihood that Jon has inadequate myelination due to his premature birth, poor myelination may be the underlying neurological explanation for why tasks like Visual-Auditory Learning are difficult for Jon.

Nonetheless, Jon's apparent low average LTM encoding ability may primarily be a specific LTM processing deficiency and not due to some weak WM functions. Either way, his deficit in encoding accounts for the academic learning problems he has been experiencing. Clearly, his intervention program should include methods that enhance LTM encoding.

LTM Retrieval Fluency. LTM retrieval fluency subtests were administered primarily to rule out the possibility that LTM retrieval problems were contributing to Jon's learning and memory problems. He obtained mid-average scores on both Retrieval Fluency and Rapid Picture Naming from the WJ III COG. His score of 105 on Rapid Picture Naming is encouraging because it indicates that his difficulty acquiring and recalling sight words is not due to a specific retrieval problem.

Processing Speed. Because of its strong relations with WM, it is always important to assess the client's processing speed. For Jon, processing speed is not part of the problem. He obtained mid-average processing speed scores on both WJ III COG subtests. Observations of Jon support this finding, as he is always quick to respond unless he has not retained the information.

Phonological Processing. Although Jon's WJ III COG Phonemic Awareness cluster score was mid-average at 102, it was nonunitary. He had a 112 in Sound Blending and an 88 in Incomplete Words. His strong performance on Sound Blending indicates that he can retain and blend phonemes and syllables when they are provided to him. His difficulty with Incomplete Words indicates that he has difficulty with auditory closure, detecting phonemes, recognizing phonemes, and segmenting words into phonemes, all important abilities for reading decoding and spelling.

Jon's below average performance on the phonological processing subtest of Incomplete Words (a score of 88) is consistent with his low STM phonological component score of 85. However, given that all of his other auditory and phonological processing scores are mid-average, it may well be that he does not have a phonological processing weakness per se. Rather, it may be that his deficient phonological STM is having a negative impact on his phonological processing.

Furthermore, all of the other closely related cognitive processes that influence phonological processing appear to be functioning in the mid-average range. For example, his oral language and auditory processing scores are mid-average.

EXAMPLE OF A WRITTEN INTERPRETATION

Jon's case is used to illustrate how the WM interpretation section of a formal assessment report should be written. In this case, two LTM processes are also included. The WM template that this example is based on can be found in the online resources. The remainder of this section illustrates how Jon's results might be interpreted in a formal, written psychological assessment report.

A selective-testing, multibattery approach was used to test Jon's working memory components, long-term memory processes, and related cognitive processes. Subtests and composites that measure these abilities were selected from the Woodcock-Johnson III Tests of Cognitive Abilities (WJ III COG), the Woodcock-Johnson III Tests of Achievement (WJ III ACH), the WISC-IV Integrated, and the Wide Range Assessment of Memory and Learning (WRAML2). All of the memory composite and subtest scores obtained by the examinee, along with some closely related cognitive processes, were combined into one memory processes analysis, using the Working Memory Analysis Worksheet.

These are the steps that were used to conduct the analysis and determine Jon's memory strengths and weaknesses:

1. All composite and subtest scores were converted to standard scores with a mean of 100 and a standard deviation of 15.
2. When more than one composite or subtest was used to measure a memory component or a cognitive process, the mean of the scores involved was calculated and used to represent the level of functioning for that component or process. These scores are referred to as "process" or "component" scores.
3. Jon's WJ III COG General Intellectual Ability score of 98 was used to predict his performance on the components and processes.
4. Discrepancies were determined by subtracting the predicted score from each memory component or cognitive process score.
5. Normative weaknesses were identified when scores were below 90, and normative strengths were identified when scores were above 109.
6. Discrepancies of greater than 12 points were labeled as intra-individual strengths or weaknesses.
7. Scores that were both a normative weakness and an intra-individual weakness were labeled as deficits, and scores that were both a normative strength and an intra-individual strength were labeled as assets.

Working memory is the limited capacity to retain information while simultaneously processing the same or other information for a short period. Short-term memory, which lasts for only a few seconds, is considered a subcomponent of working memory. Short-term memory is the storage dimension of working memory. It is divided into phonological short-term memory and visual-spatial short-term memory. The working memory components are the processing components that utilize what is being temporarily held in the short-term storage components. The three processing components of working memory are verbal, visual-spatial, and executive.

Phonological Short-Term Memory

Phonological short-term memory briefly stores (for just a few seconds) sounds and words that are heard. Phonological short-term memory is important for the development of oral language and basic reading skills. For example, vocabulary development depends heavily on adequate phonological short-term memory. Jon's phonological short-term memory was measured with subtests from the WJ III COG and the WISC-IV Integrated (see his table of scores). When Jon's memory component score of 85 for phonological short-term memory is compared with other individuals the same age, his level of functioning in phonological short-term memory can be considered a normative weakness. When Jon's score is compared with his overall level of cognitive ability, he appears to have a significant intra-individual weakness in phonological short-term memory. Because Jon has both types of weaknesses, his phonological short-term memory is considered a deficit. Thus, it appears that Jon has significant difficulty with the short-term storage of phonological, auditory, and verbal information. This deficiency is most likely related to Jon's difficulty with acquiring basic reading skills.

The level of functioning indicated by Jon's phonological short-term memory score is consistent with other assessment data gathered during interviews, observations, and testing. Jon's teachers and parents have reported that Jon has difficulty remembering new sight words, how to spell words, and how to decode words. Also, during testing Jon did not display any signs that he was using rehearsal to remember the sequence of items presented to him.

Visual-Spatial Short-Term Memory

Visual-spatial short-term memory briefly stores (for just a few seconds) visual images, visual patterns, and perception of objects, as well as their movement and location. Visual-spatial short-term memory is important for coordinated physical movement. In school, it is related with the development of arithmetic and mathematical skills. For example, understanding geometrical figures depends on visual-spatial short-term memory. Jon's visual-spatial short-term memory was tested with subtests from the WJ III COG and the WISC-IV Integrated. When Jon's memory component score of 98 is compared with other individuals the same age, his level of functioning in visual-spatial short-term memory is mid-average. When his score is compared with his overall cognitive ability level, he has neither an intra-individual strength nor weakness in visual-spatial short-term memory.

The level of functioning indicated by Jon's visual-spatial short-term memory score is consistent with other assessment data gathered during interviews, observations, and additional testing. For example, Jon's average performance in mathematics is consistent with his visual-spatial short-term memory ability.

Verbal Working Memory

Verbal working memory manipulates and transforms verbal information that is being held in short-term memory or has been retrieved from long-term memory. For example, verbal working memory is engaged during reading comprehension and written expression. Jon's verbal working memory was tested with the Story Recall subtest from the WJ III ACH. When Jon's score of 89 is compared with other individuals the same age, his level of functioning is considered a weakness because it is below the average range. When Jon's score is compared with his overall level of cognitive ability, he appears to have neither an intra-individual strength nor weakness in verbal working memory.

The normative weakness indicated by Jon's score in a measure of verbal working memory is consistent with other assessment data gathered during interviews, observations, and additional testing. Jon has difficulties with both reading comprehension and written expression. He can express ideas orally, but then can't express them in writing. Also, Jon's parents report that Jon often forgets oral directions at home.

Visual-Spatial Working Memory

Visual-spatial working memory manipulates and transforms visual-spatial information that is being held in short-term memory or has been retrieved from long-term memory. For example, visual-spatial working memory is required in order to imagine what an object will look like if it is rotated. Jon's visual-spatial working memory was tested with the Spatial Span Backward subtest from the WISC-IV Integrated. When his transformed standard score of 110 is compared with other individuals the same age, his level of functioning in visual-spatial working memory can be considered a strength. When Jon's score is compared with his overall cognitive ability, he appears to have a significant intra-individual strength in visual-spatial working memory. Because Jon has both types of strengths, his visual-spatial working memory is considered an asset.

The level of functioning indicated by Jon's visual-spatial working memory score is consistent with other assessment data gathered during interviews, observations, and additional testing. Jon's strengths in visual-spatial working memory are consistent with his average skills in mathematics. Also, Jon's score on visual-spatial processing, as measured by the WJ III COG, is in the upper end of the average range.

Executive Working Memory

Executive working memory is engaged whenever there is processing of information that is unrelated to the information being held in brief storage. It is also involved when a task requires the integration of verbal and visual-spatial information. Executive working memory is the control center for working and short-term memory. For example, executive working memory is responsible for filtering out information that is not related to the task at hand. Jon's executive working memory was assessed with the Working Memory cluster of the WJ III COG. When Jon's score of 94 for executive working memory is compared with other individuals the same age, his level of functioning in executive working memory can be considered neither a strength nor a weakness. When his score is compared with his overall level of cognitive ability, he has neither an intra-individual strength nor weakness in executive working memory.

The level of functioning indicated by Jon's executive working memory score is consistent with other assessment data. Reports from parents and observations reveal that Jon has well-developed executive skills in general. Also, Jon does not seem to have any problems with inhibition or attentional control.

Encoding

Encoding is the process of transferring information from short-term memory into long-term memory. The formation of new memories and the initial learning of new material depend on the process of encoding. Jon's encoding ability was measured with the Visual-Auditory Learning subtest from the WJ III COG and the Verbal Learning subtest from the WRAML2. Jon's standard scores on the two subtests were a 76 and a transformed score of 95, respectively. The Visual-Auditory Learning subtest is a more complex and challenging task because new stimuli are added on each trial, rather than repeating the same stimuli in each trial, as in the Verbal Learning subtest. Although Jon's overall score on Verbal Learning was average, he was slow to initially learn the words. He recalled only 3 of 13 on the first two trials, whereas average 8-year-olds recall 4.9 and 6.3 words respectively. However, in the remaining two trials he recalled seven and nine words, an average retention for someone his age. Thus, the score of 95 is a little misleading. In a situation where new material is presented only once, it is likely that Jon will not learn (encode) as much of the information as his peers. Jon's slow start at learning the words is probably due to his weak phonological STM storage.

When Jon's averaged score of 86 for encoding is compared with other individuals the same age, his level of functioning in encoding can be considered a weakness. When Jon's score is compared with his overall cognitive ability, he appears to have a significant intra-individual weakness. Because Jon has both types of weaknesses, his long-term memory encoding is considered a deficit. Jon's history of academic learning difficulties is consistent with a deficit in encoding.

Retrieval Fluency

Retrieval fluency is the ability to quickly recall information that is stored in long-term memory. Retrieval can be automatic and unconscious, or it can be conscious and controlled. Individuals who lack retrieval fluency are often unable to retrieve information on demand or are slow to retrieve it. Jon's retrieval fluency was tested with the Retrieval Fluency and Rapid Picture Naming subtests from the WJ III COG. Jon obtained mid-average scores on both subtests, resulting in a memory process score of 108 for long-term retrieval fluency. When Jon's score for retrieval fluency is compared with other individuals the same age, his retrieval fluency is neither a strength nor a weakness. When Jon's score is compared with his overall cognitive ability level, it is neither strength nor a weakness. Jon's retrieval fluency is consistent with his mid-average processing speed score of 102.

Summary

Based on the analysis of Jon's memory and processing scores, he displays a pattern of strengths and weaknesses that can account for the academic learning problems that he is experiencing. Jon has normative weaknesses (below average scores) in phonological short-term memory, verbal working memory, and long-term memory encoding. He has a normative strength (above average score) in visual-spatial working memory. Jon has intra-individual weaknesses in phonological short-term memory and in long-term memory encoding. In contrast, he has an intra-individual strength in visual-spatial working memory. Jon has deficits in phonological short-term memory and long-term memory encoding, while demonstrating an asset in visual-spatial working memory. For the remaining memory components and processes, his scores are within the average range and are neither intra-individual strengths nor weaknesses.

Jon's profile of working memory scores is that of an individual whose weaknesses within working memory lie with the storage aspects, rather than with working memory processing. The more complex the task and the more processing in addition to storage that is required, the better Jon performs. This is indicated by his higher scores in verbal working memory versus phonological short-term memory and in visual-spatial working memory versus visual-spatial short-term memory.

JON'S INTERVENTIONS

Even though the majority of Jon's WM abilities were in the average range, it was recommended that he complete WM training and learn some LTM strategies as well. The first reason for this recommendation was his deficit in phonological STM, and the second reason was his deficit in LTM encoding. It was believed that strengthening Jon's phonological STM would improve his phonetic decoding skills and his LTM encoding because he would be able to retain more phonological information and retain it for a longer period of time. Jon's executive WM was targeted because strengthening it and making him more strategic might help him to compensate for his deficits in phonological STM and LTM encoding. The parents accepted the recommendations, and a WM training program was implemented. At the same time, Jon received one-on-one tutoring in reading for 2 hours per week. A couple months after the memory evaluation was completed and these services were initiated, Jon's school classified him as having a reading disability and began providing typical school-based special education services.

Parent Training Model

Not only did Jon's parents agree to WM interventions, but they agreed to be trained so they could practice the exercises and strategies with Jon at home on a regular basis. Over the course of six 1-hour sessions they learned how to administer the WM exercises and to teach and encourage Jon to use some basic strategies. During the sessions, the trainer would briefly model the methods with Jon, as the parents observed. This would be followed by discussion with the parents, including helping them understand the purpose of the methods and why the methods should be helpful. Also, written guidelines and procedures were provided to them, and they acquired any training materials that were needed.

Jon's mother implemented the WM home-based training program with remarkable fidelity and consistency. Over a period of 6 months, she practiced WM exercises and strategies with Jon for 20–30 minutes per day, 6 days a week. She documented everything she did with Jon, including the span lengths he was achieving. As this proceeded she observed and reported improvements in Jon's performance.

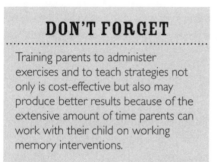

DON'T FORGET

Training parents to administer exercises and to teach strategies not only is cost-effective but also may produce better results because of the extensive amount of time parents can work with their child on working memory interventions.

A parent-training model is one approach to WM training, an approach developed and advocated by this author. This training model has its pros and cons. Many initially interested parents will be unable to carry through. The understanding, training regimen, and time required of parents are often too much. For parents who succeed and persist, home-based WM training saves families time and money, because minimal contact with a professional memory trainer is required. It also can be very effective, increase the chance that the training will occur for a long enough interval, and improve the chances for long-term maintenance.

Jon's Exercises and Strategies

Several WM exercises and strategies, as well as some LTM strategies, were implemented with Jon. All of these were managed and taught by his mother on a regular basis. Brief descriptions of the methods and the rationale for them follow. For more details on these procedures, see Chapters 7 and 8 and the online resources.

Rehearsal Practice

This method was selected because of Jon's deficits in phonological STM and LTM encoding. Automated, subvocal rehearsal strengthens the ability to retain information in phonological STM. Research has documented that training children to systematically rehearse improves their learning and memory. In addition to increasing Jon's phonological span, the objectives were to improve his ability to maintain a sequence while repeating it and to have rehearsal become an automated, subvocal procedure for him.

When provided with various types of stimuli, such as letters, numbers, and monosyllabic words, Jon was to repeat them five times while maintaining the sequence. After five repetitions, the trainer was to ask Jon to recall them a final time. The emphasis for this part of the training was the correct application of rehearsal procedures and maintaining the sequence, rather than how long a span Jon could recall. As Jon became more proficient with rehearsing aloud, he was to whisper while rehearsing, and then finally rehearse the sequence silently in his head before producing the final response. At the subvocalizing level, the trainer is to ask him if he is rehearsing.

Three main types of rehearsal methods were applied. For the first, the entire list of stimuli was presented orally at once, and then Jon repeated the list five times. The second approach was cumulative rehearsal. For this one, the items were presented orally one at a time, and Jon added each to his list in a cumulative fashion. After each new item was introduced, he was given time to rehearse the updated list. For the third method, the trainer did not present items orally but rather displayed a card with a letter or number on it. Jon then rehearsed these items in a cumulative manner.

Increasing Span

Related to the rehearsal exercises, some practice simply involved trying to increase phonological span. For these, similar stimuli were presented orally, but Jon was not required nor given time to rehearse. After the list of items was presented, he was to immediately reply. The goal was to increase the accuracy and length of his phonological span.

Chunking

Chunking is an unconscious and consciously applied strategy that also can enhance phonological STM and LTM encoding. For this strategy, three types of stimuli were used. For the first, Jon was to practice pairing numbers that were presented to him, such as making 3, 6, 3, 4 into "36, 24" and even chunking some three-digit items, such as "3, 6, 3" into "363." Second, Jon was to chunk letters in words into syllable chunks. For example, with the word "sunset," he would say the letters "s-u-n." Then he would pause before saying the letters "s-e-t" as a chunk. Word sequences were used for a third variation. For example, when given four words, such as "cat, horse, dog, cow," he would rehearse them in pairs and pause between the pairs, such as "cat-horse" and then "dog-cow."

Semantic Clustering

Semantic clustering involves grouping words or objects into categories based on meaning. The strategy is not for WM, but rather is intended to enhance LTM encoding and subsequent LTM retrieval.

Organizing information into meaningful groupings makes it easier to remember more information, because items that should be associated are consciously associated during encoding. Thus, they are more likely to be closely linked in LTM storage. During recall, the individual can activate the category of the forgotten items and then run through items in that category until he "recognizes" them as the forgotten items.

This was first taught and practiced with small objects, such as toys, that could be grouped by functional characteristics, such as toys with wheels, animals, building materials, and so forth. The items are presented all mixed together, and then the trainee must organize them into groups. After the sorting is complete, the trainee names each group and then is directed to memorize the names of the groups and not focus as much on trying to remember the individual items in each group. The same procedures were used when the stimuli were words, presented on separate pieces of paper.

Visualizing

The purpose of visualizing is to dual encode and to capitalize on Jon's visual-spatial WM strength. Also, for most people, visual-spatial information and imagery are easier to recall than verbal information. Visualizing practice was applied when parents were reading to Jon or when he was reading material himself. After reading each paragraph, Jon was to pause and visualize or continue visualizing what was just read. After he had a picture in his mind, he was directed to verbalize it.

Counting Dots

The purpose of this exercise is to practice simultaneously processing and retaining information. It is also an introductory exercise for learning how to switch between rehearsing and processing. Cards are presented with a varying number of randomly displayed dots on them. Jon was to count the dots on each card. Then, after a series of cards had been counted, he was to recall in sequence the number of dots that were on each card. Counting the dots is the processing portion of the activity. To teach switching, Jon was required to rehearse the number of dots in a cumulative fashion before going on to count dots on each subsequent card.

Math Flash Cards

This exercise is similar to counting dots, but the processing can be more challenging. Arithmetic flash cards are used as the stimuli. They can be addition, subtraction, multiplication, or division facts, as long as the trainee knows the facts at least fairly well. When each card is displayed, the trainee is to express the problem and answer aloud. In between the presentation of cards, the trainee is to rehearse the answers in a cumulative fashion. When the span level the trainee is at is reached, the trainee recalls the answers in sequence. Again, this task requires updating the rehearsal set, as well as switching back and forth between rehearsing and processing the next math fact.

N-Back

The details for practicing *n*-back are described in Chapter 7. Because it is so challenging, *n*-back is known for strengthening executive WM. It is especially effective because the trainee must continually update, inhibit, and switch. Because Jon was only 8 years old, this exercise was used minimally. At first, blocks of different colors were used as the stimuli. Later a deck of playing cards was used. Between the presentation of the items, Jon was required to rehearse aloud.

Listening Span

The Listening Span activity was included because becoming more proficient at this task might improve Jon's verbal WM and his reading comprehension. The exercise involves recalling the sequence of the last words in orally presented questions. The processing portion of the task is answering the question. For example, the trainee must answer yes or no to "Do cows drive cars?" and then to "Do houses have rooms?" Then, after the series of questions, the trainee must say, "Cars, rooms," and so on. Again, the trainee is required to rehearse the last words in a cumulative fashion between questions.

Elaboration

Elaboration was the most challenging strategy taught to Jon and his parents and the one that was practiced the least. The purpose of elaboration is to support LTM encoding and retrieval through making conscious associations between new material and related prior knowledge. It may also enhance reading comprehension when integrated with a reading comprehension strategy. This was the tactic recommended for Jon, and it was used when he read fiction. The steps included:

(1) helping him activate relevant LTM networks by previewing the story; (2) having him discuss what he thinks the story will be about; (3) asking him to predict what will happen in the story or pose questions he would like answered in the story; (4) pausing after each paragraph or page to discuss the new information; and (5) when finished, asking him if it ended as he predicted and asking him what he learned from reading the story.

Metamemory

Addressing metamemory was also part of Jon's intervention. During the initial sessions, the professional memory trainer talked with Jon about how memory works. With age-appropriate language and concepts, different types of memory were discussed, including STM versus LTM, verbal versus visual-spatial, and personal versus factual. The second part of the discussion was about Jon's individual memory strengths and weaknesses. Also, as new exercises and strategies were introduced, the trainer talked with Jon about how and why these methods might help Jon improve his memory. For example, when Jon tried semantic clustering for the first time, his delayed recall was 100%, compared with only 60% for nonstrategic efforts to memorize a list of words. This improvement in recall was used to illustrate for Jon how being more strategic could improve his memory performance.

After the initial training sessions were completed, the parent took responsibility for further development of metamemory. Based on the trainer's advice, she would talk with Jon about why they were doing the WM exercises and strategies and why they were important. Jon was told that the exercises, which were referred to as "brainwork," would make his brain stronger and allow him to learn and remember better. It was also stressed that a stronger memory might make reading and comprehending easier. As the training progressed, the parent followed up with discussions about Jon's abilities so that he better understood his memory strengths and weaknesses. The result was that Jon fully cooperated with the memory training at home and seemed motivated to improve his performance.

DON'T FORGET

Regardless of the client's developmental age, metamemory should be addressed whenever working memory training is part of an intervention.

Another case (not Jon's) of an elementary age male with a variety of memory problems illustrates the benefits of emphasizing metamemory development. The mother, who conducted memory training at home, provided the written feedback about the metamemory gains that both she and her child experienced during the intervention. The mother wrote, "I have learned the components and functions of STM, working memory, long-term memory and retrieval; from information intake, how the processes interconnect and what can interfere with the system. I can discuss semantic memory, episodic memory, central executive functions, verbal memory, visual/spatial memory, encoding, consolidation, and the retrieval process. My son has become very adept at self-monitoring. He is proficient at evaluating his own performance and a memory strategy's effectiveness. He is very comfortable switching to something else if the situation warrants. He has a working knowledge of memory systems and we have also discussed what happens in his brain. Together, he and I learned his relative memory strengths (visual, spatial, episodic) and his relative weaknesses (verbal/semantic and word/language retrieval). We continue to explore how to use his strengths to mitigate the weaker areas."

First Postintervention Assessment

After 6 months with all the previously discussed interventions in place, Jon was re-evaluated by the author of this book. In general, Jon demonstrated significant improvements in most memory areas and in his reading skills. For parents, teachers, and students, improvement in academic skills is the bottom line. Without positive far transfer effects from WM exercises and strategies, their value can be questioned. Although Jon demonstrated significant improvement in WM, the effect that WM training had on his academic skills will remain unknown because tutoring in reading had been going on concurrently and because Jon had begun receiving special education services.

When students are re-evaluated with standardized tests, standard scores seldom change significantly, even when the student is making adequate or normal progress. In Jon's case, different achievement scales were used for pre- and postintervention testing. The WIAT-III was the premeasure and the WJ III ACH was the postmeasure. Therefore, a 12 to 15 point difference should be expected if the change is to be considered significant. Applying this guideline, Jon had significant gains in basic reading skills and reading comprehension, with increases of 14 standard score points in each. However, his spelling standard score did not change at all (see Rapid Reference 9.2).

Jon's memory components and processes were retested with the WJ III COG, the same scale that was used for the initial evaluation. When considering change within the same battery, standard score differences between 8 and 12 points are usually statistically significant. Jon's results were generally encouraging (see Rapid Reference 9.3). His visual-spatial STM improved 8 points, his executive WM improved 10 points, and his LTM encoding improved 10 points.

≡ Rapid Reference 9.2 Changes in Jon's Academic Skills

Academic Skill	Pre-Intervention Score	Post-Intervention Score	Change
Basic reading skills	83	97	+14
Reading comprehension	79	93	+14
Spelling	83	83	0

Only phonological STM remained unchanged. Reports from his teachers were consistent with his gains in LTM encoding. They reported that his initial learning had improved, requiring less repetition and review. They also reported that his reading fluency and mathematics skills had improved significantly. Mathematics is known to have a strong connection with visual-spatial and executive WM.

The lack of gain in phonological STM was consistent with his unchanged spelling score, as the two phonologically based skills are highly related. However, Jon's reading skills improved significantly without a concomitant increase in phonological STM, a skill highly related with basic reading skills. Although the gains in basic reading skills could not be attributed to phonological STM, Jon's stronger executive WM may have had some influence on his improved reading comprehension. For instance, the training exercises that involved his abilities to update, shift, and inhibit may have improved those specific executive WM processes. Such processes are also essential for effective reading comprehension. Also, Jon's stronger executive WM may have had some influence on his basic reading skills. Perhaps his stronger executive WM and training in WM strategies resulted in more frequent and effective use of strategies when phonological STM was called on during reading decoding.

Second Postintervention Assessment

Following the first re-evaluation, Jon continued to receive reading disability services at school, and he also continued to receive 2 hours of one-on-one tutoring in reading per week. However, immediately following the first reevaluation, the WM exercises conducted by his parents were dropped. It was recommended that he complete online WM exercises on a regular basis to maintain his WM gains. However, this did not happen.

Rapid Reference 9.3 Changes in Jon's Memory Scores

Memory Component or Process	Pre-Intervention Score	End of Intervention Score	Change	Six Months Postintervention	Change from End of Intervention	Change from Pre-Intervention to 6 Months Postintervention
Phonological STM	85	84	−1	89	+5	+4
Visual-spatial STM	98	106	+8	106	0	+8
Executive WM	94	104	+10	86	−18	−8
LTM encoding	86	94	+8	84	−10	−2

Six months later, a second re-evaluation was conducted. Although Jon had maintained his gains in reading skills, his scores in executive WM and LTM encoding declined significantly from the time of the first re-evaluation. At the same time, his functioning levels in phonological STM and visual-spatial STM remained constant (see Rapid Reference 9.3).

> # CAUTION
> ....
> The gains accomplished during working memory training may not be enduring unless the trainee continues to engage his working memory in ways that continue to challenge it.

At first glance, these declines seem discouraging. Researchers have often questioned the longevity of the gains reported in WM training research. Generally, studies don't conduct long-term follow-up, but there have been a couple of studies that reported maintenance of WM gains for 6 to 18 months postintervention (E. Dahlin et al., 2008; Holmes et al., 2009). This case study indicates that WM training gains may not persist in children unless something is done to maintain them. The analogy of weight training applied to WM training helps make sense of this phenomenon. As one conducts weight training with heavier and heavier weights, the muscles grow and become stronger. When one terminates weight training and does nothing to maintain the growth, the muscles will become weaker again.

A viable option for maintaining training gains might be performing WM exercises periodically, such as doing a refresher round of exercises several times a year. However, this is only a conjecture; further research is needed. The crucial issue that needs to be determined by research is whether WM gains can be maintained by efforts other than WM training exercises themselves. That is, if the individual progresses to more challenging cognitive activities as a result of WM training, and then he continues with these challenging cognitive activities, can WM gains not be maintained?

Jon's case sheds some light on this question. Reports from Jon's mother and reading tutor, as well as observations of Jon, reveal that he is not interested in cognitively challenging activities and tries to avoid them. For example, he does not read books unless directed to. So, Jon's decline might have been due to his lack of ongoing efforts to engage in cognitively challenging activities that would place high demands on WM.

Some psychologists who conduct WM training have reported approximately 80% success rate to this author. These reports are consistent with the author's experience and summary reports from Cogmed. However, the long-term efficacy of WM training exercises and other WM interventions remains an unanswered question.

Despite the case of Jon and the limited empirical evidence for both maintenance and generalization, this author still advocates for the evidence-based WM exercises and interventions reviewed in this book. Although the improvements in WM performance may not persist after the training sessions and other interventions end, there are still other worthwhile enduring benefits (many of which cannot be assessed with standardized tests) that frequently occur, including:

- Improved academic skills, such as improved reading and math.
- A better ability to focus and divide attention.
- Increased metamemory self-awareness, such as understanding one's memory strengths and weaknesses.
- A better understanding of how to cope with WM challenges, such as knowing when to use a strategy.
- The development of more effective study skills that compensate for memory weaknesses.
- Improved academic performance, such as completing school assignments more efficiently.
- Additional data on the individual's WM functioning that was gathered during the intervention.
- An increased willingness by the trainee's teachers to provide appropriate accommodations and modifications.

 **TEST YOURSELF**

1. **When the results of the Working Memory Analysis Worksheet are included in an assessment report, it is most important that the report include:**
   (a) The equations used to determine discrepancies
   (b) An explanation of what the procedures involved
   (c) A listing of all the subtest scores
   (d) A review of the examinee's history

2. **A "deficit" occurs when:**
   (a) More than one subtest score is deficient
   (b) A score is below average
   (c) A score is an intra-individual weakness
   (d) A score is both below average and an intra-individual weakness

3. **An important research question that remains to be answered is:**
   (a) How long the effects of working memory training last
   (b) The relationship between encoding and working memory
   (c) How long short-term memory lasts
   (d) Whether parents can be effective working memory trainers

4. **Which working memory exercise or strategy is the most fundamental?**
   (a) Chunking
   (b) Elaboration
   (c) Rehearsal
   (d) N-back

5. **Which component involves primarily storage rather than processing?**
   (a) Visual-spatial short-term memory
   (b) Verbal working memory
   (c) Executive working memory
   (d) Visual-spatial working memory

Answers: 1. b; 2. d; 3. a; 4. c; 5. a

Appendix A

Scaled Score to Standard Score Conversion Table With Percentiles

Table A.1 Scaled Score to Standard Score Conversion With Percentiles

Scaled Score (M = 10; SD = 3)	Standard Score (M = 100; SD = 15)	Percentile Rank
19	145	99
	144	99
	143	99
	142	99
	141	99
18	140	99
	139	99
	138	99
	137	99
	136	99
17	135	99
	134	99
	133	99
	132	98
	131	98
16	130	98
	129	97
	128	97
	127	96
	126	96
15	125	95
	124	95
	123	94
	122	93
	121	92
14	120	91
	119	90
	118	88
	117	87

(continued)

Table A.1 (*Continued*)

Scaled Score (M = 10; SD = 3)	Standard Score (M = 100; SD = 15)	Percentile Rank
	116	86
13	115	84
	114	82
	113	81
	112	79
	111	77
12	110	75
	109	73
	108	70
	107	68
	106	66
11	105	63
	104	61
	103	58
	102	55
	101	53
10	100	50
	99	47
	98	45
	97	42
	96	39
9	95	37
	94	34
	93	32
	92	30
	91	27
8	90	25
	89	23
	88	21
	87	19
	86	18
7	85	16
	84	14
	83	13
	82	12
	81	10
6	80	9
	79	8
	78	7
	77	6
	76	5

Table A.1 (*Continued*)

Scaled Score (M = 10; SD = 3)	Standard Score (M = 100; SD = 15)	Percentile Rank
5	75	5
	74	4
	73	4
	72	3
	71	3
4	70	2
	69	2
	68	2
	67	1
	66	1
3	65	1
	64	1
	63	1
	62	1
	61	1
2	60	1
	59	1
	58	1
	57	1
	56	1
1	55	1

Appendix B

T-Score to Standard Score Conversion Table

"Consistent scoring" means that low *T*-scores are similar to low standard scores, and high *T*-scores are similar to high standard scores. "Reverse scoring" means high *T*-scores are indicative of low ability and low *T*-scores are indicative of high ability. Use the Consistent Scoring column to transform *T*-scores from scales such as the DAS-II. Use the Reverse Scoring column for converting scores from the BASC-2, BRIEF, CPPS, and similar reverse-scored scales.

In the Reverse Scoring column the standard score's distance from the mean has been reversed. For example, a *T*-score of 60 is one standard deviation above the mean, but with reverse scoring, the distance from the mean has been reversed so that a *T*-score of 60 has a standard score that is one standard deviation below the mean.

Table B.1 *T*-Score to Standard Score Conversion

Consistent Scoring		Reverse Scoring	
T-Score	Standard Score	*T*-Score	Standard Score
20	55	30	130
21	56	31	129
22	58	32	127
23	59	33	125
24	61	34	124
25	62	35	122
26	64	36	121
27	65	37	119
28	67	38	118
29	68	39	116
30	70	40	115
31	71	41	113
32	73	42	112
33	75	43	110
34	76	44	109

Table B.1 (*Continued*)

Consistent Scoring		Reverse Scoring	
T-Score	Standard Score	T-Score	Standard Score
35	78	45	107
36	79	46	106
37	81	47	104
38	82	48	103
39	84	49	102
40	85	50	100
41	87	51	98
42	88	52	97
43	90	53	96
44	91	54	94
45	93	55	93
46	94	56	91
47	96	57	90
48	97	58	88
49	98	59	87
50	100	60	85
51	102	61	84
52	103	62	82
53	104	63	81
54	106	64	79
55	107	65	78
56	109	66	76
57	110	67	75
58	112	68	73
59	113	69	71
60	115	70	70
61	116	71	68
62	118	72	67
63	119	73	65
64	121	74	64
65	122	75	62
66	124	76	61
67	125	77	59
68	127	78	58
69	129	79	56
70	130	80	55
71	132	81	53
72	133	82	52

(*continued*)

Table B.1 (*Continued*)

Consistent Scoring		Reverse Scoring	
T-Score	Standard Score	*T*-Score	Standard Score
73	135	83	50
74	136	84	49
75	138	85	47
76	139		
77	141		
78	142		
79	144		
80	145		

Appendix C

Working Memory Composites and Subtests Sorted by Scale

Table C.1 Working Memory Composites and Subtests Sorted by Scale*

Scale	WM Component	Composite	Composite's Subtests	Noncomposite Subtests
CAS-II	Verbal WM			Sentence Questions
CAS-II	Verbal WM			Sentence Repetition
CAS-II	Visual-Spatial STM			Figure Memory
CAS-II	Visual-Spatial STM			Visual Digit Span
CHAMP	Verbal WM			Instructions
CHAMP	Visual-Spatial STM			Objects
CHAMP	Visual-Spatial WM			Places
CPPS	Executive WM			Working Memory
CTOPP	Phonological STM	Phonological Memory		
CTOPP	Phonological STM		Memory for Digits	
CTOPP	Phonological STM		Nonword Repetition	
CTOPP 2	Phonological STM	Phonological Memory		
CTOPP 2	Phonological STM		Memory for Digits	
CTOPP 2	Phonological STM		Nonword Repetition	
DAS-II	Executive WM	Working Memory		
DAS-II	Executive WM		Recall of Digits Backward	
DAS-II	Executive WM		Recall of Sequential Order	
DAS-II	Phonological STM			Recall of Digits Forward
DAS-II	Visual-Spatial STM			Recall of Designs
DAS-II	Visual-Spatial STM			Recognition of Pictures
D-REF Parent	Executive WM	Attention/Working Memory		

D-REF Teacher	Executive WM	Attention/Working Memory	
KABC-II	Executive WM		Word Order
KABC-II	Phonological STM		Number Recall
KABC-II	Visual-Spatial STM		Face Recognition
KABC-II	Visual-Spatial STM		Hand Movements
Leiter 3	Visual-Spatial STM		Forward Memory
Leiter 3	Visual-Spatial WM		Reverse Memory
NEPSY-II	Phonological STM		Repetition of Nonsense Words Total Score
NEPSY-II	Verbal WM		Narrative Memory Free Recall Total Score
NEPSY-II	Verbal WM		Sentence Repetition Total Score
NEPSY-II	Verbal WM		Word List Interference Repetition Total Score
NEPSY-II	Visual-Spatial STM		Memory for Designs Total Score
NEPSY-II	Visual-Spatial STM		Memory for Faces Total
PAL-II	Executive WM		Quantitative Working Memory
PAL-II	Executive WM		Spatial Working Memory Oral
PAL-II	Phonological STM		Letters
PAL-II	Phonological STM		Words

(continued)

Table C.1 *(Continued)*

Scale	WM Component	Composite	Composite's Subtests	Noncomposite Subtests
PAL-II	Verbal WM			Sentences: Listening
PAL-II	Verbal WM			Sentences: Writing
PAL-II	Visual-Spatial WM			Spatial Working Memory Drawing
TAPS-3	Executive WM			Number Memory Reversed
TAPS-3	Phonological STM			Number Memory Forward
TAPS-3	Phonological STM			Word Memory
TAPS-3	Verbal WM			Sentence Memory
TOMAL-2	Executive WM			Digits Backward
TOMAL-2	Executive WM			Letters Backward
TOMAL-2	Phonological STM			Digits Forward
TOMAL-2	Phonological STM			Letters Forward
TOMAL-2	Verbal WM			Memory for Stories
TOMAL-2	Visual-Spatial STM			Abstract Visual Memory
TOMAL-2	Visual-Spatial STM			Facial Memory
TOMAL-2	Visual-Spatial STM			Manual Imitation
TOMAL-2	Visual-Spatial STM			Memory for Location
TOMAL-2	Visual-Spatial STM			Visual Sequential Memory
WAIS-IV	Executive WM			Arithmetic
WAIS-IV	Executive WM			Digit Span Backward
WAIS-IV	Executive WM			Digit Span Sequencing
WAIS-IV	Executive WM			Letter-Number Sequencing
WAIS-IV	Phonological STM			Digit Span Forward
WIAT III	Verbal WM			Sentence Repetition

Test	Construct			Subtest
WISC-IV Integrated	Executive WM			Letter-Number Sequencing PA
WISC-IV Integrated	Phonological STM			Letter Span Nonrhyming
WISC-IV Integrated	Phonological STM			Letter Span Rhyming
WISC-IV Integrated	Visual-Spatial STM			Spatial Span Forward
WISC-IV Integrated	Visual-Spatial STM			Visual Digit Span
WISC-IV Integrated	Visual-Spatial WM			Spatial Span Backward
WISC-V	Executive WM			Digit Span Backward
WISC-V	Executive WM			Digit Span Sequencing
WISC-V	Executive WM			Letter-Number Sequencing
WISC-V	Phonological STM			Digit Span Forward
WISC-V	Visual-Spatial STM			Picture Span
WJ III ACH	Executive WM	Working Memory		Understanding Directions
WJ III ACH	Verbal WM			Story Recall
WJ III COG	Executive WM		Auditory Working Memory	
WJ III COG	Executive WM		Numbers Reversed	
WJ III COG	Executive WM			
WJ III COG	Phonological STM			Memory for Words
WJ III COG	Visual-Spatial STM			Picture Recognition
WJ III DS	Verbal WM	Working Memory		Memory for Sentences
WJ III NU ACH	Executive WM			Understanding Directions
WJ III NU COG	Executive WM		Auditory Working Memory	
WJ III NU COG	Executive WM		Numbers Reversed	
WJ III NU COG	Executive WM			

(continued)

263

Table C.1 (Continued)

Scale	WM Component	Composite	Composite's Subtests	Noncomposite Subtests
WJ III NU COG	Phonological STM			Memory for Words
WJ III NU COG	Visual-Spatial STM			Picture Recognition
WJ IV ACH	Verbal WM			Reading Recall
WJ IV COG	Executive WM	Short-Term Working Memory		
WJ IV COG	Executive WM		Numbers Reversed	Memory for Words
WJ IV COG	Executive WM		Object-Number Sequencing	Story Recall
WJ IV COG	Executive WM		Verbal Attention	Picture Recognition
WJ IV COG	Phonological STM			Understanding Directions
WJ IV COG	Verbal WM			Sentence Repetition
WJ IV COG	Visual-Spatial STM			Logical Memory I
WJ IV ORAL	Executive WM			Designs I
WJ IV ORAL	Verbal WM			Visual Reproduction I
WMS-IV	Verbal WM			
WMS-IV	Visual-Spatial STM			
WMS-IV	Visual-Spatial STM			
WMS-IV	Visual-Spatial WM	Visual Working Memory		
WMS-IV	Visual-Spatial WM		Spatial Addition	
WMS-IV	Visual-Spatial STM		Symbol Span	
WNV	Visual-Spatial STM			Recognition
WPPSI-IV	Visual-Spatial STM	Working Memory	Picture Memory	
WPPSI-IV	Visual-Spatial STM		Zoo Locations	
WPPSI-IV	Visual-Spatial STM			
WRAML2	Executive WM	Working Memory		

WRAML2	Executive WM	Symbolic Working Memory	Number/Letter
WRAML2	Executive WM	Verbal Working Memory	Sentence Memory
WRAML2	Phonological STM		Story Memory
WRAML2	Verbal WM		Design Memory
WRAML2	Verbal WM		Finger Windows
WRAML2	Visual-Spatial STM		Picture Memory
WRAML2	Visual-Spatial STM		
WRAML2	Visual-Spatial WM		

*This table is also in the online resources.

Annotated Bibliography

Alloway, T. P., & Gathercole, S. E. (Eds.). (2006). *Working memory and neurodevelopmental disorders*. New York, NY: Psychology Press.

This edited text outlines the working memory profiles of individuals with a range of neurodevelopmental disorders, such as autism, ADHD, Down syndrome, dyslexia, learning disabilities, and specific language impairment. It also examines the relations between working memory and reading and arithmetic.

Baddeley, A. D. (1986). *Working memory*. New York, NY: Oxford University Press.

For working memory researchers and those developing expertise in working memory, this volume is a must-have resource. Baddeley describes his model of working memory in detail while reviewing the research supporting each component of his model. Much subsequent research has supported the model, but the research foundations are clearly explained in this work. Only the concept of episodic working memory, which was developed later, is missing.

Cowan, N. (2005). *Working memory capacity*. New York, NY: Erlbaum.

In this book, Cowan explains the evidence supporting his theoretical model of working memory, and contrasts the model with competing perspectives, such as Baddeley's. Cowan makes the case for his embedded-processes model that distinguishes between the focus of attention in working memory and recently activated portions of long-term memory. The work also explains the capacity limits of working memory, reviews the research regarding these limitations, and accounts for the limitations from several perspectives.

Dehn, M. J. (2008). *Working memory and academic learning: Assessment and intervention*. Hoboken, NJ: Wiley.

This is the author's initial book on working memory. Much of the information is similar to the current work, except that the current book has updated information as needed. The main differences between the two works are that the original explores theoretical models in more depth, reviews the research in more depth, and examines measurement instruments in more depth.

Dehn, M. J. (2010). *Long-term memory problems in children and adolescents: Assessment, intervention, and effective instruction.* Hoboken, NJ: Wiley.

This book examines long-term memory functions in children from a neuroscience and neuropsychological perspective. After reviewing risk factors and detailing memory processes such as consolidation, this text outlines procedures for diagnostic testing of long-term memory functions. It concludes with evidence-based recommendations for enhancing long-term memory in the classroom and with reviews of evidence-based interventions for individuals and small groups.

Dehn, M. J. (2011). *Helping students remember: Exercises and strategies to strengthen memory.* Hoboken, NJ: Wiley.

This is a practical workbook designed to assist students whose academic learning is suffering due to a memory deficit or ineffective utilization of their memory capabilities. This workbook provides numerous evidence-based strategies and exercises to strengthen both working and long-term memory. The workbook is divided into two levels: the lower level for grades 3 to 6 and the upper level for grades 7 to 12. It includes detailed directions for the instructor or memory trainer, as well as reproducible worksheets for trainees.

Klingberg, T. (2009). *The overflowing brain: Information overload and the limits of working memory.* New York, NY: Oxford University Press.

Klingberg, the author of the computerized working memory training program known as Cogmed, explores the limitations and possibilities of the brain in regards to working memory. Although relevant research is included, this very readable and engaging book is primarily about everyday memory challenges and how individuals should try to find a balance between demand and capacity.

Melby-Lervåg, M., & Hulme, C. (2013). Is working memory training effective? A meta-analytic review. *Developmental Psychology, 49*(2), 270–291. doi:10.1037/a0028228

This systematic meta-analytic review of 23 well-designed studies on computerized working memory training programs found that the programs produced reliable short-term improvements in working memory skills. For verbal working memory, these near-transfer effects were not sustained at follow-up, whereas for visuospatial working memory, limited evidence suggested that such effects might be maintained. More importantly, there was no convincing evidence of the generalization of working memory training to other skills (nonverbal and verbal ability, inhibitory processes in attention, word decoding, and arithmetic). The authors conclude that memory training programs appear to produce short-term, specific training effects that do not generalize. This publication garnered much attention and focused the controversy regarding working memory training because the findings cast doubt on both the clinical relevance of working memory training programs and their utility as methods of enhancing cognitive functioning in typically developing children and healthy adults.

Morrison, A. B., & Chein, J. M. (2011). Does working memory training work? The promise and challenges of enhancing cognition by training working memory. *Psychonomic Bulletin Review, 18,* 46–60.

This article favorably reviews working memory training and provides details on several training methods that have been utilized in research studies. The review found that training-related increases in WM capacity have been successfully demonstrated across a wide range of subject populations, but different training techniques seem to produce different results. In particular, core WM training studies seem to produce more far-reaching transfer effects, likely because they target domain-general mechanisms of WM. The authors are optimistic about the value of WM training, but also acknowledge several limitations that need to be addressed.

References

Ackerman, P. L., Beier, M. E., & Boyle, M. O. (2002a). Individual differences in working memory within a nomological network of cognitive and perceptual speed abilities. *Journal of Experimental Psychology: General, 131*, 567–589.

Ackerman, P. L., Beier, M. E., & Boyle, M. O. (2002b). Working memory and intelligence: The same or different constructs? *Psychological Bulletin, 131*, 30–60.

Adams, W., & Sheslow, W. (2003). *Wide Range Assessment of Memory and Learning–Second Edition*. Wilmington, DE: Wide Range.

Alderson, R. M., Rapport, M. D., Hudec, K. L, Sarver, D. E., & Kofler, M. J. (2010). Competing core processes in Attention-Deficit/Hyperactivity Disorder (ADHD): Do working memory deficiencies underlie behavioral inhibition deficits? *Child Psychology, 38*, 497–507.

Alloway, T. P. (2011). *Improving working memory: Supporting students' learning*. London: SAGE.

Alloway, T. P., & Alloway, R. G. (2009). The efficacy of working memory training in improving crystallized intelligence. *Nature Proceedings*. hdl:10101/npre.2009.3697.1

Alloway, T. P., & Alloway, R. G. (2010). Investigating the predictive roles of working memory and IQ in academic achievement. *Journal of Experimental Child Psychology, 106*, 20–29.

Alloway, T. P., & Gathercole, S. E. (Eds.). (2006). *Working memory and neurodevelopmental disorders*. New York, NY: Psychology Press.

Alloway, T. P., Gathercole, S. E., Adams, A. M., & Willis, C. (2005). Working memory abilities in children with special educational needs. *Educational & Child Psychology, 22*, 56–67.

Alloway, T. P., Gathercole, S. E., & Kirkwood, H. J. (2008). *Working Memory Rating Scale (WMRS)*. London, England: Pearson Assessment.

Alloway, T. P., Gathercole, S. E., & Pickering, S. J. (2006). Verbal and visuo-spatial short-term and working memory in children: Are they separable? *Child Development, 77*, 1698–1716.

Anderson, J. R. (1983). *The architecture of cognition*. Cambridge, MA: Harvard University Press.

Andersson, U., & Lyxell, B. (2007). Working memory deficit in children with mathematical disabilities: A general or specific deficit? *Journal of Experimental Child Psychology, 96*, 197–228.

Ashcraft, M., & Kirk, E. P. (2001). The relationships among working memory, math anxiety, and performance. *Journal of Experimental Psychology: General, 130*, 224–237.

Baars, B. J., & Franklin, S. (2003). How conscious experience and working memory interact. *Trends in Cognitive Sciences, 7*, 166–172.

Babikian, T., & Asarnow, R. (2009). Neurocognitive outcomes and recovery after pediatric TBI: Meta-analytic review of the literature. *Neuropsychology, 23*, 283–296.

Backman, L., & Nyberg, L. (2013). Dopamine and training-related working-memory improvement. *Neuroscience and Biobehavioral Reviews, 37*, 2209–2219.

Baddeley, A. D. (1986). *Working memory*. New York, NY: Oxford University Press.

Baddeley, A. D. (1990). The development of the concept of working memory: Implications and contributions of neuropsychology. In G. Vallar & J. Shallice (Eds.), *Neuropsychological impairments of short-term memory* (pp. 54–73). New York, NY: Cambridge University Press.

Baddeley, A. D. (1996a). The concept of working memory. In S. E. Gathercole (Ed.), *Models of short-term memory* (pp. 1–27). East Sussex, UK: Erlbaum.

Baddeley, A. D. (1996b). Exploring the central executive. *Quarterly Journal of Experimental Psychology, 49A*, 5–28.

Baddeley, A. D. (2000). The episodic buffer: A new component in working memory? *Trends in Cognitive Sciences, 4*, 417–423.

Baddeley, A. D. (2003a). Working memory and language: An overview. *Journal of Communication Disorders, 36*, 189–208.

Baddeley, A. D. (2003b). Working memory: Looking back and looking forward. *Nature Reviews: Neuroscience, 4*, 829–839.

Baddeley, A. D. (2006). Working memory: An overview. In S. J. Pickering (Ed.), *Working memory and education* (pp. 1–31). Burlington, MA: Academic Press.

Baddeley, A. D., & Hitch, G. J. (1974). Working memory. In G. A. Bower (Ed.), *Recent advances in learning and motivation* (Vol. 8, pp. 47–89). New York, NY: Academic Press.

Bahrick, H. P. (2000). Long-term maintenance of knowledge. In E. Tulving & F. I. M. Craik (Eds.), *The Oxford handbook of memory* (pp. 347–362). New York, NY: Oxford University Press.

Baldo, J. V., & Dronkers, N. F. (2006). The role of inferior parietal and inferior frontal cortex in working memory. *Neuropsychology, 20,* 529–538.

Banikowski, A. K., & Mehring, T. A. (1999). Strategies to enhance memory based on brain-research. *Focus on Exceptional Children, 32,* 1–16.

Barkley, R. A. (1997a). *ADHD and the nature of self-control*. New York, NY: Guilford Press.

Barkley, R. A. (1997b). Behavioral inhibition, sustained attention and executive functions: Constructing a unifying theory of ADHD. *Psychological Bulletin, 121,* 65–94.

Barrouillet, P., Bernardin, S., Portrat, S., Vergauwe, E., & Camos, V. (2007). Time and cognitive load in working memory. *Journal of Experimental Psychology: Learning, Memory, & Cognition, 33,* 570–585.

Barrouillet, P., Gavens, N., Vergauwe, E., Gaillard, V., & Camos, V. (2009). Working memory span development: A time-based resource-sharing model account. *Developmental Psychology, 45,* 477–490.

Barrouillet, P., & Lepine, R. (2005). Working memory and children's use of retrieval to solve addition problems. *Journal of Experimental Child Psychology, 91,* 183–204.

Barrouillet, P., Portrat, S., & Camos, V. (2011). On the law relating processing to storage in working memory. *Psychological Review, 118,* 175–192.

Bayliss, D. M., Jarrold, C., Baddeley, A. D., & Gunn, D. M. (2003). The complexities of complex span: Explaining individual differences in working memory in children and adults. *Journal of Experimental Psychology: General, 132,* 71–92.

Bedard, A-C., Martinussen, R., Ickowicz, A., & Tannock, R. (2004). Methylphenidate improves visual-spatial memory in children with attention-deficit/hyperactivity disorder. *Journal of the American Academy of Child and Adolescent Psychiatry, 43,* 260–280.

Berninger, V. W., & Richards, T. L. (2002). *Brain literacy for educators and psychologists*. San Diego, CA: Academic Press.

Briscoe, J., Gathercole, S. E., & Marlow, N. (2001). Everyday memory and cognitive ability in children born very prematurely. *Journal of Child Psychology and Psychiatry, 42,* 749–754.

Broadbent, N. J., Clark, R. E., Zola, S., & Squire, L. R. (2002). The medial temporal lobe and memory. In L. R. Squire & D. L. Schacter (Eds.), *Neuropsychology of memory* (3rd ed., pp. 3–23). New York, NY: Guilford Press.

Broadley, I., MacDonald, J., & Buckley, S. (1994). Are children with Down's syndrome able to maintain skills learned from a short-term memory training programme? *Down Syndrome: Research and Practice, 2,* 116–122.

Brown, D. A., & Hulme, C. (1996). Nonword repetition, STM, and word age-of-acquisition: A computational model. A model and a method. In S. E. Gathercole (Ed.), *Models of short-term memory* (pp. 129–148). East Sussex, UK: Erlbaum.

Brown, S. C., & Craik, F. I. M. (2000). Encoding and retrieval of information. In E. Tulving & F. I. M. Craik (Eds.), *The Oxford handbook of memory* (pp. 93–107). New York, NY: Oxford University Press.

Brown, T. E., Reichel, P. C., & Quinlan, D. M. (2009). Executive function impairments in high IQ adults with ADHD. *Journal of Attention Disorders, 13,* 161–167.

Buehner, M., Krumm, S., Ziegler, M., & Pluecken, T. (2006). Cognitive abilities and their interplay: Reasoning, crystallized intelligence, working memory components, and sustained attention. *Journal of Individual Differences, 27,* 57–72.

Buehner, M., Mangels, M., Krumm, S., & Ziegler, M. (2005). Are working memory and attention related constructs? *Journal of Individual Differences, 26,* 121–131.

Bull, R., & Espy, K. A. (2006). Working memory, executive functioning, and children's mathematics. In S. J. Pickering (Ed.), *Working memory and education* (pp. 93–123). Burlington, MA: Academic Press.

Bull, R., & Johnston, R. S. (1997). Children's arithmetic difficulties: Contributions from processing speed, item identification, and short-term memory. *Journal of Experimental Child Psychology, 65,* 1–24.

Bunge, S. A., & Wright, S. B. (2007). Neurodevelopmental changes in working memory and cognitive control. *Current Opinion in Neurobiology, 17,* 243–250.

Bus, A., & Van IJzendoorn, M. (1999). Phonological awareness and early reading: A meta-analysis of experimental training studies. *Journal of Educational Psychology, 91,* 403–414.

Buschkuehl, M., Jaeggi, S. M., & Jonides, J. (2012). Neuronal effects following working memory training. *Developmental Cognitive Neuroscience, 25,* S167–S179.

Cain, K., Oakhill, J., & Bryant, P. (2004). Children's reading comprehension ability: Concurrent prediction by working memory, verbal ability, and component skills. *Journal of Educational Psychology, 96,* 31–42.

Carmen, D. V. (2012). Working memory deficits in math learning difficulties: A meta-analysis. *International Journal of Developmental Disabilities, 58,* 67–84.

Carney, R. N., Levin, M. E., & Levin, J. R. (1993). Mnemonic strategies: Instructional techniques worth remembering. *Teaching Exceptional Children, 25,* 24–30.

Carretti, B., Borella, E., Cornoldi, C., & De Beni, R. (2009). Role of working memory in explaining the performance of individuals with specific reading comprehension difficulties: A meta-analysis. *Learning and Individual Differences, 19,* 246–251.

Carroll, J. B. (1993). *Human cognitive abilities: A survey of factor-analytic studies.* Cambridge, UK: Cambridge University Press.

Chun, M. M., Golomb, J. D., & Turk-Browne, N. B. (2011). A taxonomy of internal and external attention. *Annual Review of Psychology, 62,* 73–101. doi:10.1146/annurev.psych.093008.100427

Clark, J., & Klecan-Aker, J. (1992). Therapeutic strategies for language disordered children: The impact of visual imagery on verbal encoding in vocabulary instruction. *Journal of Childhood Communication Disorders, 14,* 129–145.

Cohen-Mimran, R., & Sapir, S. (2007). Deficits in working memory in young adults with reading disabilities. *Journal of Communication Disorders, 40,* 168–183.

Colom, R., Rebollo, I., Palacios, A., Juan-Espinosa, M., & Kyllonen, P. C. (2004).Working memory is (almost) perfectly predicted by *g*. *Intelligence, 32,* 277–296.

Comblain, A. (1994). Working memory in Down's syndrome: Training the rehearsal strategy. *Down Syndrome: Research and Practice, 2,* 123–126.

Compton, D. L., Fuchs, L. S., Fuchs, D., Lambert, W., & Hamlett, C. L. (2012). The cognitive and academic profiles of reading and mathematics learning disabilities. *Journal of Learning Disabilities, 45,* 79–95.

Conlin, J. A., & Gathercole, S. E. (2006). Lexicality and interference in working memory in children and adults. *Journal of Memory and Language, 55,* 363–380.

Conlin, J. A., Gathercole, S. E., & Adams, J. W. (2005). Children's working memory: Investigating performance limitations in complex span tasks. *Journal of Experimental Child Psychology, 90,* 303–317.

Conners, F. A., Rosenquist, C. J., & Taylor, L. A. (2001). Memory training for children with Down syndrome. *Down Syndrome: Research and Practice, 7,* 25–33.

Conway, A. R. A., Cowan, N., & Bunting, M. F. (2001). The cocktail party revisited: The importance of working memory capacity. *Psychonomic Bulletin & Review, 8,* 331–335.

Conway, A. R. A., Cowan, N., Bunting, M. F., Therriault, D. J., & Minkoff, S. R. B. (2002). A latent variable analysis of working memory capacity, short-term memory capacity, processing speed, and general fluid intelligence. *Intelligence, 30,* 163–183.

Conway, A. R. A., Kane, M. J., & Engle, R. W. (2003). Working memory capacity and its relation to general intelligence. *Trends in Cognitive Sciences, 7,* 547–552.

Conway, A. R. A., Macnamara, B. N., & Engel de Abreu, P. M. J. (2013). Working memory and intelligence: An overview. In T. P. Alloway & R. G. Alloway (Eds.), *Working memory: The connected intelligence* (pp. 13–36). New York, NY: Psychology Press.

Conway, R. N., & Ashman, A. (1989). Teaching planning skills in the classroom: The development of an integrated model. *International Journal of Disability, Development and Education, 36,* 225–240.

Cook, N. M. (1989). The applicability of verbal mnemonics for different populations: A review. *Applied Cognitive Psychology, 3,* 3–22.

Corkin, S. (1984). Lasting consequences of bilateral medial temporal lobectomy: Clinical course and experimental findings in H.M. *Seminars in Neurology, 4*(2), 249–259. doi:10.1055/s-2008-1041556.

Cornish, K., Wilding, J., & Grant, C. (2006). Deconstructing working memory in developmental disorders of attention. In S. J. Pickering (Ed.), *Working memory and education* (pp. 157–188). Burlington, MA: Academic Press.

Cowan, N. (1995). *Attention and memory: An integrated framework.* Oxford Psychology Series, 26. New York, NY: Oxford University Press.

Cowan, N. (1999). An embedded-process model of working memory. In A. Miyake & P. Shah (Eds.), *Models of working memory: Mechanisms of active maintenance and executive control* (pp. 62–101). Cambridge, UK: Cambridge University Press.

Cowan, N. (2001). The magical number 4 in short-term memory: A reconsideration of mental storage capacity. *Behavioral and Brain Sciences, 24,* 87–185.

Cowan, N. (2005). *Working memory capacity.* New York, NY: Erlbaum.

Craig, F. I. M., & Lockhart, R. S. (1972). Levels of processing: A framework for memory research. *Journal of Verbal Learning and Verbal Behavior, 11,* 671–684.

Crain, S., Shankweiler, D., Macaruso, P., & Bar-Shalom, E. (1990). Working memory and comprehension of spoken sentences: Investigations of children with reading disorder. In G. Vallar & J. Shallice (Eds.), *Neuropsychological impairments of short-term memory* (pp. 477–509). New York, NY: Cambridge University Press.

Dahlin, E., Nyberg, L., Backman, L., & Neely, A. S. (2008). Plasticity of executive functioning in young and older adults: Immediate training gains, transfer, and long-term maintenance. *Psychology and Aging, 23,* 720–730.

Dahlin, K. I. E. (2011). Effects of working memory training on reading in children with special needs. *Reading and Writing, 24,* 479–491.

Daneman, M., & Carpenter, P. A. (1980). Individual differences in working memory and reading. *Journal of Verbal Learning and Verbal Behavior, 19,* 450–466.

Daneman, M., & Merikle, P. M. (1996). Working memory and language comprehension: A meta-analysis. *Psychonomic Bulletin and Review, 3,* 422–433.

Daneman, M., & Tardiff, T. (1987). Working memory and reading skill reexamined. In M. Coltheart (Ed.), *Attention and performance XII: The psychology of reading* (pp. 491–508). Hove, UK: Erlbaum.

David, C. V. (2012). Working memory deficits in math learning disabilities: A meta-analysis. *International Journal of Developmental Disabilities, 58,* 67–84.

De Abreu, E., & Pascale, M. J. (2011). Working memory in multilingual children: Is there a bilingual effect? *Memory, 19,* 529–537.

De Beni, R., Borella, E., & Carretti, B. (2007). Reading comprehension in aging: The role of working memory and metacomprehension. *Aging, Neuropsychology, and Cognition, 14,* 189–212.

De Beni, R., & Palladino, P. (2000). Intrusion errors in working memory tasks: Are they related to reading comprehension ability. *Learning and Individual Differences, 12,* 131–145.

De Beni, R., Pazzaglia, F., Meneghetti, C., & Mondoloni, A. (2007). Working memory components and imagery instructions in the elaboration of a spatial mental model. *Psychological Research, 71,* 373–382.

Dehn, M. J. (2008). *Working memory and academic learning: Assessment and intervention.* Hoboken, NJ: Wiley.

Dehn, M. J. (2010). *Long-term memory problems in children and adolescents: Assessment, intervention, and effective instruction.* Hoboken, NJ: Wiley.

Dehn, M. J. (2011). *Helping students remember: Exercises and strategies to strengthen memory.* Hoboken, NJ: Wiley.

Dehn, M. J. (2012). *Children's Psychological Processes Scale.* Onalaska, WI: Schoolhouse Educational Services.

Dehn, M. J. (2014a). The Children's Psychological Processes Scale (CPPS): Factor structure and correlations with performance-based measures. *Journal of Attention Disorders, 18,* 305–317.

Dehn, M. J. (2014b). *Essentials of processing assessment* (2nd ed.). Hoboken, NJ: Wiley.

Dehn, M. J. (2014c). Interventions for students with memory difficulties. In J. T. Mascolo, V. C. Alfonso, & D. P. Flanagan (Eds.), *Essentials of planning, selecting, and tailoring interventions for unique learners* (pp. 357–386). Hoboken, NJ: Wiley.

Dehn, M. J. (2014d). *The memory processes analyzer*. Onalaska, WI: Schoolhouse Educational Services.

Dehn, M. J. (2014e). Supporting and strengthening working memory in the classroom to enhance executive functioning. In S. Goldstein & J. A. Naglieri (Eds.), *Handbook of executive functioning* (pp. 495–508). New York, NY: Springer.

de Jong, P. F. (1998). Working memory deficits of reading disabled children. *Journal of Experimental Child Psychology, 70,* 75–96.

de Jong, P. F. (2006). Understanding normal and impaired reading development: A working memory perspective. In S. J. Pickering (Ed.), *Working memory and education* (pp. 33–60). Burlington, MA: Academic Press.

de Jong, T. (2010). Cognitive load theory, educational research, and instructional design: Some food for thought. *Instructional Science, 38,* 105–134.

DeLuca, J., Schultheis, M. T., Madigan, N. K., Christodoulou, C., & Averill, A. (2000). Acquisition versus retrieval deficits in traumatic brain injury: Implications for memory rehabilitation. *Archives of Physical Medicine and Rehabilitation, 81,* 1327–1333.

D'Esposito, M. (2007). From cognitive to neural models of working memory. *Philosophical Transactions of the Royal Society of London, Series B, Biological Sciences, 362,* 761–772.

D'Esposito, M., Detre, J. A., Alsop, D. C., Shin, R. K., Atlas, S., & Grossman, M. (1995). The neural basis of the central executive system of working memory. *Nature, 378,* 279–281.

Desrocher, M. & Rovet, J. (2004). Neurocognitive correlates of Type I Diabetes Mellitus in childhood. *Child Neuropsychology, 10,* 36–52.

Duff, S. C., & Logie, R. H. (2001). Processing and storage in working memory span. *Quarterly Journal of Experimental Psychology, 54A,* 31–48.

Dunlosky, J., & Bjork, R. A. (Eds.). (2008). *Handbook of metamemory and memory*. New York, NY: Psychology Press.

Dunning, D. L., Holmes, J., & Gathercole, S. E. (2013). Does working memory training lead to generalized improvements in children with low working memory? A randomized controlled trial. *Developmental Science, 16,* 915–925.

Dye, M. W., Green, C. S., & Bavelier, D. (2009). Increasing speed of processing with action video games. *Current Directions in Psychological Science, 18,* 321–326.

Elliott, C. D. (2006). *Differential Ability Scales–Second Edition.* San Antonio, TX: PsychCorp.

Elliott, J. G., Gathercole, S. E., Alloway, T. P., Holmes, J., & Kirkwood, H. (2010). An evaluation of a classroom-based intervention to help overcome working memory difficulties and improve long-term academic achievement. *Journal of Cognitive Education and Psychology, 9,* 227–250.

Ellis, N. C., & Hennelley, R. A. (1980). A bilingual word-length effect: Implications for intelligence testing and the relative ease of mental calculation in Welsh and English. *British Journal of Psychology, 71,* 43–52.

Elzinga, B. M., Bakker, A., & Bremner, J. D. (2005). Stress-induced cortisol elevations are associated with impaired delayed, but not immediate recall. *Psychiatry Research, 134,* 211–223.

Emilien, G., Durlach, C., Antoniadis, E., Van Der Linden, M., & Maloteaux, J-M. (2004). *Memory: Neuropsychological, imaging, and psychopharmacological perspectives.* New York, NY: Psychology Press.

Engle, R. W. (1996). Working memory and retrieval: An inhibition-resource approach. In J. T. E. Richardson, R. W. Engle, L. Hasher, R. H. Logie, E. R. Stoltzfus, & R. T. Zacks (Eds.), *Working memory and human cognition* (pp. 89–119). New York, NY: Oxford University Press.

Engle, R. W. (2002). Working memory capacity as executive attention. *Current Directions in Psychological Science, 11*(1), 19–23.

Engle, R. W., Cantor, J. J., & Carullo, J. J. (1992). Individual differences in working memory and comprehension: A test of four hypotheses. *Journal of Experimental Psychology: Learning, Memory, and Cognition, 18,* 972–992.

Engle, R. W., Carullo, J. J., & Collins, K. W. (1991). Individual differences in working memory for comprehension and following directions. *Journal of Educational Research, 84,* 253–262.

Engle, R. W., Kane, M. J., & Tuholski, S. W. (1999). Individual differences in working memory capacity and what they tell us about controlled attention, general fluid intelligence and functions of the prefrontal cortex. In A. Miyake & P. Shah (Eds.), *Models of working memory: Mechanisms of active maintenance and executive control* (pp. 102–134). Cambridge, UK: Cambridge University Press.

Engle, R. W., Tuholski, S. W., Laughlin, J. E., & Conway, A. R. A. (1999). Working memory, short-term memory, and general fluid intelligence: A latent-variable approach. *Journal of Experimental Psychology: General, 128,* 309–331.

Ericsson, K. A., & Kintsch, W. (1995). Long-term working memory. *Psychological Review, 102,* 211–245.

Frisco-van den Bos, I., van der Ven, S. H. G., Kroesbergen, E. H., & van Luit, J. E. H. (2013). Working memory and mathematics in primary school children: A meta-analysis. *Educational Research Review, 10,* 29–44.

Fry, A. F., & Hale, S. (1996). Processing speed, working memory, and fluid intelligence: Evidence for a developmental cascade. *Psychological Science, 7,* 237–241.

Gagne, E. D., Yekovich, C. W., & Yekovich, F. R. (1993). *The cognitive psychology of school learning* (2nd ed.). New York, NY: HarperCollins College.

Garcia-Madruga, J. A., Elosua, M. R., Gil, L., Gomez-Veiga, I., Vila, J. O., Orjales, I., … Duque, G. (2013). Reading comprehension and working memory's executive processes: An intervention study in primary school students. *Reading Research Quarterly, 48,* 155–174.

Gathercole, S. E. (1999). Cognitive approaches to the development of short-term memory. *Trends in Cognitive Sciences, 3,* 410–419.

Gathercole, S. E., & Adams, A-M. (1993). Phonological working memory in very young children. *Developmental Psychology, 29,* 770–778.

Gathercole, S. E., & Alloway, T. P. (2004). Working memory and classroom learning. *Dyslexia Review, 15,* 4–9.

Gathercole, S. E., & Alloway, T. P. (2008). *Working memory and learning: A practical guide for teachers.* Los Angeles, CA: SAGE.

Gathercole, S. E., & Baddeley, A. D. (1989). Evaluation of the role of phonological STM in the development of vocabulary in children: A longitudinal study. *Journal of Memory and Language, 28,* 200–213.

Gathercole, S. E., & Baddeley, A. D. (1990). The role of phonological memory in vocabulary acquisition: A study of young children learning new names. *British Journal of Psychology, 81,* 439–454.

Gathercole, S. E., & Baddeley, A. D. (1993). *Working memory and language*. East Sussex, UK: Lawrence Erlbaum.

Gathercole, S. E., & Pickering, S. J. (2000). Assessment of working memory in six- and seven-year-old children. *Journal of Educational Psychology, 92,* 377–390.

Gathercole, S. E., Pickering, S. J., Ambridge, B., & Wearing, H. (2004). The structure of working memory from 4–15 years of age. *Developmental Psychology, 40,* 177–190.

Geary, D. C. (2011, September 26). Cognitive predictors of achievement growth in mathematics: A 5-year longitudinal study. *Developmental Psychology*. Advance online publication. doi:10.1037/a0025510

Geary, D. C., Hoard, M. K., Byrd-Craven, J., & DeSoto, M. C. (2004). Strategy choices in simple and complex addition: Contributions of working memory and counting knowledge for children with mathematical disability. *Journal of Experimental Child Psychology, 88,* 121–151.

Gershberg, F. B., & Shimamura, A. P. (1995). Impaired use of organizational strategies in free recall following frontal lobe damage. *Neuropsychologia, 33,* 1305–1333.

Gersten, R. (1985). Direct instruction with special education students: A review of evaluation research. *Journal of Special Education, 19,* 41–58.

Gersten, R., & Keating, T. (1987). Long-term benefits from direct instruction. *Educational Leadership, 44,* 28–29.

Giap, B. T., Jong, C. N., Ricker, J. H., Cullen, N. K., & Zafonte, R. D. (2000). The hippocampus: Anatomy, pathophysiology, and regenerative capacity. *Journal of Head Trauma and Rehabilitation, 15,* 875–894.

Gibson, B. S., Gondoli, D. M., Flies, A. C., Dobrzenski, B. A., & Unsworth, N. (2010). Application of the dual-component model of working memory in ADHD. *Child Neuropsychology, 16,* 60–79.

Gibson, B. S., Kronenberger, W. G., Gondoli, D. M., Johnson, A. C., Morrissey, R. A., & Steeger, C. M. (2012). Component analysis of simple span vs. complex span adaptive working memory exercises: A randomized, controlled trial. *Journal of Applied Research in Memory and Cognition, 1,* 179–184.

Gill, C. B., Klecan-Aker, J., Roberts, T., & Fredenburg, K. A. (2003). Following directions: Rehearsal and visualization strategies for children with specific language impairment. *Child Language Teaching and Therapy, 19,* 85–104.

Gillon, G. T. (2004). *Phonological awareness*. New York, NY: Guilford Press.

Giofre, D., Mammarella, I. C., & Cornoldi, C. (2013). The structure of working memory and how it relates to intelligence in children. *Intelligence, 41,* 396–406.

Gioia, G. A., Isquith, P. K., Guy, S. C., & Kenworthy, L. (2000). *Behavior Rating Inventory of Executive Function*. Lutz, FL: Psychological Assessment Resources.

Goff, D. A., Pratt, C., & Ong, B. (2005). The relations between children's reading comprehension, working memory, language skills and components of reading decoding in a normal sample. *Reading and Writing, 18,* 583–616.

Goldman-Rakic, P. S. (1992). Working memory and the mind. *Scientific American, 267*(3), 111–117.

Gray, S. A., Chaban, P., Martinussen, R., Goldberg, R., Gotlieb, H., Kronitz, R., … Tannock, R. (2012). Effects of computerized working memory training program on working memory, attention, and academics in adolescents with severe LD and comorbid ADHD: A randomized controlled trial. *Journal of Child Psychology and Psychiatry, 53,* 1277–1284.

Green, C. S., & Bavelier, D. (2008). Exercising your brain: A review of human brain plasticity and training-induced learning. *Psychology and Aging, 23,* 692–701.

Green, C. T., Long, D. L., Green, D., Losif, A. M., Dixon, J. F., Miller, M. R., … Schweitzer, J. B. (2012). Will working memory training generalize to improve off-task behavior in children with attention-deficit/hyperactivity disorder? *Neurotherapeutics, 9,* 639–648.

Gropper, R. J., Gotlieb, H., Kronitz, R., & Tannock, R. (2014). Working memory training in college students with ADHD or LD. *Journal of Attention Disorders, 18,* 331–345.

Gutierrez-Clellen, V. F., Calderon, J., & Weismer, S. E. (2004). Verbal working memory in bilingual children. *Journal of Speech, Language, and Hearing Research, 47,* 863–876.

Haist, F., Shimamura, A. P., & Squire, L. R. (1992). On the relationship between recall and recognition memory. *Journal of Experimental Psychology: Learning, Memory, and Cognition, 18,* 691–702.

Hale, J. B., & Fiorello, C. A. (2004). *School neuropsychology: A practitioner's handbook*. New York, NY: Guilford Press.

Halford, G. S., Wilson, W. H., & Phillips, S. (2001). Processing capacity limits are not explained by storage limits. *Behavioral and Brain Sciences, 24,* 123–124.

Hanten, G., Bartha, M., & Levin, H. S. (2001). Metacognition following pediatric traumatic brain injury: A preliminary study. *Developmental Neuropsychology, 18,* 383–398.

Harris, J. R. (1996). Verbal rehearsal and memory in children with closed head injury: A quantitative and qualitative analysis. *Journal of Communication Disorders, 29,* 79–93.

Harris, K. R., Friedlander, B. D., Saddler, B., Frizzelle, R., & Graham, S. (2005). Self-monitoring of attention versus self-monitoring of academic performance: Effects among students with ADHD in the general education classroom. *Journal of Special Education, 39,* 145–156.

Hartsuiker, R. J., & Barkuysen, P. N. (2006). Language production and working memory: The case of subject-verb agreement. *Language and Cognitive Processes, 21,* 181–204.

Hasher, L., & Zacks, R. T. (1979). Automatic and effortful processes in memory. *Journal of Experimental Psychology: General, 108,* 356–388.

Hedden, T., & Yoon, C. (2006). Individual differences in executive processing predict susceptibility to interference in verbal working memory. *Neuropsychology, 20,* 511–528.

Henry, L. A. (2001). How does the severity of a learning disability affect working memory performance? *Memory, 9,* 233–247.

Henry, L. A., & Millar, S. (1993). Why does memory span improve with age? A review of the evidence for two current hypotheses. *European Journal of Cognitive Psychology, 5,* 241–287.

Hershey, T., Lillie, R., Sadler, M., & White, N. H. (2003). Severe hypoglycemia and long-term spatial memory in children with type 1 diabetes mellitus: A retrospective study. *Journal of the International Neuropsychological Society, 9,* 740–750.

Hester, R., & Garavan, H. (2005). Working memory and executive function: The influence of content and load on the control of attention. *Memory & Cognition, 33,* 221–233.

Hitch, G. J. (1990). Developmental fractionation of working memory. In G. Vallar & J. Shallice (Eds.), *Neuropsychological impairments of short-term memory* (pp. 221–246). New York, NY: Cambridge University Press.

Hitch, G. J., Halliday, S., Schaafstal, A. M., & Schraagen, M. C. (1988). Visual working memory in young children. *Memory & Cognition, 16,* 120–132.

Hitch, G. J., Towse, J. N., & Hutton, U. (2001). What limits children's working memory capacity? Theoretical accounts and applications for scholastic development. *Journal of Experimental Psychology: General, 130,* 183–198.

Holmes, J., & Adams, J. W. (2006). Working memory and children's mathematical skills: Implications for mathematical development and mathematics curricula. *Educational Psychology, 26,* 339–366.

Holmes, J., Gathercole, S. E., & Dunning, D. L. (2009). Adaptive training leads to sustained enhancement of poor working memory in children. *Developmental Science, 12,* F9–F15.

Hudec, K. L., Alderson, R. M., Kasper, L. J., & Patros, C. H. G. (2014). Working memory contributes to elevated motor activity in adults with ADHD: An examination of the role of central executive and storage/rehearsal processes. *Journal of Attention Disorders, 18,* 357–368.

Hulme, C., & Mackenzie, S. (1992). *Working memory and severe learning difficulties.* East Sussex, UK: Lawrence Erlbaum.

Hutton, U. M. Z., & Towse, J. N. (2001). Short-term memory and working memory as indices of children's cognitive skills. *Memory, 9,* 383–394.

Imbo, I., & Vandierendonck, A. (2007). The development of strategy use in elementary school children: Working memory and individual differences. *Journal of Experimental Child Psychology, 96,* 284–309.

Imbo, I., Vandierendonck, A., & Vergauwe, E. (2007). The role of working memory in carrying and borrowing. *Psychological Research, 71,* 467–483.

Jaeggi, S. M., Buschkuehl, M., Jonides, J., & Perrig, W. J. (2008). Improved fluid intelligence with training on working memory. *Proceedings of the National Academy of Sciences, USA, 105*(19), 6829–6833. doi:10.1073/pnas.0801268105

Jaeggi, S. M., Buschkuehl, M., Jonides, J., & Shah, P. (2012). Cogmed and working memory training—Current challenges and the search for underlying mechanisms. *Journal of Applied Research in Memory and Cognition, 1,* 211–213.

Jang, J., Schunn, C. D., & Nokes, T. J. (2011). Spatially distributed instructions improve learning outcomes and efficiency. *Journal of Educational Psychology, 103,* 60–72.

Johnson, W., Logie, R. H., & Brockmole, J. R. (2010). Working memory tasks differ in factor structure across age cohorts: Implications for dedifferentiation. *Intelligence, 38,* 513–528.

Jonides, J., Smith, E. E., Marshuetz, C., & Koeppe, R. A. (1998). Inhibition in verbal working memory revealed by brain activation. *Proceedings of the National Academy of Sciences, U.S.A, 95,* 8410–8413.

Just, M. A., & Carpenter, P. A. (1992). A capacity theory of comprehension: Individual differences in working memory. *Psychological Review, 99,* 122–149.

Kail, R. (2007). Longitudinal evidence that increases in processing speed and working memory enhance children's reasoning. *Psychological Science, 18,* 312–313.

Kail, R., & Hall, L. K. (2001). Distinguishing short-term memory from working memory. *Memory & Cognition, 29,* 1–9.

Kamhi, A. G., & Pollock, K. E. (2005). *Phonological disorders in children: Clinical decision making in assessment and intervention.* Baltimore, MD: Brookes.

Kane, M. J., Conway, A. R. A., Bleckley, M. K., & Engle, R. W. (2001). A controlled-attention view of working memory capacity. *Journal of Experimental Psychology: General, 130,* 169–183.

Kane, M. J., & Engle, R. W. (2000). Working-memory capacity, proactive interference, and divided attention: Limits on long-term memory retrieval. *Journal of Experimental Psychology: Learning, Memory, and Cognition, 26,* 336–358.

Kane, M. J., & Engle, R. W. (2002). The role of prefrontal cortex in working-memory capacity, executive attention, and general fluid intelligence: An individual-differences perspective. *Psychonomic Bulletin and Review, 9,* 637–671.

Kane, M. J., Hambrick, D. Z., Tuholski, S. W., Wilhelm, O., Payne, T. W., & Engle, R. W. (2004). The generality of working memory capacity: A latent-variable approach to verbal and visuospatial memory span and reasoning. *Journal of Experimental Psychology: General, 133,* 189–217.

Kar, B. C., Dash, U. N., Das, J. P., & Carlson, J. (1993). Two experiments on the dynamic assessment of planning. *Learning and Individual Differences, 5,* 13–29.

Karpicke, J. D., & Roediger, H. L., III (2007). Expanding retrieval practice promotes short-term retention, but equally spaced retrieval enhances long-term retention. *Journal of Experimental Psychology: Learning, Memory, and Cognition, 33,* 704–719.

Kasper, L. J., Alderson, R. M., & Hudec, K. L. (2012). Moderators of working memory deficits in children with attention-deficit/hyperactivity disorder (ADHD): A meta-analytic review. *Clinical Psychology Review, 32,* 605–617.

Kaufman, A. S., & Kaufman, N. L. (2004). *Kaufman Assessment Battery for Children–Second Edition.* Circle Pines, MN: AGS.

Keith, T. Z., Fine, J. G., Taub, G. E., Reynolds, M. R., & Kranzler, J. H. (2006). Higher order, multi-sample, confirmatory factor analysis of the Wechsler Intelligence Scale for Children—Fourth Edition: What does it measure? *School Psychology Quarterly, 12,* 89–107.

Kellogg, R. T., Olive, T., & Piolat, A. (2007). Verbal, visual, and spatial working memory in written language production. *Acta Psychologica, 124,* 382–297.

Kirschner, P. A. (2002). Cognitive load theory: Implications of cognitive load theory on the design of learning. *Learning and Instruction, 12,* 1–10.

Klimesch, W. (1994). *The structure of long-term memory: A connectivity model of semantic processing.* Hillsdale, NJ: Erlbaum.

Klingberg, T. (2009). *The overflowing brain: Information overload and the limits of working memory.* New York, NY: Oxford University Press.

Klingberg, T. (2010). Training and plasticity of working memory. *Trends in Cognitive Sciences, 14,* 317–324.

Klingberg, T., Fernell, E., Olesen, P., Johnston, M., Gustafsson, P., Dahlstrom, K., … Westerberg, H. (2005). Computerized training of working memory in children with ADHD—A controlled, randomized, double-blind trial. *Journal of the American Academy of Child and Adolescent Psychiatry, 44,* 177–186.

Klingberg, T., Forssberg, H., & Westerberg, H. (2002). Training of working memory in children with ADHD. *Journal of Clinical and Experimental Neuropsychology, 24,* 781–791.

Koriat, A. (2000). Control processes in remembering. In E. Tulving & F. I. M. Craik (Eds.), *The Oxford handbook of memory* (pp. 333–346). New York, NY: Oxford University Press.

Korkman, M., Kirk, U., & Kemp, S. (2007). *NEPSY-II: A developmental neuropsychological assessment.* San Antonio, TX: Psychological Corporation.

Kroesbergen, E. H., Van Luit, J. E., & Naglieri, J. A. (2003). Mathematical learning disabilities and PASS cognitive processes. *Journal of Learning Disabilities, 36,* 574–582.

Kyllonen, P. C. (1996). Is working memory capacity Spearman's *g*? In I. Dennis & P. Tapsfield (Eds.), *Human abilities: Their nature and measurement* (pp. 49–76). Mahwah, NJ: Erlbaum.

Kyllonen, P. C., & Christal, R. E. (1990). Reasoning ability is (little more than) working-memory capacity?! *Intelligence, 14,* 389–433.

Lauer, R. E., Giordani, B., Boivin, M. J., Halle, N., Glasgow, B., Alessi, N. E., … Berent, S. (1994). Effects of depression on memory performance and metamemory in children. *Journal of the American Academy of Child and Adolescent Psychiatry, 33,* 679–685.

Leather, C. V., & Henry, L. A. (1994). Working memory span and phonological awareness tasks as predictors of early reading ability. *Journal of Experimental Child Psychology, 58,* 88–111.

LeBlanc, M. D., & Weber-Russell, S. (1996). Text integration and mathematical connections: A computer model of arithmetic word problem solving. *Cognitive Science, 20,* 357–407.

Leonard, L. B., Weismer, S. E., Miller, C. A., Francis, D. J., Tomblin, J. B., & Kail, R. V. (2007). Speed of processing, working memory, and language impairment in children. *Journal of Speech, Language, and Hearing Research, 50,* 408–428.

Levin, H. S., Fletcher, J. M., Kusnerik, L., & Kufera, J. A. (1996). Semantic memory following pediatric head injury: Relationship to age, severity of injury, and MRI. *Cortex, 32,* 461–478.

Liefooghe, B., Barrouillet, P., Vandierendonck, A., & Camos, V. (2008). Working memory costs of task switching. *Journal of Experimental Psychology: Learning, Memory, and Cognition, 34,* 478–494.

Linden, D. E. J. (2007). The working memory networks of the human brain. *Neuroscientist, 13,* 257–267.

Linderholm, T., & Van Den Broek, P. (2002). The effects of reading purpose and working memory capacity on the processing of expository text. *Journal of Educational Psychology, 94,* 778–784.

Loomes, C., Rasmussen, C., & Pei, J. (2008). The effect of rehearsal training on working memory span of children with fetal alcohol spectrum disorder. *Research in Developmental Disabilities, 29,* 113–124.

Loosli, S. V., Buschkuehl, M., Perrig, W. J., & Jaeggi, S. M. (2012). Working memory training improves reading processes in typically developing children. *Child Neuropsychology, 18,* 62–78.

Luciana, M., Conklin, H. M., Hooper, C. J., & Yarger, R. S. (2005). The development of nonverbal working memory and executive control processes in adolescents. *Child Development, 76,* 697–712.

MacDonald, M. C., & Christiansen, M. H. (2002). Reassessing working memory: Comment on Just and Carpenter (1992) and Waters and Caplan (1996). *Psychological Review, 109,* 35–54.

Mackey, A. P., Hill, S. S., Stone, S. I., & Bunge, S. A. (2011). Differential effects of reasoning and speed training in children. *Developmental Science, 14,* 582–590.

Martin, N. A., & Brownell, R. (2005). *Test of Auditory Processing Skills, Third Edition.* Novato, CA: Academic Therapy.

Martinussen, R., Hayden, J., Hogg-Johnson, S., & Tannock, R. (2005). A meta-analysis of working memory impairments in children with attention-deficit/hyperactivity disorder. *Journal of the American Academy of Child and Adolescent Psychiatry, 44,* 377–384.

Martinussen, R., & Tannock, R. (2006). Working memory impairments in children with attention-deficit hyperactivity disorder with and without comorbid language learning disorders. *Journal of Clinical and Experimental Neuropsychology, 28,* 1073–1094.

Masoura, E. V. (2006). Establishing the link between working memory function and learning disabilities. *Learning Disabilities: A Contemporary Journal, 4,* 29–41.

Mastropieri, M. A., Sweda, J., & Scruggs, T. E. (2000). Putting mnemonic strategies to work in an inclusive classroom. *Learning Disabilities Research & Practice, 15,* 69–74.

McCabe, D. P., Roediger, H. L., McDaniel, M. A., Balota, D. A., & Hambrick, D. Z. (2010). The relationship between working memory capacity and executive functioning: Evidence for a common executive attention construct. *Neuropsychology, 24,* 222–243.

McClelland, J. L., McNaughton, B. L., & O'Reilly, R. C. (1995). Why there are complementary learning systems in the hippocampus and neocortex: Insights from the successes and failures of connectionist models of learning and memory. *Psychological Review, 102,* 419–457.

McCloskey, G. (2015). *McCloskey Executive Functions Scale.* Onalaska, WI: Schoolhouse Educational Services.

McCloskey, G., & Perkins, L. A. (2013). *Essentials of executive functions assessment.* Hoboken, NJ: Wiley.

McCloskey, G., Perkins, L. A., & Van Divner, B. (2009). *Assessment and intervention for executive function difficulties.* New York, NY: Taylor & Francis.

McElree, B. (1998). Attended and non-attended states in working memory: Accessing categorized structures. *Journal of Memory and Language, 38,* 225–252.

McGrew, K. S., LaForte, E. M., & Schrank, F. A. (2014). *Technical manual Woodcock-Johnson IV*. Rolling Meadows, IL: Riverside.

McGrew, K. S., & Wendling, B. J. (2010). Cattell-Horn-Carroll cognitive-achievement relations: What we have learned from the past 20 years of research. *Psychology in the Schools, 47,* 651–675. doi:10.1002/pits.20497

McLean, J. F., & Hitch, G. J. (1999). Working memory impairments in children with specific arithmetic learning difficulties. *Journal of Experimental Child Psychology, 74,* 240–260.

McNamara, D. S., & Scott, J. L. (2001). Working memory capacity and strategy use. *Memory & Cognition, 29,* 10–17.

Melby-Lervåg, M., & Hulme, C. (2013). Is working memory training effective? A meta-analytic review. *Developmental Psychology, 49*(2), 270–291. doi:10.1037/a0028228

Metha, M. A., Owen, A. M., Sahakian, B. J., Mavaddat, N., Pickard, J. D., & Robbins, T. W. (2000). Methylphenidate enhances working memory by modulating discrete frontal and parietal lobe regions in the human brain. *Journal of Neuroscience, 20*(6), 1–6.

Milner, B., Squire, L. R., & Kandel, E. R. (1998). Cognitive neuroscience and the study of memory. *Neuron, 20,* 445–468.

Minear, M., & Shah, P. (2006). Sources of working memory deficits in children and possibilities for remediation. In S. J. Pickering (Ed.), *Working memory and education* (pp. 273–307). Burlington, MA: Academic Press.

Morales, J., Calvo, A., & Bialystok, E. (2013). Working memory development in monolingual and bilingual children. *Journal of Experimental Child Psychology, 114,* 187–202.

Morrison, A. B., & Chein, J. M. (2011). Does working memory training work? The promise and challenges of enhancing cognition by training working memory. *Psychonomic Bulletin Review, 18,* 46–60.

Moscovitch, M., Nadel, L., Winocur, G., Gilboa, A., & Rosenbaum, R. S. (2006). The cognitive neuroscience of remote episodic, semantic, and spatial memory. *Current Opinion in Neurobiology, 16,* 179–190.

Moser, D. D., Fridriksson, J., & Healy, E. W. (2007). Sentence comprehension and general working memory. *Clinical Linguistics & Phonetics, 21,* 147–156.

Naglieri, J. A. (1999). *Essentials of CAS assessment.* New York, NY: Wiley.

Naglieri, J. A., Das, J. P., & Goldstein, S. (2014). *Cognitive Assessment System, Second Edition.* Austin, TX: PRO-ED.

Naglieri, J. A., & Goldstein, S. (2013). *Comprehensive Executive Function Inventory.* North Tonawanda, NY: Multi-Health Systems.

Naglieri, J. A., & Gottling, S. H. (1997). Mathematics instruction and PASS cognitive processes: An intervention study. *Journal of Learning Disabilities, 30,* 513–520.

Naglieri, J. A., & Johnson, D. (2000). Effectiveness of a cognitive strategy intervention to improve math calculation based on the PASS theory. *Journal of Learning Disabilities, 33,* 591–597.

Naglieri, J. A., & Pickering, E. B. (2010). *Helping children learn: Intervention handouts for use in school and home* (2nd ed.). Baltimore, MD: Brookes.

Nairne, J. S. (2002). Remembering over the short-term: The case against the standard model. *Annual Review of Psychology, 53,* 53–81.

National Reading Panel. (2000). *Teaching children to read: An evidence-based assessment of the scientific research literature on reading and its applications for reading instruction.* Washington, DC: National Institute of Child Health and Human Development.

Nelson, C. A. (1995). The ontogeny of human memory: A cognitive neuroscience perspective. *Developmental Psychology, 31,* 723–738.

Normand, S., & Tannock, R. (2014). Screening for working memory deficits in the classroom: The psychometric properties of the working memory rating scale in a longitudinal school-based study. *Journal of Attention Disorders, 18,* 294–304.

Oberauer, K. (2002). Access to information in working memory: Exploring the focus of attention. *Journal of Experimental Psychology: Learning, Memory, and Cognition, 28,* 411–421.

Olesen, P. J., Westerberg, H., & Klingberg, T. (2004). Increased prefrontal and parietal activity after training of working memory. *Nature Neuroscience, 7,* 75–79.

Olivers, C. N. L., Meijer, F., & Theeuwes, J. (2006). Feature-based memory-driven attentional closure: Visual working memory content affects visual attention. *Journal of Experimental Psychology, 32,* 1243–1265.

Ornstein, P. A., Grammer, J. K., & Coffman, J. L. (2010). Teachers' "mnemonic style" and the development of skilled memory. In H. S. Waters & W. Schneider (Eds.), *Metacognition, strategy use, and instruction* (pp. 23–53). New York, NY: Guilford Press.

Ornstein, P. A., Naus, M. J., & Stone, B. P. (1977). Rehearsal training and developmental differences in children's memory. *Child Development, 46,* 818–830.

O'Shaughnessy, T., & Swanson, H. L. (1998). Do immediate memory deficits in students with learning disabilities in reading reflect a developmental lag or deficit? *Learning Disability Quarterly, 21,* 123–148.

O'Sullivan, J. T., & Howe, M. L. (1998). A different view of metamemory with illustrations from children's beliefs about long-term retention. *European Journal of Psychology of Education, 13,* 9–28.

O'Sullivan, J. T., & Pressley, M. (1984). Completeness of instruction and strategy transfer. *Journal of Experimental Child Psychology, 38,* 275–288.

Paas, F., Renkl, A., & Sweller, J. (2004). Cognitive load theory: Instructional implications of the interaction between information structures and cognitive architecture. *Instructional Science, 32,* 1–8.

Palmer, S. (2000). Phonological recoding deficit in working memory of dyslexic teenagers. *Journal of Research in Reading, 23,* 28–40.

Parente, R., & Herrmann, D. (1996). Retraining memory strategies. *Topics in Language Disorders, 17,* 45–57.

Pascoe, L., Roberts, G., Doyle, L. W., Lee, K. J., Thompson, D. K., Seal, M. L., ... Anderson, P. J. (2013). Preventing academic difficulties in preterm children: A randomized controlled trial of an adaptive working memory training intervention—IMPRINT study. *Pediatrics, 13,* 144. Retrieved from http://www.biomedcentral.com/1471–2431/12/144

Passolunghi, M. C., & Siegel, L. S. (2001). Short-term memory, working memory, and inhibitory control in children with difficulties in arithmetic problem-solving. *Journal of Experimental Child Psychology, 80,* 44–57.

Passolunghi, M. C., & Siegel, L. S. (2004). Working memory and access to numerical information in children with disability in mathematics. *Journal of Experimental Child Psychology, 88,* 348–367.

Pavio, A., & Csapo, K. I. (1969). Concrete-image and verbal memory codes. *Journal of Experimental Psychology, 80,* 279–285.

Pennington, B. F., Bennetto, L., McAleer, O., & Roberts, R. J. (1996). Executive functions and working memory: Theoretical and measurement issues. In G. R. Lyon & N. A. Krasnegor (Eds.), *Attention, memory, and executive function* (pp. 327–348). Baltimore, MD: Brookes.

Perrig, W. J., Hollenstein, M., & Oelhafen, S. (2009). Can we improve fluid intelligence with training on working memory in persons with intellectual disabilities? *Journal of Cognitive Education and Psychology, 8,* 148–164.

Pickering, S. J., & Gathercole, S. E. (2004). Distinctive working memory profiles in children with special educational needs. *Educational Psychology, 24,* 393–408.

Pickering, S. J., Gathercole, S. E., Hall, M., & Lloyd, S. A. (2001). Development of memory for pattern and path: Further evidence for the fractionation of visuo-spatial memory. *Quarterly Journal of Experimental Psychology, 54A,* 397–420.

Pliszka, S. R. (2003). *Neuroscience for the mental health clinician.* New York, NY: Guilford Press.

Prabhakaran, V., Narayanan, K., Zhao, Z., & Gabrieli, J. D. E. (2000). Integration of diverse information in working memory within the frontal lobe. *Nature Neuroscience, 3,* 85–90.

Prebler, A.-L., Krajewski, K., & Hasselhorn, M. (2013). Working memory capacity in preschool children contributes to the acquisition of school relevant precursor skills. *Learning and Individual Differences, 23,* 138–144.

Pressley, M., Johnson, C. J., & Symons, S. (1987). Elaborating to learn and learning to elaborate. *Journal of Learning Disabilities, 20,* 76–91.

Quinlan, D. M., & Brown, T. E. (2003). Assessment of short-term verbal memory impairments in adolescents and adults with ADHD. *Journal of Attention Disorders, 6,* 143–152.

Rabipour, S., & Raz, A. (2012). Training the brain: Fact and fad in cognitive and behavioral remediation. *Brain and Cognition, 79,* 159–179.

Radvansky, G. A., & Copeland, D. E. (2006). Memory retrieval and interference: Working memory issues. *Journal of Memory and Language, 55,* 33–46.

Ranganath, C., Johnson, M. K., & D'Esposito, M. (2003). Prefrontal activity associated with working memory and episodic long-term memory. *Neuropsychologia, 41,* 378–389.

Rapport, M. D., Bolden, J., Kofler, M. J., Sarver, D. E., Raiker, J. S., & Alderson, R. M. (2009). Hyperactivity in boys with attention deficit/hyperactivity disorder (ADHD): A ubiquitous core symptom or manifestation of working memory deficits? *Journal of Abnormal Child Psychology, 37,* 521–534.

Rapport, M. D., Orban, S. A., Kofler, M. J., & Friedman, L. M. (2013). Do programs designed to train working memory, other executive functions, and attention benefit children with ADHD? A meta-analytic review of cognitive, academic, and behavioral outcomes. *Child Psychology Review, 33,* 1237–1252.

Rasmussen, C., & Bisanz, J. (2005). Representation and working memory in early arithmetic. *Journal of Experimental Child Psychology, 91,* 137–157.

Reber, P. J., & Kotovksy, K. (1997). Implicit learning in problem solving: The role of working memory capacity. *Journal of Experimental Psychology: General, 126,* 178–203.

Reid, R., Schartz, M., & Trout, A. L. (2005). Self-regulation interventions for children with attention deficit/hyperactivity disorder. *Exceptional Children, 71,* 361–377.

Reynolds, C. R., & Voress, J. K. (2007). *Test of Memory and Learning–Second Edition*. Austin: TX: PRO-ED.

Richardson, J. T. E. (1996). Evolving concepts of working memory. In J. T. E. Richardson, R. W. Engle, L. Hasher, R. H. Logie, E. R. Stoltzfus, & R. T. Zacks (Eds.), *Working memory and human cognition* (pp. 3–30). New York, NY: Oxford University Press.

Riggs, K. J., McTaggart, J., Simpson, A., & Freeman, R. P. J. (2006). Changes in the capacity of visual working memory in 5- to 10-year-olds. *Journal of Experimental Child Psychology, 95,* 18–26.

Ritchie, D., & Karge, B. D. (1996). Making information memorable: Enhanced knowledge retention and recall through the elaboration process. *Preventing School Failure, 41,* 28–33.

Roche, J. D., & Johnson, B. D. (2014). Cogmed working memory training product review. *Journal of Attention Disorders, 18,* 379–384.

Roid, G. H. (2003). *Stanford-Binet Intelligence Scales–Fifth Edition*. Itasca, IL: Riverside.

Roman, M. J., Delis, D. C., Willerman, L., Magulac, M., Demadura, T. L., de la Peña, J. L., … Walsh, J. (1998). Impact of pediatric traumatic brain injury on components of verbal memory. *Journal of Clinical and Experimental Psychology, 20,* 245–258.

Rose, N. S., & Craik, F. I. (2012). A processing approach to the working memory/long-term memory distinction: Evidence from the levels-of-processing span task. *Journal of Experimental Psychology: Learning, Memory, & Cognition, 38,* 1019–1029.

Rosen, V. M., & Engle, R. W. (1997). The role of working memory capacity in retrieval. *Journal of Experimental Psychology: General, 126,* 211–227.

Rosenshine, B., & Stevens, R. (1986). Teaching functions. In M. C. Wittrock (Ed.), *Handbook of research on teaching* (3rd ed., pp. 376–391). Washington, DC: American Educational Research Association.

Ryan, C. M., Freed, M. I., Rood, J. A., Cobitz, A. R., Waterhouse, B. R., & Strachan, M. W. (2006). Improving metabolic control leads to better working memory in adults with type 2 diabetes. *Diabetes Care, 29,* 345–351.

Ryan, L. M., & Warden, D. L. (2003). Post concussion syndrome. *International Review of Psychiatry, 15,* 310–316.

Rypma, B., & D'Esposito, M. (1999). The roles of prefrontal brain regions in components of working memory: Effects of memory load and individual differences. *Proceedings of the National Academy of Sciences, USA, 96,* 6558–6563.

Savage, R., Cornish, K., Manly, T., & Hollis, C. (2006). Cognitive processes in children's reading and attention: The role of working memory, divided attention, and response inhibition. *British Journal of Psychology, 97,* 365–385.

Savage, R., Lavers, N., & Pillay, V. (2007). Working memory and reading difficulties: What we know and what we don't know about the relationship. *Educational Psychology Review 19,* 185–221.

Schacter, D. L. (1996). *Searching for memory: The brain, the mind, and the past.* New York, NY: Basic Books.

Schacter, D. L. (1999). The seven sins of memory: Insights from psychology and cognitive neuroscience. *American Psychologist, 54,* 182–203.

Schecklmann, M., Ehlis, A.-C., Plichta, M. M., Dresler, T., Heine, M., Boreatti-Hummer, A., … Fallgatter, A. J. (2014). Working memory and response inhibition as one integral phenotype of adult ADHD? A behavioral and imaging correlational investigation. *Journal of Attention Disorders, 17*(6), 470–482.

Schneider, J. W., & McGrew, K. S. (2012). The Cattell-Horn-Carroll (CHC) model of intelligence. In D. P. Flanagan, & P. L. Harrison (Eds.), *Contemporary intellectual assessment* (3rd ed., pp. 99–144). New York, NY: Guilford Press.

Schneider, W. (2010). Metacognition and memory development in childhood and adolescence. In H. S. Waters & W. Schneider (Eds.), *Metacognition, strategy use, and instruction* (pp. 54–84). New York, NY: Guilford Press.

Schrank, F. A., Mather, N., & McGrew, K. S. (2014a). *Woodcock-Johnson IV Tests of Achievement.* Rolling Meadows, IL: Riverside.

Schrank, F. A., Mather, N., & McGrew, K. S. (2014b). *Woodcock-Johnson IV Tests of Oral Language.* Rolling Meadows, IL: Riverside.

Schrank, F. A., McGrew, K. S., & Mather, N. (2014). *Woodcock-Johnson IV Tests of Cognitive Abilities.* Rolling Meadows, IL: Riverside.

Schwabe, L., Bohringer, A., & Wolf, O. T. (2009). Stress disrupts context-dependent memory. *Learning and Memory, 16,* 110–113.

Scruggs, T. E., & Mastropieri, M. A. (1990). The case for mnemonic instruction: From laboratory research to classroom applications. *Journal of Special Education, 24,* 7–32.

Scruggs, T. E., Mastropieri, M. A., & Sullivan, G. S. (1994). Promoting relational thinking: Elaborative interrogation for students with mild disabilities. *Exceptional Children, 60,* 450–457.

Seigneuric, A., & Ehrlich, M. (2005). Contribution of working memory capacity to children's reading comprehension: A longitudinal investigation. *Reading and Writing, 18,* 617–656.

Seigneuric, A., Ehrlich, M., Oakhill, J. V., & Yuill, N. M. (2000). Working memory resources and children's reading comprehension. *Reading and Writing: An Interdisciplinary Journal, 13,* 81–103.

Service, E. (1992). Phonology, working memory, and foreign language learning. *Quarterly Journal of Experimental Psychology, 45A,* 21–50.

Shaywitz, S. E. (2003). *Overcoming dyslexia: A new and complete science-based program for overcoming reading problems at any level.* New York, NY: Knopf.

Shelton, J. T., Elliott, E. M., Matthews, R. A., Hill, B. D., & Gouvier, W. D. (2010). The relationships of working memory, secondary memory, and general fluid intelligence: Working memory is special. *Journal of Experimental Psychology: Learning, Memory, and Cognition, 36,* 813–820.

Sherman, E. M., & Brooks, B. L. (2015). *Child and Adolescent Memory Profile.* Lutz, FL: Psychological Assessment Resources.

Shipstead, Z., Hicks, K. L., & Engle, R. W. (2012). Cogmed working memory training: Does the evidence support the claims? *Journal of Applied Research in Memory and Cognition, 1,* 185–193.

Siegel, D. J. (1999). *The developing mind.* New York, NY: Guilford Press.

Siegel, L. S., & Ryan, E. B. (1989). The development of working memory in normally achieving and subtypes of learning disabilities. *Child Development, 60,* 973–980.

Simons, J. S., & Spiers, H. J. (2003). Prefrontal and medial temporal lobe interactions in long-term memory. *Neuroscience, 4,* 637–648.

Smith, E. E., & Jonides, J. (1997). Working memory: A view from neuroimaging. *Cognitive Psychology, 33,* 5–42.

Smith-Spark, J. H., & Fisk, J. E. (2007). Working memory functioning in developmental dyslexia. *Memory, 15,* 34–56.

Soderqvist, S., Bergman Nutley, S., Peyrard-Janvid, M., Matsson, H., Humphreys, K., Kere, J., & Klingberg, T. (2011). Dopamine, working memory, and training induced plasticity: Implications for developmental research. *Developmental Psychology, 48,* 836–843.

Soto, D., Heinke, D., Humphreys, G. W., & Blanco, M. J. (2005). Early involuntary top-down guidance of attention from working memory. *Journal of Experimental Psychology: Human Perception and Performance, 31,* 248–261.

Speece, D. L. (1987). Information subtypes of learning disabled readers. *Learning Disabilities Research, 2,* 91–102.

Spencer-Smith, M., & Klingberg, T. (2015). Benefits of working memory training program for inattention in daily life: A systematic review and meta-analysis. *PLOS ONE, 10,* doi:10.1371/journal.pone.0119522.

St. Clair-Thompson, H. L. (2007). The influence of strategies upon relationships between working memory and cognitive skills. *Memory, 15,* 353–365.

St. Clair-Thompson, H. (2011). Executive functions and working memory behaviours in children with a poor working memory. *Learning and Individual Differences, 21,* 409–414.

St. Clair-Thompson, H., Stevens, R., Hunt, A., & Bolder, E. (2010). Improving children's working memory and classroom performance. *Educational Psychology, 30,* 203–219.

Sub, H. M., Oberauer, K., Wittmann, W. W., Wilhelm, O., & Schulze, R. (2002). Working-memory capacity explains reasoning ability—And a little bit more. *Intelligence, 30,* 261–288.

Swanson, H. L. (1994). Short-term and working memory: Do both contribute to our understanding of academic achievement in children and adults with learning disabilities? *Journal of Learning Disabilities, 27,* 34–50.

Swanson, H. L. (1999). Instructional components that predict treatment outcomes for students with learning disabilities: Support for a combined strategy and direct instruction model. *Learning Disabilities Research, 14,* 129–140.

Swanson, H. L. (2000). Are working memory deficits in readers with learning disabilities hard to change? *Journal of Learning Disabilities, 33,* 551–566.

Swanson, H. L. (2006). Cross-sectional and incremental changes in working memory and mathematical problem solving. *Journal of Educational Psychology, 98,* 265–281.

Swanson, H. L. (2011). Working memory, attention, and mathematical problem solving: A longitudinal study of elementary school children. *Journal of Educational Psychology, 103,* 821–837.

Swanson, H. L., & Alexander, J. (1997). Cognitive processes as predictors of word recognition and reading comprehension in learning disabled and skilled readers: Revisiting the specificity hypothesis. *Journal of Educational Psychology, 89,* 128–158.

Swanson, H. L., & Beebe-Frankenberger, M. (2004). The relationship between working memory and mathematical problem solving in children at risk and not at risk for serious math difficulties. *Journal of Educational Psychology, 96,* 471–491.

Swanson, H. L., & Berninger, V. W. (1995). The role of working memory in skilled and less skilled readers' comprehension. *Intelligence, 21,* 83–108.

Swanson, H. L., & Berninger, V. W. (1996). Individual differences in children's working memory and writing skill. *Journal of Experimental Child Psychology, 63,* 358–385.

Swanson, H. L., Cochran, K. F., & Ewers, C. A. (1990). Can learning disabilities be determined from working memory performance? *Journal of Learning Disabilities, 23,* 59–67.

Swanson, H. L., Howard, C. B., & Saez, L. (2006). Do different components of working memory underlie different subgroups of reading disabilities? *Journal of Learning Disabilities, 39,* 252–269.

Swanson, H. L., & Howell, M. (2001). Working memory, short-term memory, and speech rate as predictors of children's reading. *Journal of Educational Psychology, 93,* 720–734.

Swanson, H. L., & Jerman, O. (2007). The influence of working memory on reading growth in subgroups of children with disabilities. *Journal of Experimental Child Psychology, 96,* 249–283.

Swanson, H. L., Jerman, O., & Zheng, X. (2008). Growth in working memory and mathematical problem solving in children at risk and not at risk for serious math difficulties. *Journal of Educational Psychology, 100*(2), 343–379.

Swanson, H. L., Orosco, M. J., Lussier, C. M., Gerber, M. M., & Guzman-Orth, D. A. (2011). The influence of working memory and phonological processing on English language learner children's bilingual reading and language acquisition. *Journal of Educational Psychology, 103,* 838–856.

Swanson, H. L., & Sachse-Lee, C. (2001). Mathematical problem solving and working memory in children with learning disabilities: Both executive and phonological processes are important. *Journal of Experimental Child Psychology, 79,* 294–321.

Swanson, H. L., Zheng, X., & Jerman, O. (2009). Working memory, short-term memory, and learning disabilities: A selective metaanalysis of the literature. *Journal of Learning Disabilities, 42,* 260–287.

Tageuchi, H., Sekiguchi, A., Taki, Y., Yokoyama, S., Yomogida, Y., Komuro, N., … Kawashima, R. (2010). Training of working memory impacts structural connectivity. *Journal of Neuroscience, 30,* 3297–3303.

Tamm, L., Hughes, C., Ames, L., Pickering, J., Silver, C. H., Stavinoha, P., … Emslie, G. (2010). Attention training for school-aged children with ADHD: Results of an open trial. *Journal of Attention Disorders, 14,* 86–94.

Temple, C. M. (2004). Developmental amnesias and acquired amnesias of childhood. In A. D. Baddeley, M. D. Kopelman, & B. A. Wilson (Eds.), *The essential handbook of memory disorders for clinicians* (pp. 91–112). Hoboken, NJ: Wiley.

Torgesen, J. K. (1996). Model of memory from an information processing perspective: The special case of phonological memory. In G. R. Lyon & N. A. Krasnegor (Eds.), *Attention, memory, and executive function* (pp. 157–184). Baltimore, MD: Paul H. Brookes.

Torgesen, J. K., & Goldman, T. (1977). Rehearsal and short-term memory in reading disabled children. *Child Development, 48,* 56–60.

Towse, J. N., Hitch, G. J., & Hutton, U. (1998). A reevaluation of working memory capacity in children. *Journal of Memory and Language, 39,* 195–217.

Tronsky, L. N. (2005). Strategy use, the development of automaticity, and working memory involvement in complex multiplication. *Memory & Cognition, 33,* 927–940.

Turley-Ames, K. J., & Whitfield, M. M. (2003). Strategy training and working memory task performance. *Journal of Memory and Language, 49,* 446–468.

Turner, J. E., Henry, L. A., & Smith, P. T. (2000). The development of the use of long-term knowledge to assist short-term recall. *Quarterly Journal of Experimental Psychology, 53A,* 457–478.

Turner, M. L., & Engle, R. W. (1989). Is working memory capacity task dependent? *Journal of Memory and Language, 28,* 127–154.

Unsworth, N., Brewer, G. A., & Spillers, G. J. (2013). Working memory capacity and retrieval from long-term memory: The role of controlled search. *Memory and Cognition, 41,* 242–254.

Unsworth, N., & Engle, R. W. (2007). The nature of individual differences in working memory capacity: Active maintenance in primary memory and controlled search from secondary memory. *Psychological Review, 114,* 104–132.

Vanderberg, R., & Swanson, H. L. (2007). Which components of working memory are important in the writing process? *Reading and Writing, 20,* 721–752.

Van der Molen, M. J., Van Luit, J. E., Van der Molen, M. W., Klugkist, I., & Jongmans, M. J. (2010). Effectiveness of a computerized working memory training in adolescents with mild to borderline intellectual disabilities. *Journal of Intellectual Disability Research, 54,* 433–447.

Van Der Sluis, S., Van Der Leij, A., & De Jong, P. F. (2005). Working memory in Dutch children with reading- and arithmetic-related LD. *Journal of Learning Disabilities, 38,* 207–221.

van Ewijk, H., Heslenfeld, D. J., Luman, M., Rommelse, N. N., Hartman, C. A., Hoekstra, P., … Oosterlaan, J. (2014). Visuospatial working memory in ADHD patients, unaffected siblings, and healthy controls. *Journal of Attention Disorders, 18,* 369–378.

van Gog, T., Ericsson, K. A., Rikers, R. M., & Paas, F. (2005). Instructional design for advanced learners: Establishing connections between the theoretical frameworks of cognitive load and deliberate practice. *Educational Technology Research and Development, 53,* 73–81.

Van Merrienboer, J. J. G., Kirschner, P. A., & Kester, L. (2003). Taking the load off a learner's mind: Instructional design for complex learning. *Educational Psychologist, 38,* 5–13.

Verhaeghen, P., Cerella, J., & Basak, C. (2004). A working-memory work-out: How to expand the focus of serial attention from one to four items, in ten hours or less. *Journal of Experimental Psychology: Learning, Memory, and Cognition, 30,* 1322–1337.

Visu-Petra, L., Cheie, L., & Miu, A. C. (2013). Working memory and anxiety: Exploring the interplay of individual differences across development. In T. P. Alloway & R. G. Alloway (Eds.), *Working memory: The connected intelligence* (pp. 209–238). New York, NY: Psychology Press.

Wagner, R. K. (1996). From simple structure to complex function: Major trends in the development of theories, models, and measurements of memory. In G. R. Lyon & N. A. Krasnegor (Eds.), *Attention, memory, and executive function* (pp. 139–156). Baltimore, MD: Brookes.

Wagner, R. K., Torgesen, J. K., Rashotte, C. A., & Pearson, N.A. (2013). *Comprehensive Test of Phonological Processing, Second Edition.* Austin, TX: Pro-Ed.

Wang, S., & Gathercole, S. E. (2013). Working memory deficits in children with reading difficulties: Memory span and dual task coordination. *Journal of Experimental Child Psychology, 115,* 188–197.

Was, C. A., & Woltz, D. J. (2006). Reexamining the relationship between working memory and comprehension: The role of available long-term memory. *Journal of Memory and Language, 56,* 86–102.

Watts, F. N., Morris, L., & MacLeod, A. K. (1987). Recognition memory in depression. *Journal of Abnormal Psychology, 96,* 273–275.

Wechsler, D. (2003). *Wechsler Intelligence Scale for Children, Fourth Edition.* San Antonio, TX: Psychological Corporation.

Wechsler, D. (2008). *Wechsler Adult Intelligence Scale, Fourth Edition.* San Antonio, TX: Pearson.

Wechsler, D. (2009). *Wechsler Memory Scale, Fourth Edition.* San Antonio, TX: Pearson.

Wechsler, D. (2012). *Wechsler Preschool and Primary Scales of Intelligence, Fourth Edition.* Bloomington, MN: Pearson.

Wechsler, D. (2014). *Wechsler Intelligence Scale for Children, Fifth Edition.* Bloomington, MN: Pearson.

Wechsler, D., Kaplan, E., Fein, D., Kramer, J., Morris, R., Delis, D., & Maerlender, A. (2004). *Wechsler Intelligence Scale for Children Fourth Edition—Integrated.* San Antonio, TX: Psychological Corporation.

Westerberg, H., Jacobaeus, H., Hirvikoski, T., Clevberger, M.-L., Ostensson, A., Bartfai, A., & Klingberg, T. (2007). Computerized working memory training after stroke—A pilot study. *Brain Injury, 21,* 21–29.

White, W. A. T. (1988). A meta-analysis of the effects of direct instruction in special education. *Education and Treatment of Children, 11,* 364–374.

Wilson, B. A. (2009). *Memory rehabilitation: Integrating theory and practice.* New York, NY: Guilford Press.

Wilson, K. M., & Swanson, H. L. (2001). Are mathematics disabilities due to a domain-general or a domain-specific working memory deficit? *Journal of Learning Disabilities, 34,* 237–248.

Wixted, J. T. (2004). The psychology and neuroscience of forgetting. *Annual Review of Psychology, 55,* 235–269.

Wolters, C. A., Yu, S. L., Hagen, J. W., & Kail, R. (1996). Short-term memory and strategy use in children with insulin-dependent diabetes mellitus. *Journal of Consulting and Clinical Psychology, 64,* 1397–1405.

Wright, I., & Limond, J. (2004). A developmental framework for memory rehabilitation in children. *Pediatric Rehabilitation, 7,* 85–96.

Wu, K. K., Anderson, V., & Castiello, U. (2006). Attention-deficit/hyperactivity disorder and working memory: A task switching paradigm. *Journal of Clinical and Experimental Neuropsychology, 28,* 1288–1306.

Yasik, A. E., Saigh, P. A., Oberfield, R. A., & Halamandaris, P. V. (2007). Posttraumatic stress disorder: Memory and learning performance in children and adolescents. *Biological Psychiatry, 61,* 382–388.

Zec, R. F., Zellers, D., Belman, J., Miller, J., Matthews, J., Ferneau-Belman, D., ... Robbs, R. (2001). Long-term consequences of severe closed head injury on episodic memory. *Journal of Clinical and Experimental Neuropsychology, 23,* 671–691.

Zinke, K., Zeintl, M., Rose, N. S., Putzmann, J., Pydde, A., & Kliegel, M. (2014). Working memory training and transfer in older adults: Effects of age, baseline performance, and training gains. *Developmental Psychology, 50,* 304–315.

About the Author

Milton J. Dehn earned his BA in psychology from the University of Minnesota, his MS in school psychology from Moorhead State University, and his doctorate in educational psychology from the University of South Dakota (1992). Dr. Dehn taught for 13 years in the School Psychology Program at the University of Wisconsin-La Crosse, where he also served as program director. In 2003, he cofounded Schoolhouse Tutoring and Schoolhouse Educational Services. Dr. Dehn has practiced as a school psychologist in four Midwestern states and is currently a private practice school psychologist in Wisconsin. For the past 10 years he has specialized in memory assessment, consultation, training, and interventions for children, adolescents, and adults with working memory and long-term memory problems. Dr. Dehn has several publications on children's memory problems. He is a frequently requested speaker at state, national, and international conferences, where he presents on assessment and intervention for working memory and long-term memory impairments.

About the Online Resources

Thank you for choosing the *Essentials of Psychological Assessment* series. *Essentials of Working Memory Assessment and Intervention* includes downloadable resources designed to enhance your education and practice.

To access your resources, please follow these steps:

Step 1 Go to www.wiley.com/go/psyessresources

Step 2 Enter your email address, the password provided below, and click "submit"

      Password: memory2015

Step 3 Select and download the listed resources

If you need any assistance, please contact Wiley Customer Care 800-762-2974 (U.S.), 317-572-3994 (International) or visit www.wiley.com.

CONTENT INCLUDED IN THE ONLINE RESOURCES

Chapter 2

Rapid Reference 2.2 Specific Working Memory Components Most Highly Related With Cognitive Processes
Definitions of Cognitive Processes Related to Working Memory

Chapter 3

Rapid Reference 3.3 Brain Regions With Reported Activation During Working Memory Processes
Brain Structures Involved With Working Memory

Chapter 4

Cognitive Processes Significantly Related With Specific Academic Skills
Rapid Reference 4.3 Working Memory Components Most Highly Related With Specific Academic Skills by Age

Chapter 5

Chapter 7

Chapter 8

Appendixes

Appendix A Scaled Score to Standard Score Conversion Table With
    Percentiles
Appendix B *T*-Score to Standard Score Conversion Table
Appendix C Working Memory Composites and Subtests Sorted by Scale
Working Memory Report Template
Working Memory Analysis Worksheet With Excel Calculations

Index